Preparing for the Coming Glory

The Valley of Dry Bones

Olatunde Olaniyi Ola-Daniel

Unless otherwise indicated, all Scriptures are taken from the King James Version of the Bible.

Scripture quotations marked MSG are taken from THE MESSAGE, copyright © 1993, 2002, 2018 by Eugene H. Peterson. Used by permission of NavPress. All rights reserved. Represented by Tyndale House Publishers, Inc.

(Each time the pronoun *he* is used in the entire book, it refers to both male and female. All Scriptures used in this book are from King James Version except otherwise stated)

Preparing for the Coming Glory
The Valley of Dry Bones
Copyright © 2025 by Olatunde Olaniyi Ola-Daniel
ISBN:

Published by Word and Spirit Publishing
P.O. Box 701403
Tulsa, Oklahoma 74170
wordandspiritpublishing.com

Printed in the United States of America. All rights reserved under International Copyright Law. Content and/or cover may not be reproduced in whole or in part in any form without the expressed written consent of the Publisher.

Contents

1. The Era of the Glory of God 1
2. The Journey 17
3. God's Plan 27
4. The Call to Holiness 47
5. The Making of the Champions 79
6. The Wilderness Experience 101
7. The Isolation 129
8. The School of Waiting 143
9. The Valley of Dry Bones 209
10. The Expected Point 233
11. The PHD Program 255

1

The Era of the Glory of God

I believe the Church is about to move into a time I will call the hour of the glory of God. For convenience's sake, let's call it the "glory era." This will be the finest hour of the Church. Many of our forefathers (Peter, Paul, James, and so on) looked forward to this time. They wished they could have been part of the army that will carry the Church into her finest hour. It will be a great privilege to be alive and to be a Christian in this time. The glory era is completely different from the era in which we currently are living. In this current era, God is with us, but His tabernacle is located outside the camp. Anyone who wishes to seek Him has to go outside the camp to meet Him. It is not an easy journey to undertake. That is why only few have done so. Those few are considered the superstars of the Church. But in the glory era, God will have to bring His tabernacle into the camp. This has serious implications.

This book will help to prepare us to be part of the army of God that will take the battle to the enemy's gate in this, finest hour of the Church.

Preparing for the Coming Glory

These are those who will taste of the glory of God in a brighter form than the world has ever known. The latter rain must, of necessity, be greater than the former. The outpouring the Church is about to experience is like nothing we have ever seen or experienced before. What we read about in the book of Acts will pale in comparison to what God is about to do. But in order to give a foundation to this preparation, we must consider the operations of God's glory in different eras.

Now then, let's look at the differences between the Old Testament and the New Testament eras. Many people have tagged the Old Testament era as the era of judgment, while they tagged the New Testament era as the era of grace and mercy. In the Old, the people could not handle the terribleness of God, so they requested that God should speak to them through a middle man. God agreed to their demands and restricted the priesthood to one family—the descendants of Aaron, Moses' brother. No one could approach the Holy of Holies other than the priest. And even the priest could not approach unworthily. The judgment would be instant if he did. But in the New Testament, many people think, God, through the Holy Spirit, has come to dwell among us, and so He shows grace and mercy and overlooks our sins. *I am sorry to announce to you that that is not entirely true.* The God of the Old Testament is the same God we meet in the New Testament. He will and can never change.

In the Body of Christ today, most people don't want to do away with their sins. From the followers to the leaders, all live their lives according to the dictates of their flesh, the world, and self. Some have even called for a review of the commands of the Bible, calling it archaic and not relevant to today's situations. This is to justify their lifestyles, as it is becoming increasingly difficult to live a life of purity and holiness in our world. Someone once asked me a question along this line. The person pointed out some great ministers by name and asked why God was still promoting their ministry and why they still demonstrated the gifts of the Spirit, even when they had publicly been caught in sin. The answer is easy and straightforward. The gift is not a show of the strength of their relationship with God. It is just a gift, meant to demonstrate the goodness of God to humanity. God's permitting the use of the gift in the life given to sin is not a stamp of God's approval of that sin. That is why God's tabernacle cannot be in the midst of His people at this time—He cannot stand sin. Hence, in order to avoid instant judgment, God has moved His tabernacle outside of the camp, like He did in the Old Testament.

In the coming glory era, God wants to bring into the Kingdom the greatest harvest of all time. There will be demonstrations of the gift and power of the Holy Spirit like we have never seen before. The power of God will be so raw and easily attainable that the atheist community and the world at large will have to publicly admit that there is a God who loves humanity. But the current Church is not capable of emanating such glory. In order for the Church to be able to attain such spiritual heights, God must bring His tabernacle within. The prophet Ezekiel (the man who prophesied the rise of the end-time army) puts it this way:

> *My tabernacle also shall be with them: yea, I will be their God, and they shall be my people. And the heathen shall know that I the* Lord *do sanctify Israel, when my sanctuary shall be in the midst of them for evermore.*
>
> Ezekiel 37:27–28

At that time, when God brings His tabernacle into the midst of His people, the world will have to admit that there is only one true God, and that Jesus Christ is His Son. They will be forced to come to terms with the fact that there is no other way under heaven through which man can be saved, other than the name of Jesus. There will be no doubt in anyone's heart that the only path to heaven is through Jesus. Notice what it says in verse 28: The holiness emanating from the Church will be impeccable. No one will be able to find any error in any individual who is a part of this Church, in order to bring an offense against God. The entire Body will be so sanctified that the world will see holiness in every single member of the Church. They will be forced to agree that this lifestyle of holiness is beyond human reach. There must be a God in their midst who is constantly sanctifying them.

In order for God to bring the current Church to that state of purity and 0-/j'0pkjp-=][‘=-]'pholiness, God has to take the Church through the refiner's fire to prepare her for the glory. We must understand that when this happens, the size of the Church will be shrunk to the barest minimum. Think about that. I am sure many questions will arise in many hearts. Why can't the current Church be the glorious Church? Wouldn't that bring in more of a harvest than when the population is drastically reduced? The answer to the last question is no. God is not looking for quantity; He is looking for quality. God doesn't want the coming harvest to take the form and character of the current people in the Church. The majority of us in the Church still live in sin, and many see nothing wrong with many things God Himself has called an abomination. God will have to separate the wheat from the chaff so that the wheat can be useful in the hand of the Master. The chaff is of no use. Look at how the Master Himself put it:

> *As therefore the tares are gathered and burned in the fire; so shall it be in the end of this world. The Son of man shall send forth his angels, and they shall gather out of his kingdom all things that offend, and them which do iniquity.*
>
> —Matthew 13:40-41

The Era of the Glory of God

Consider the above passage. Notice the last phrase of verse 40. It tells us the era to which Jesus was referring—the end of this world, the time we call the end times. Verse 41 tells us exactly how Jesus will bring about the refiner's fire. He will send His angels. These are not regular angels. These are seraphim. This is the same group of angels the prophet Isaiah saw in Isaiah 6. They are custodians of God's refiner's fire. In verse 7 of Isaiah 6, these angels passed the prophet through the refiner's fire to purge him of all sins. After the experience, he was equipped to carry a higher dimension of God's glory. It is these same angels about whom Jesus is speaking in the above passage. They will be unleashed on the Church. When they come into our midst, they will bring their refiner's fire, and the least of us will be equipped to carry as much glory as prophet Isaiah did. After their job is done, God can bring His tabernacle into our midst. Now then, in Matthew 13:41, notice what the Master says about the result of the angels' activity. It will separate those given to holiness from those given to offense and sin. Those who offend and do iniquity will be pushed out of the Kingdom, and those who live a holy life will be purged and empowered to live a holier life. The refiner's fire is a double-edged sword. On one hand, it purges those who live a godly life from ungodliness and makes them more holy. On the other hand, it destroys those who are hypocrites, who trample on the grace of God. By the time they are done with their job, the size of the Church will be a tiny fraction of what it is today.

Now then, apart from the rain of revival God wants to pour on the Church in these last days, there are other reasons the Church must come under the covering of the coming glory. Anyone who is not under this covering cannot survive this era. Even though it is the finest era of the Church, it will also be the worst era of humanity. The evil the devil is about to unleash on humanity is second to none since the world was created. Jesus Himself told us that this evil has never been and will never be (Matthew 24:21). The world will witness diseases that have never been seen among humans. These are diseases engineered by the enemy to bring about his wicked agenda. The political system of many nations will be restructured in order to accommodate the coming one-world government of the antichrist. Only those under the glory dome will survive.

In the glory era (which is the finest hour of the Church and the worst time for the world), demonic activities will be at their peak. Currently, the demonic activities on the earth are somewhat restricted. Although they are right now on the rise because we are approaching the glory era, it is not at a level where we can see raw demonic activities taking place on the streets unchecked. Some demonic activities still take place under disguise and cover. They cover their activities under science, culture, a lifestyle choice, the pursuit of happiness, etc. The Church can still survive living in sin. But a time is coming when the enemy will no longer be shy with his processes. In that time, men will witness demons walking in the streets. At that time, if God is not in the midst of the Church, many will not survive the raw attack that will be leveled against the Church. Anyone who is not found under the shadow of the Almighty (Psalm 91) will automatically be made a victim of demonic oppression and control.

Also, the deception we see in our world today is nothing compared to what is coming. Today, many things we hold on to as truth are complete lies. Just in the last five years, we have seen many nations that have believed in lies. No one could decipher the truth. It is as if the whole world has been bewitched and all are reading from the same script. Anyone who tries to speak the truth is completely silenced. Every news station is propagating the same lies as if they are mouthpieces for a false god. Science has been redefined to follow the narrative of a demigod. What we use to know as good is now called bad. What we use to call bad is now known as good. This is just a summary of our world today. But this is child's play compared to the level of deception the devil will bring in the next era. In fact, it will be so bad that Jesus gives that era a theme. The theme He gave is *deception*.

> *And Jesus answered and said unto them, Take heed that no man deceive you.*
>
> —Matthew 24:4

Consider the above passage. It starts with the words "and Jesus answered." That means He is answering a question. If you read from the beginning of that chapter, you will learn that the question before Jesus was whether He could tell them the sign that would accompany the glory era, which comes about in the last days. The first answer Jesus gave to this question was this: Be careful not to be deceived by any. The deception of the devil will be at an all-time high at that time, so much so that many will believe the antichrist was working through the true power of God. The whole world will stand in awe of him. The intensity of deception today is very low, yet many Christians cannot discern the mind of God in what is happening around them. When the intensity gets high, do you think majority in the current Church will survive? Sadly, the answer is no. Unless God comes within the Church, many will be doomed for hell or experience God's mercy by going home early.

When the glory of God descends, no man can stand. The glory of God comes with the power and weight of the Spirit. It comes with fire. The glory is a double-edged sword. The same glory will refine someone to be pure gold while it also destroys another as fire consumes all on its way. When the glory comes into the Church, some will be refined, but many will be destroyed. Let's take a look at one or two examples in the Scriptures to have an idea of what happens when God decides to invade the space of man with His glory:

> *It came even to pass, as the trumpeters and singers were as one, to make one sound to be heard in praising and thanking the* L*ord; and when they lifted up their voice with the trumpets and cymbals and instruments of musick, and praised the* L*ord, saying, For he is good; for his mercy endureth for ever: that then the house was filled with a cloud, even the house of the* L*ord; so that the priests could not stand to minister by reason of the cloud: for the glory of the* L*ord had filled the house of God.*
>
> —2 Chronicles 5:13–14

The above passage gives us an idea of what we should expect in the glory era. God has pitched His tent outside the camp of Israel. Anyone who wishes to seek the Lord must go out of the camp. But in the Old Testament, when the Temple was built, the whole nation was led by their leaders to invite God into their space. God graciously decided to honor the invitation. When God appeared in His glory, not one of them could stand. When He appears, His glory is so heavy to bear that you need to build some spiritual muscle and stamina in order to be able to withstand it.

It was the glory of God that raised Jesus Christ from the dead (Romans 6:4). Look at what happened when the glory of God appeared in the grave where Jesus was laid:

> *His countenance was like lightning, and his raiment white as snow: and for fear of him the keepers did shake, and became as dead men.*
>
> —Matthew 28:3–4

The Era of the Glory of God

Can you see that? In the first passage we considered, the men involved were believers. They were in the service of God when the glory descended. They were unable to stand, but they fell in awe of the weight of the glory of God. But in the second case, the men involved were unbelievers. When the glory came, it almost destroyed them. They were as men who were dead. Can you see the difference?

Natural man cannot withstand the glory of God. The current Church is filled with carnal men. If God were to bring His tabernacle into our midst now, many would die. The era of the glory is beautiful for true followers, but it spells doom for fake followers. Unfortunately, there are more fake followers in our midst than true followers. Sin cannot survive in the atmosphere of the glory of God. When God is in the midst, He cannot tolerate sin, no matter how hard He tries. If He must move in, sin *must*, of a necessity, move out. If sin does not move out, death must occur. God is the same both in the Old Testament and in the New. Many preachers have erroneously taught that the God of the Old Testament knew no mercy while the God of the New Testament is a God of mercy and grace. That statement is very far from the truth. God is the same yesterday, today, and forever. He hated sin and disobedience then; He hates it now. In order to clear up any doubt on this issue, let's consider two passages, one from the Old Testament and the other from the New to show the severity of God:

> *And Nadab and Abihu, the sons of Aaron, took either of them his censer, and put fire therein, and put incense thereon, and offered strange fire before the Lord, which he commanded them not. And there went out fire from the Lord, and devoured them, and they died before the Lord.*
>
> —Leviticus 10:1-2

Preparing for the Coming Glory

Let's give a little background to the above passage for a better understanding. This was a time when Israel told God they could not tolerate His presence. They would rather God speak to them through a third party. God then instituted the office of the priest. The priests would go out of the camp to the tabernacle to meet with God on behalf of the people. But God did not reduce His standard for the priests. The people could get away with sin because they did not have to approach God directly. But the priest did not have that "luxury." God's standard remains high for any who must approach. The young men Nadab and Abihu, mentioned in the passage above, were among the first people anointed to the office of priest in Israel. The eyes of all the nation were on them. Only they could approach God from among their peers. That was a thing of prestige. They made a name among the people. Talk about them went around the camp of over three million people. Many parents wished their children would be given such an opportunity. They walked the streets with their shoulders high. They were schooled on what to do and what not to do. They were to approach with fear and trembling. The rule remained, only do what He said to do. Whatever you would do without His direction would amount to nothing. After many weeks of being schooled, these men went into the presence of God to make the offerings. Definitely, they wanted to prove to the onlookers that they were special. They had a name among the people to uphold, and they schemed to stand up to that name. The smoke of their offerings approached the throne of heaven easily. But when the smoke of their sacrifice approached the throne of God, it was considered strange. Heaven did not call for it. The vessels presenting it were not offering it with a pure motive. They came with shoulders high, hoping to make a greater name for themselves among the people. Sin lay at their doorstep. They had just been recently elevated above their peers, and they were glorified with beautiful clothing that carried precious stones. Was it pride that built up within them that was on display? Whatever it was, God responded with fire. The fire of God can do two things, depending on the vessel. If the motive is pure and the vessel is clean, the fire of God will purify. But if the motive is bad and the vessel is not clean, the fire of God will destroy. That's exactly what happened to these two: they perished under the consuming fire. When God is in the midst of the people, there is no playing around. One must approach with utmost fear and trembling. Someone might say, Where was the love of the Father here, spoken about in the Scriptures? Look at how Paul answers that question:

> *Behold therefore the goodness and severity of God: on them which fell, severity; but toward thee, goodness, if thou continue in his goodness: otherwise thou also shalt be cut off.*
>
> —Romans 11:22

Notice what Paul said in the above passage. There is what is called the goodness of God (which we classify as the love of God) *and* the severity of God. Notice for whom the severity of God is reserved; it is reserved for those who refuse to live a life pleasing to God after all necessary resources have been made available for such an individual. Notice also that the goodness of God is reserved for those who "continue" in a lifestyle of holiness. The word *continue* must not be left out when dealing with such matters. Notice what happens if someone who has lived in holiness all his life stops doing so; he shall be cut off. This is the Bible. This is a true representation of the position of God concerning His people and the matter of sin. God truly is love. But we must also understand the severity of God. The glory era is going to be the finest hour of the Church. But it will also come with judgment for any wrongdoing in the Church.

Someone might say, "Oh, what happened to Nadab and Abihu is the Old Testament . . . that was not in the era of mercy. In the Old Testament, there was no remission of sins, only the covering of sins. In the New Testament, Christ came and died for our sins, so the grace and mercy of God will always prevail over His judgment." Let us see how true that statement is:

> *But a certain man named Ananias, with Sapphira his wife, sold a possession, and kept back part of the price, his wife also being privy to it, and brought a certain part, and laid it at the apostles' feet.*
>
> —Acts 5:1–2

Let's give a little background to this passage for a better understanding. After Jesus died and was resurrected, He sent the Holy Spirit to head a newly created body called the Church. The Holy Spirit came with power and might on the Day of Pentecost, and since then He has been directing the affairs of the Church. In the Old Testament, God was in the Temple, but in the New Testament, the Holy Spirit, the head of the Church, dwells among His people. He is the representation of the Godhead in the midst of God's people. Now that Jesus has come to show us the way to live a life pleasing to God, the Holy Spirit, who is also God, can now comfortably live in our midst. Hence, in the early days of the Church, God moved His tabernacle from outside the camp to within the camp. He started to direct the affairs of the Church from within. You don't need to go out of the camp anymore to seek Him. He is within. Not only has the Church been considering how to please God, but also God has made available a new heart for anyone who would yield to the Spirit. That heart carries the laws of God within it, and with that heart, we can perfectly please God. These things that God has made available to the Church are what made God comfortably bring back His tabernacle into the camp of His people. Now the people of God have all the necessary tools to please God in the exact way that Jesus did.

Now then, back to the above passage; the passage starts with 'But.' That tells us we need to look at the previous chapter to have a correct understanding of what the author is referring to.

> *And Joses, who by the apostles was surnamed Barnabas, (which is, being interpreted, The son of consolation,) a Levite, and of the country of Cyprus, having land, sold it, and brought the money, and laid it at the apostles' feet.*
>
> —Acts 4:36–37

The passage above includes the last two verses of chapter 4. Here we find the reason for the "but" at the beginning of chapter 5. By this time, the population of the Church was over five thousand believers. This man, Joses, stood out from among the crowd for his donations to the Church. His name spread far and wide among the people. He was so loved by the leadership of the Church that he was even given a nickname. Every time there was a gathering of the Church, the leaders never failed to celebrate this man. This was the genesis of the problem for the new characters introduced in chapter 5. They wanted such accolades as well. They wanted the crowds to celebrate them. They wanted to stand out above everyone else. They wanted to be mentioned in the services. And so they schemed. They brought a strange offering to the Lord. They placed it on the altar while the leaders were watching. But the head of the Church saw it all when they were scheming in the secret place:

Preparing for the Coming Glory

> *But Peter said, Ananias, why hath Satan filled thine heart to lie to the Holy Ghost, and to keep back part of the price of the land?*
>
> —Acts 5:3

Notice what Peter said to them. They did not lie to the leaders of the Church. They actually lied to the head of the Church—the Holy Spirit. He was in the midst of the Church, and He would not tolerate such behavior. Now then, we can see that the error of Ananias and Sapphira was not very different from the error made by Nadab and Abihu in the Old Testament. The only difference is that they are in different dispensations. The Old was a dispensation in which the blood of bulls and rams covered the sins of the people of God. Hence, there was instant and fast judgment. But in the New dispensation, the blood of Jesus Christ not only covers our sins, but it actually washes them off and makes us white as snow. The error of Ananias and Sapphira took place under the dispensation of the New. This is supposed to be the era of grace and mercy, though, right? Christ died for our sins. The Father was supposed to overlook their act because of what Jesus did on the cross and forgive them, right? That is what we expect to happen. But let's see what actually took place:

> *And Ananias hearing these words fell down, and gave up the ghost: and great fear came on all them that heard these things.*
>
> —Acts 5:5

Consider the above passage. It is not drawn from the Old Testament. It is drawn from the New. Can you see the instant judgment that came from God? God was in the midst of the Church. The glory of God cannot tolerate sin. The consuming fire of God must be released for instant judgment. It is a law. No amount of sacrifice can reverse it. The only other way is for God to take His tabernacle out of the camp again and only permit those who understand how to strike a balance between the *love* of God and the *severity* of God, who know how to conduct their lives accordingly, to approach. God was the same before the Old Testament, He was the same in the Old Testament, He was the same in the New Testament, He is the same today, and He will be the same forever (Hebrews 13:8). Nothing and no one can change Him.

2

The Journey

The Preparation

The glory must descend whether we like it or not, whether we are ready or not. God will get His victory either with few or with many. Hence, it is in our own interest to be part of what God is doing in these last days. However, God has extended His mercy to many by creating a training institution where those who are willing to be part of His end-time army can learn the ways of God and then be enrolled in His end-time workforce. God has raised a committee of Watchers who will orchestrate the lives of any who is willing to go through series of events that help lead to conformity with the ways of God. He has structured our paths on earth to be a journey with Him.

God revealed to the prophet Ezekiel how He plans to raise this end-time army. When Ezekiel saw the raw materials from where God plans to raise the army, all the strength in his body vanished. The situation looked hopeless. But we know that what is impossible with man is possible with God. The hopelessness can become a shining light of hope if we learn to allow God to be the sole director of the affairs of our lives. The ultimate purpose of God is to drive everyone who wants to be a tool in His hand into a valley. That valley is filled with bones. And not just bones, but completely dry bones. Bones that are so dry that a little strike on the ground would make them break into pieces. Hence, when you look at the valley, you will see many bones. The bones are so mixed together that you don't know which belongs to whom:

> *The hand of the* L*ord* *was upon me, and carried me out in the spirit of the* L*ord**, and set me down in the midst of the valley which was full of bones, and caused me to pass by them round about: and, behold, there were very many in the open valley; and, lo, they were very dry.*
>
> —Ezekiel 37:1–2

The Journey down the Valley

In the above Scripture, the prophet Ezekiel was not shown how the bones got to the valley. He was not shown which bones belonged to whom. The bones had no identity. Everything that would have allowed him to identify who owned which was completely stripped from each bone. He just saw the scattered, broken, and completely dry bones. These bones are without identity or ambition; they are without flesh or self. Though in the world but completely seprated from the world and its lust.

From generation to generation, God looks for people to represent Him. Someone who can be a spokesperson, someone who can represent the interests of the Kingdom, a true ambassador, through whom many come to the knowledge of Christ. But unfortunately, very rarely does God find a handful of people who can truly represent His Kingdom. This is probably because God will stop at nothing to prune those interested in representing His Kingdom so they come out sparkling as gold.

The Institution of the Refiner's Fire

The first step into the world of Christianity is to be born again. Look at how Jesus put it in John 3:3:

Jesus answered and said unto him, Verily, verily, I say unto thee, Except a man be born again, he cannot see the kingdom of God.

Unfortunately, the vast majority of Christians remain at this location. This location is not the intention of heaven for anyone who wants to come into the fold. Notice what Jesus said in the passage above. Being born again only affords you the opportunity of seeing the Kingdom of God. That is not the ultimate reason why Christ came. He didn't need to come for us to only be able to peek into the Kingdom of God. The intention of God is for us to go beyond peeking. In fact, the place of peeking is a dangerous place to be. Because, in that place, eternity is not guaranteed. Look at how Jesus Himself puts it in this passage:

For God so loved the world, that he gave his only begotten Son, that whosoever believeth in him should not perish, but have everlasting life.

—John 3:16

Preparing for the Coming Glory

Notice how Jesus framed that statement. First, it is a matter of *whosoever*. That means the offer is available to every human being who has existed since that statement was made. That offer was not made to only those who go to church or only the Israelites. It was not made to those who live in certain countries. It was not made only to people who are familiar with Christianity. It was made to *all* humans *everywhere* regardless of the national religion of the country where he/she is from, regardless of their background or socioeconomic status, regardless of race or color—that *whosoever* is for *all*. That statement was made over two thousand years ago. Every single human who has passed through the earth since then could have tapped in to that statement. Those currently in hell now are also covered by that statement.

Now, let's consider another word in that statement that is a little shocking: Whosoever believes in Him *should* not perish. One might wonder why Jesus used such a word in the matter of eternity. It seems to me, from that statement, that the matter of eternity is not a guarantee even if you take that initial step of believing. *Should* not perish. What it means to me is that anyone who believes in the work that Jesus did on the cross should not perish. That is a probability. There are other words that could have been used in that statement to seal the fate of the person. For example, Jesus could have said: Whosoever believes in Me *will* not perish. This is a more certain statement. He could have also said, Whosoever believes in Me *cannot* perish. That is more guaranteed than the other two. It means that no matter what I do or don't do, all I need in order to gain eternity is to believe in Jesus. Once I do that, eternity is guaranteed. But Jesus says that if you believe, you *should* not perish. If we relate this verse (verse 16) to verse 3, which we considered earlier, we will notice that believing is an initial step. It affords you the opportunity to see. The place of seeing is not the place of experience. They are two

The Journey

different things. In fact, there is a world of difference between seeing and experiencing. You cannot compare someone who saw a movie with someone who acted in the movie, and neither can you compare someone who saw a beautiful garden on Instagram to someone who visited the same garden in person. The intention of Christ is not for us to see the Kingdom, and it is not for us to just believe in the Son of God. His intention is to go beyond believing and seeing. His intention is for us to enter and be a part. Enter and experience. His intention for us is to believe so much that our believing will drive us to take deliberate steps that will usher us into the Kingdom of God.

This is why the doctrine that says once you are saved, nothing you do or do not do can make you lose your salvation (once saved, forever saved) is not from God. Someone can say, "Oh no, you've got it all wrong. If a man has a son, no matter how wayward the son is, he is still the son of his father." Yes, it is true, he is still the son of his father. But there is no reasonable father who will commit his estate or conglomerate to the hands of a wayward son. If earthly fathers will not do that, God will also not do that. Look at the following passage:

> *A wise servant shall have rule over a son that causeth shame, and shall have part of the inheritance among the brethren.*
> —Proverbs 17:2

Notice how the wisest king who ever lived put it. A wise servant is far better than a foolish son. The servant who shows himself worthy can get the inheritance that originally belonged to a son. Just in case you need proof from the New Testament, let us consider Galatians 4:1:

> *Now I say, That the heir, as long as he is a child, differeth nothing from a servant, though he be lord of all.*

Preparing for the Coming Glory

According to Paul in the above passage, if an heir to the throne is a child, there is no difference between him and a slave. Being born again, which is the initial step into the world of God, can only make you a child in the Kingdom. Necessary growth steps have to be taken in order for important matters of the Kingdom to be handed over to you.

The truth of the matter is that God will leave no stone unturned and no ground of compromise for any vessel who wants to be a part of His agenda. It will interest you to know that even Jesus had to go through God's school of making (the institute of the refiner's fire), before He was presented to the world. Let's look at a popular passage that summarizes it, Isaiah 9:6:

> *For unto us a child is born, unto us a son is given: and the government shall be upon his shoulder: and his name shall be called Wonderful, Counsellor, The mighty God, The everlasting Father, The Prince of Peace*

Let us consider a quick and summarized analysis of the above passage. The passage starts with the words "unto us." Who is "us"? "Us" is the world. Remember what we read in John 3:16 ("For God so loved the world, that He gave His Son . . .")? Good. Now go back to the above passage (Isaiah 9:6) and notice that the Child was born unto us, but He was not given unto us until He became a Son. Can you see the next statement that follows? "Unto us a Son is given": A child cannot bear the government on his shoulder. Even though the salvation of the world was a matter of urgency for God, the urgency did not stop God from waiting until Jesus became a Son. If God does that for Jesus, then not one of us can escape the process if we want to amount to anything in the hand of God.

The Journey

We have been given an account of the event that occurred when the Child was born unto us. It was a remarkable event. Angels appeared to many people to announce the birth. Wise men saw the sIgn in the heavens. Many people saw the vision of how God presented the Child to the world. Some, like Simeon and Anna, defied death because they had been promised to witness the event. As remarkable as the event was, it didn't automatically translate to Jesus bearing the government on His shoulder. God was never under pressure to give us the Child. He had to wait for thirty years. Those thirty years were designed to bring out the Son from the Child. When heaven was satisfied with the quality of man that Jesus had become, heaven gladly fulfilled the second part of Isaiah 9:6: "Unto us a Son is given." Look at the presentation ceremony here, in Matthew 3:16–17:

> *And Jesus, when he was baptized, went up straightway out of the water: and, lo, the heavens were opened unto him, and he saw the Spirit of God descending like a dove, and lighting upon him: and lo a voice from heaven, saying, This is my beloved Son, in whom I am well pleased.*

As Jesus went through the school designed for Him, He passed everything thrown at Him. At that point, God was confident that Jesus could conduct business on His behalf. Look at how God presented Him in the above passage (verse 17). God called Him, "My beloved Son." That was the day when Jesus was announced to the world. That was the day when He was given to the world. That very day, Jesus was given the seal of the Spirit, an endowment for all who must represent the interest of the Kingdom.

Preparing for the Coming Glory

Somebody might say, Oh, this is heresy. Jesus was God, and He did not need to go through any process to bring out the Son in Him. Well, let's search the Scriptures to see if that is true. Read Philippians 2:6–7:

> *... who, being in the form of God, thought it not robbery to be equal with God: but made himself of no reputation, and took upon him the form of a servant, and was made in the likeness of men.*

In the above passage, we can clearly see that even though Jesus was equal with God, He set that particular glory and portfolio aside and took on human flesh and frailties in order to save us. Hence, it is unscriptural to say that Jesus didn't need to go through any process to become who the Father wanted Him to be. Notice the last phrase in the above passage: Jesus was made in the likeness of men. It was a man who lost the Garden; it was a Man who must get it back. A man sinned against God; a Man must pay the price for the sin, not an angel or God. Let us consider two other passages to back up our claim. Look at Hebrews 5:7–9:

> *... who in the days of his flesh, when he had offered up prayers and supplications with strong crying and tears unto him that was able to save him from death, and was heard in that he feared; though he were a Son, yet learned he obedience by the things which he suffered; and being made perfect, he became the author of eternal salvation unto all them that obey him.*

This passage is loaded with truths. Time will not permit to do justice to it. But let us do our best to give a summarized version of it. First, it should be noted that these three verses refer to Jesus. If you start reading from verse 14 of chapter 4, you will see where Paul started the conversation. He was talking about Jesus being our great High Priest. Now then, coming back to verse 7 of chapter 5, notice how that verse was introduced: "In the days of His flesh." It was talking about Jesus being human like us, subjected to all the temptations we are subject to and having experienced what we are experiencing. He had to learn to submit Himself to God in perfect obedience even though He was the Son. Unconditional obedience is the number-one demand heaven will place on all who want to go far with God. Now, look at verse 9. It started with "Jesus was made perfect." What could that mean? When Jesus was in heaven, He was perfect and sinless. But when He came to the world for our sake, He had to leave that glory in heaven and go through the ranks to learn perfection afresh. This was the condition for Him to be the Author of our eternal salvation. This automatically leaves us without excuse in case someone wants to say, "But Jesus was perfect because He was the Son of God." We can see from this passage that Jesus left that status in heaven before coming to the earth.

Now then, let's look at the second passage, Hebrews 4:15:

For we have not an high priest which cannot be touched with the feeling of our infirmities; but was in all points tempted like as we are, yet without sin.

Notice the words "which cannot be touched with the feeling of our infirmity." What could that mean? Jesus can empathize with our weaknesses, not just sympathize. It is a world of difference. To empathize is to feel exactly what someone else feels, either to a lesser or higher degree because you have experienced the same. But to sympathize is to merely understand someone's emotion from your own perspective, not necessarily because you have been there before, but perhaps because you have seen someone or read about someone who had been there before.

Preparing for the Coming Glory

Let me give you an example of a common mistake we make. Let's say someone has recently lost a loved one. Many people, when comforting such, may say words like "I understand what you are going through at this moment." If such a fellow has never lost a loved one, there is no way he can understand what the one grieving is going through. To truly understand what someone is going through is to have gone through it yourself. So, when that passage says that Jesus understands exactly what and how we feel when we are in tribulation, that means that Jesus understands from a place of experience. Hence, this passage also clearly confirms that Jesus had to go through the drills to do the work prescribed for Him by heaven. Also note that He was tempted *in all points*. What could that mean? It means there is no kind of temptation common to man that the devil did not bring to the table to see which would appeal to Jesus. That means He was tempted to steal. The devil must have pointed out some gold to Him. This will help your ministry. Take it. The devil must have also tempted Him with sex, allowing beautiful woman to flock around Him. Whatever sin you can ever think of that is common to men, Jesus was tested with it.

3

God's Plan

God's Laid-Out Plan

Now we have seen our example, Jesus Christ. He was not spared in any way, but He went through the process in order to achieve the desire of heaven. We also have to go through the process that will bring out the "son" in us in order to be made a useful tool in the hands of the Master. God has a clear picture of what everyone who comes to Christ should be like. In order for any individual to assume the shape of God's picture for his life, he must pass through His processes. Let's look at the writings of the apostle Paul to confirm this.

> *For whom he did foreknow, he also did predestinate to be conformed to the image of his Son, that he might be the firstborn among many brethren.*
>
> —Romans 8:29

Preparing for the Coming Glory

Let's look at the above passage and try to do a little justice to it. "Those He did foreknow": that word is from the Greek word *proginosko*, which means "to have knowledge of beforehand." The next question is, who falls into this category? The answer is: every single human, born of a woman, who passed through the face of the earth, falls into this category. This picture is being extended to all humans, just as John 3:16 is extended to all human beings. Now then, among all humans, born of a woman, whoever accepts the offer given in John 3:16 now qualifies to be included in the next statement: those whose sins have been forgiven and who have been imputed with righteousness. For those people, God did predestinate. What does that mean? It means God has determined what they must become before they come in. Predestination is not what some say it is. In this case, what it means is that God has drawn a curriculum that He expects all who come through the door of salvation to undergo in order to become what He wants them to become. Predestination is not automatic, as some think. It is an expectation. If you don't work hard at it, you can't get to the expected end. Let me give an example. A college of medicine is an institution set up to create medical professionals. Some individuals sat down and determined that whoever goes through the curriculum of this college will come out as a medical professional at the other end after a certain number of years and classes passed satisfactorily. The curriculum is designed to help them achieve the goal. This goal was set before anyone ever gained admission into the school. Better put, the end goal is a predestination for *all* who enroll in the college.

From the above example, it is not right to say it is automatic for everyone who gains admission into that school to become a medical professional regardless of what they do or don't do after their admission. Neither is it right to say that the designers of such a program already know who will become a medical professional, so that no matter how hard others try, they cannot be medical professionals if they are not predetermined by the organizers to do so. These two errors are some of the interpretations given to the above passage by some. First, they say that once you get born again, God has predestined you to conform to the image of God. You don't have to do anything to become that. The other error is that they say God has already predetermined those who will be saved, meaning that no matter how hard you try, if you are not part of the group who is predestined, you cannot make the list. How wicked can that be? That sounds like God condemned some people to hell even before they were born. What is the point of Christ coming to judge the world if we are not responsible for accepting or rejecting salvation ourselves? This is far from what the passage means. If this is true, then we can conclude that God has respect for persons. He decides that some will be saved and others will go to hell. Let's look at what the apostle Paul wrote to see if this is true:

For there is no respect of persons with God.

—Romans 2:11

In the above passage, it is clear where God stands on the matter. He has no respect of persons. He has no one He favors over another. There is no arbitrary favoritism with Him. There is no special one in the agenda of God. The above verse also means that God shows no partiality. That means that what you put in with God is what you get. You draw near to Him; He will draw near to you, regardless of who you are or where you are from. With God, one person is not more important than another. Hence, it is wrong to say that God has predetermined who will make it to heaven and who will not make it. On what basis did He choose? On the basis of favor or beauty? Let's look at another passage to understand this:

Preparing for the Coming Glory

The Lord is not slack concerning his promise, as some men count slackness; but is longsuffering to us-ward, not willing that any should perish, but that all should come to repentance.

—2 Peter 3:9

This verse is also clear on the character of God. It tells why God is not slack concerning His promises. First, what promise is Peter referring to here? The promise being referred to here is God putting an end to the world, which will automatically lead to the judgment and destruction of evildoers. What is the reason given for God's supposedly slow-to-act character? He is not willing that *any* should perish. Did you see that? If the doctrine that says God has already predetermined all who will go to heaven is true, then this verse would be a lie. But we know all of Scripture is true. It is God's desire for everyone to make it to heaven because God gave Jesus to *all people*. Notice the last phrase of the above passage: "that all should come to repentance." All means *all*. If God desires *all* to come to repentance, then He would not predestine some people to go to hell.

Now that we have confirmed that the two doctrines concerning predestination are false doctrines, then we can continue with our analysis. Now then, let's go back to the college of medicine analogy. The owners of the college do not decide who will apply to attend the college. They only put out some requirements for those who are interested in attending the college. It is the responsibility of the student to ensure that he meets all admission requirements. In the same way, even though Jesus was given to the whole world, it is not God's responsibility to ensure we come to Christ. It is our responsibility to either accept or reject the Son of God. The requirements for admission has been clearly laid out in the Bible: believe in your heart and confess with your mouth. All those who meet these requirements will be admitted into the Kingdom of God.

God's Plan

This is the first step. Now then, the fact that you gained admission into the college is not a guarantee that you will graduate at all. And even when you graduate, it is not a guarantee that you will finish with good grades. The board of the college does not predetermine who will graduate and who will not. They do not predetermine who will finish with good grades and who will not. They make all the necessary help available to *all*; then they simply teach and expect all students to do what they need to do in order to excel. In the same way, God never predetermines who will conform to the image of Christ. He simply does the teaching and expects obedience from all of His students. Of course, not all students will obey. And even if all obey, the levels of obedience will differ, just like the levels of students' dedication to studying medicine differs. Look at how Paul explains it in this passage:

> *But in a great house there are not only vessels of gold and of silver, but also of wood and of earth; and some to honour, and some to dishonour. If a man therefore purge himself from these, he shall be a vessel unto honour, sanctified, and meet for the master's use, and prepared unto every good work.*
>
> —2 Timothy 20:20–21

First, Paul starts with the phrase, "in a great house." What is that "great house"? The great house is the Kingdom of God. This is the place where God's reign is unrestricted. It can also be likened to the college of medicine in our example. Members become part of the great house by believing in Christ, in the same way that applicants become members of the college by meeting the admission requirements. Now then, the next things mentioned in this passage are various kinds of vessels. "Vessels" here represent those who have accepted Christ—the students who have gained admission into the college in our example. Notice that there are various grades of vessels in the example: gold, silver, wood, and clay. This describes the various levels of endurance of each individual when they pass through stress or tribulation. Notice also that, even though all the vessels find their way into the house, not all of them become gold, silver, or wood. When we look carefully at verse 22, we see why some become honorable and others are not so honorable. Verse 22 starts with the word: "If." *If* indicates a probability. This means you become something if you do something. That also means that you may never become that thing unless you fulfill the requirement. Many passages in the Scriptures start with the word "when." For example, look at Isaiah 43:2:

When thou passest through the waters, I will be with thee; and through the rivers, they shall not overflow thee: when thou walkest through the fire, thou shalt not be burned; neither shall the flame kindle upon thee.

God says 'when' in the above passage. This means it is only a matter of time that you will pass through waters, whether you are born again or not. The only advantage the believer has in this situation is that he has an insurance policy from God that can never fail. That insurance policy guarantees that when his time comes to go through the water, he will be shielded from the adverse effects, just like Shadrach, Meshach, and Abednego were shielded from the effects of the fire. But 2 Timothy 2:21 didn't start with the word "when." It starts with "if." This means that not all will go through that situation, even though the desire of God is for all of them to experience this. Only those who decide to will go through. The passage clearly states what is needed in order for honor to be imputed: "If a man can purge himself from these . . ." In essence, what Paul is saying is that whoever wants to be an honorable vessel in the hand of the Almighty must purge himself of certain things. Nobody will be forced to purge himself. The same advice given to one is the same given to all: purge yourself. Whoever eventually becomes imputed with honor is the one who decides to follow through with the instruction. God is the God of "if any man."

Going back to Romans 8:29, you can now agree with me that when that passage says God predestines those He foreknew, it simply means that God has designed a curriculum for all those He foreknew to conform to the image of Christ. If anyone among those He foreknew decides to go through the drill, then they become what God has predestined them to become. But if anyone refuses to be part of the process, then they will not become the image God expects them to be.

The Curriculum

God has designed a curriculum for every human who passes through this earth. The curriculum is specifically tailored to fit the uniqueness of our individuality. It involves two things. Everything we pursue on earth will become an absolute waste if we don't pursue these things. The first and most important is the path to becoming like Jesus, and the second is the ministry we are supposed to fulfill. This curriculum must be achieved by all who come through the door of salvation. The consequence for not fulfilling the first is more grievous than the consequence of not fulfilling the second. In fact, heaven is more inclined toward us fulfilling the first than the second. At this time, we shall mostly explore the first—being like Christ. Let's look at Scripture to help our understanding:

> *But none of these things move me, neither count I my life dear unto myself, so that I might finish my course with joy, and the*

> *ministry, which I have received of the Lord Jesus, to testify the gospel of the grace of God.*
>
> —Acts 20:24

Notice what Paul says in the above passage. Many things were thrown at him, just like life throws many things at us today. Unfortunately, many of us are carried away by the things life throws at us. The primary purpose of these things is to distract us away from the two most important purposes in life. Paul was able to recognize the devil's strategy of deception. He clearly said in the above passage why he decided not to allow these things to distract him. First, he desired to finish his course, and second, he desired to fulfill his ministry. Paul called the first his "course," and the second, his "ministry." Matching what Paul says with what we were saying at the beginning of this chapter, we can now put a name to the two things involved in the curriculum that God has designed for everyone who comes to Him through the door of salvation. The first in the curriculum of God for us is "the course," and the second is "the ministry."

The Course and the Ministry

The word *course* in Acts 20:24 comes from the Greek word *dromos*, which means "a race, a career, the course of life or of office." In our world, we have different kinds of careers—engineering, medicine, architecture, to mention but a few. For someone to become a doctor, for example, he has to go to college, after going from kindergarten through to graduating from high school. The curriculum for such an individual in medical school will be tailored toward making him a medical doctor. It is the same way in this situation. The "course" here is Jesus. We all have one course of study in the University of God: *Jesusology*.

God's Plan

The intention of heaven is that everyone who comes into the Kingdom through the gate of salvation will go through the curriculum from kindergarten through high school, and then enroll in the University of God to study Jesusology. When such an individual manages to graduate from the university, he will be a little "Jesus," just like a medical student becomes a doctor after graduation.

After graduation from the course of Jesusology, then the individual is ready to fulfill his ministry. The word "ministry" in the passage under consideration is from the Greek word *diakonia*, which means "attendance as a servant, aid or service." Notice from the passage that the ministry was received; it was not earned. What that means is that after earning your bachelor's degree in Jesusology from the University of God, then you will be given a ministry in which you are to serve as a servant, putting into practice what you have learned. This is the expected pattern in the matters of the Kingdom. However, we don't have it like so in reality. We have many a minister in big churches and with large congregations who did not attend the University of God. This is the greatest trick of the devil that has put the Church at a great disadvantage. The devil has helped the Church to put the cart before the horse. As soon as a person attends a human-led Bible college, he goes straight into ministry without attending the University of God.

Putting the cart before the horse has many dangerous consequences. First, we should note that a minister does not actually minister the Word when he is ministering. The minister ministers substance from his being when he is ministering. Let's break that statement down: When a preacher stands in front of the congregation to speak forth the Word of God, he may have spent hours doing research on the subject he plans to speak about. He is actually not communicating the subject to the congregation, however; he is communicating his own substance to the people. The substance is who he is before God, what he has stored in his spirit. If he is a liar, even though he is sharing the Word of God, he is actually inputting a lying spirit into the congregation. If he is a fornicator, it doesn't matter what the topic of discussion is, he is inputting fornication into the software of the congregation. In this scenario, there will then be much fornication and adultery occurring in the congregation even though the Word of God is being preached. You can see how terrible that would be for the Church. Another reason why pastors not going through the University of God is dangerous for the Church is that it will be difficult for such a minister to uphold a high moral standard, and this gives a lot of room and opportunity for the world to speak things against the Church. Look at how God Himself put such a case when David sinned against Him in the matter of Uriah:

> *Howbeit, because by this deed thou hast given great occasion to the enemies of the* L<small>ORD</small> *to blaspheme, the child also that is born unto thee shall surely die.*
>
> —2 Samuel 12:14

In the above passage, God said David's act of disobedience gave the enemies of God great occasion to speak against the Lord. Did you notice that? Not the enemies of *David*. The enemies of *God*. David's act gave the enemies of God great occasion to blaspheme God Himself. That is exactly what happens in our world when a prominent minister has a moral deficiency. It gives an opening for the enemies of the Church and God Himself to blaspheme, not necessarily the enemies of the minister in question.

The most dangerous reason that we cannot afford to buy in to the trick of the devil by putting the cart before the horse is that it can cost us heaven. Anyone who does not go through the University of God is in danger of missing out on heaven, even if he is a great minister with thousands of members in his congregation. The most important thing God expects every Christian to fulfill on earth is "the course"—going through that university. Anyone who does not go through the University stands the danger of missing heaven no matter what the person's status in the Church is. Someone might say that's a ridiculous statement to make, given the fact that the person is born again. Let's examine some passages to attest to this fact. See how Jesus Himself puts it:

> *Many will say to me in that day, Lord, Lord, have we not prophesied in thy name? and in thy name have cast out devils? And in thy name done many wonderful works? And then will I profess unto them, I never knew you: depart from me, ye that work iniquity.*
>
> —Matthew 7:22-23

Let's take a little time to analyze this passage. First, He said many would make a statement to Him on Judgment Day to defend why they should be allowed to enter heaven. Look at the defense the people were putting up. The first group said they had prophesied in the name of Jesus. Notice the response of Jesus to their defense. He didn't say, "You are liars; you didn't prophesy in My name." He didn't say, "Yes, you prophesied, but you prophesied lies." What that means to me is that they actually prophesied the truth. Now, before we analyze the response of Jesus, let's look at this a little deeper. There is only one reason a Christian would be enabled to prophesy: the person is in the office of a prophet. And we know that the office of a prophet is not available to those who have not entered into the Kingdom through the door of salvation. It is an administrative gift given to the Church by the office of the Christ. So, whoever it is who is prophesying accurately in the name of Jesus must first be born again, and second, they must be a member of the Church (the Body of Christ).

The second group tells the Lord they have cast out devils in the name of Jesus. Again, it should be of note that they actually cast out these devils, because Jesus didn't deny their claim. For anyone to successfully cast out devils, it means that at one point, this fellow has been a part of the Kingdom of God. Casting out devils is a public demonstration that emphasizes the superiority of the Kingdom of light over the kingdom of darkness. Hence, we can say without a doubt that the second group were also part of the people who had stepped into the Kingdom via the door of salvation.

Now then, considering the third group, notice that they even said they did many wonderful works through the name of Jesus. That is the miracle-working power of God. Definitely these guys had been born again. In order to perform any miracle in the name of the Lord, those in this third group would have taken a step even further into the Kingdom by getting baptized in the Holy Spirit. The wonder-working power of God is packaged to the Church through the gifts of the Holy Spirit. This is the duty of th office of the Holy Spirit. That is not to say that the first two categories may not involve speaking in tongues. They could, but a person doesn't have to be baptized in the Holy Spirit to function in the administrative gift of the office of Christ; they just have to be born again. The gift of the office of Christ can be enhanced when one is baptized in the Holy Spirit, but one doesn't have to be baptized in the Holy Spirit to function in any of the gifts administered by the office of Christ. Also, for them to be able to do all the things they listed, they may have served as a minister wherever they worshiped. So, the group of people whom Jesus is talking about in the above passage is very likely to include minsters in various capacities in the Body of Christ. At the least, they were all born again at one point in time in their affiliation with the Church. Therefore, looking at the passage again, it is of note that we are talking about people who have been born again and have served in the Church in one capacity or the other for some time. But Jesus denied these people entrance to heaven.

The next logical question is, why? The Scripture does not leave us in darkness concerning the reason they were denied access. The "why" is in the statement that Jesus made. Let's look at it closely. Notice the first statement Jesus made to disqualify them: "I never knew you." This means that even though they seem to be ministering in the Church as a servant of God, the One whom they claim to serve does not know them. Second, He gave the reason He said He doesn't know them: they are workers of iniquity. Hence, we can gather from this Scripture that the reason He doesn't allow them into heaven is not because they are not born again. If that were the reason, He would have mentioned that they had rejected Christ. They didn't reject Christ. They didn't reject the offer God made to man in John 3:16. They were just workers of iniquity. Now, how does that relate to the issue at hand? Let's look at the verse following verse 23 to see if Jesus sheds any light on the reason He denies them access to heaven:

> *Therefore whosoever heareth these sayings of mine, and doeth them.*
>
> —Matthew 7:24a

Take a careful look at that verse. It starts with the word "therefore." That means we have to look for what it is *there for*. We are talking about why Jesus denied those people access to heaven. They heard the Word quite alright, but they did not put what they heard into practice. Now then, let's go back to our first example. If an individual wants to be a medical doctor, he goes to a medical school, where he is instructed on how to be a doctor. All instructions are given in the form of lectures, which are comprised of words. There may be demonstrations using cadavers or human subjects. Even in those cases, the demonstrations will be explained in words. Therefore, anyone who will turn out to be a good doctor will have to both listen to the instructions and then act on the instructions given. That's exactly what Jesus is saying here. In the University of God, enrollment is automatic, but graduation is earned. So, in essence, what Jesus is saying is that these people attended the university, but they did not follow or act on the instructions given. There are two things involved in what Jesus said: hearing the Word and then doing it.

Now then, there is still another question we need to settle. When Jesus denied access to heaven to these people, one of the reasons He gave for doing so was "I never knew you." Why would Jesus make such a statement to people whom He had clearly personally enrolled into the Kingdom? Let's do a little exploration. When the newly admitted get into medical school, they are fresh and completely ignorant about medical knowledge. But after years of diligence in attending lectures and studying, they become what the institution expects them to become—medical doctors. They speak like doctors, they dress like doctors, they walk like doctors, and they behave like doctors; they are even called doctors. When other doctors see them, they recognize these ones are doctors. When those who are not doctors see them, they also know these people are doctors. That is exactly what it is like when you attend the University of God to study Jesusology. When you graduate from the University of God, you should look exactly like Jesus. You should walk like Jesus, you should talk like Jesus, and you should behave like Jesus. Hence, when people see you, they should say, "Look at Jesus walking over there on the streets of New York." That was exactly what happened in Antioch. Let's take a look:

> *And when he had found him, he brought him unto Antioch. And it came to pass, that a whole year they assembled themselves with the church, and taught much people. And the disciples were called Christians first in Antioch.*
>
> —Acts 11:26

These guys in Antioch had been instructed by Paul, one of the best and brightest graduates from the University of God at that time. He instructed them in words for a full year. The result was remarkable. People who were not affiliated with the Church called them Christians. The word "Christian" is from the Greek word *Christianos*, which means "follower of Christ." The logical question will be, what did the people see that caused them to call them Christians? They saw Jesus in each of them.

Now then, going back to why Jesus said He never knew those people, Jesus looked at them and saw nothing of Himself in them. He knew they were Christians because He had admitted them into the Kingdom when they professed Him as Savior. But they never acknowledged Him as Lord. He was never the Lord of their lives. They did as they wanted and rejected His counsel. That was why He also said they were "workers of iniquity." So, it was not that Jesus didn't know them; it was that Jesus didn't see any part of Himself in them. The word used for "know" in the passage is the same word used for sexual intercourse between a man and a woman. The way a man "knows" his wife is different from the way the same man knows his friends. Jesus was saying to these people that He never knew them intimately because they never listened to His instructions. They never gave Him space in their lives. He was not the Lord over their affairs.

Therefore, we can clearly see how important it is to graduate from the University of God before pursuing the work of the ministry. Look at how Jesus puts it in this passage:

> *And he ordained twelve, that they should be with him, and that he might send them forth to preach.*
>
> —Mark 3:14

Jesus ordained the Twelve to do two things. What were those two things? The first was that they *"should"* be with Him, and the second is that He *"might"* send them forth. Let's take a deeper look at these two roles Jesus confined the Twelve to fulfilling. Let's see if it matches what we have been talking about. Remember how Paul put the two together in the earlier passage we considered? He called the first his "course," and the second he called his "ministry" (Acts 20:24). First, that passage says they *should* be with Him. What could that mean? It means that His greatest desire is for them to stay with Him. Many wander away from His feet, claiming that they are busy doing the things of God. The word *"should"* in that passage is a probability statement. It means that it is heaven's desire for Christians to sit at His feet, but because God will not tamper with our will, it is left up to us to actually decide to stay. We must stay with all our body, soul, and spirit. Now then, in those days, the education system was mostly comprised of a master-disciple relationship. A disciple would spend a significant amount of time with the master to learn the art or trade of the master. They spent most of their valuable time with the master, and in some cases, they actually lived with the master. This was the case with Jesus and the disciples. Hence, they were to seat at His feet to learn from Him the ways of the

God's Plan

Kingdom. After many months of being with Jesus, look at what people who hated Jesus said about them:

> *Now when they saw the boldness of Peter and John, and perceived that they were unlearned and ignorant men, they marvelled; and they took knowledge of them, that they had been with Jesus.*
>
> —Acts 4:13

Notice what the people who actually had killed Jesus said about the disciples. It was clear to all that they had learned directly at the Master's feet. These guys had attended the University of God and had graduated with flying colors. When they came out of the university, it was clear to all who saw them that they had studied Jesusology. They could see Jesus in them. That's exactly what Jesus meant when He told those people that He didn't know them. There was no evidence in them that they had been with Jesus. No part of Jesus was seen in them. This is the course we all have to take when we enter the Kingdom through the door of salvation. It is far more important than any ministry, as far as heaven is concerned.

The second part of the above passage talks about our ministry. Look at how Mark puts it: "that He might send them forth to preach." The way it is put in this passage, it appears to me that Jesus understood that the cart should not be put before the horse. It is clear that the more we look like Jesus, the more effective we will be in the work of the ministry. Notice the word that was used in that passage: *"might."* That means that sending them forth to do the work of ministry was a 50-50 chance. What is most important to heaven is being with Jesus. Doing ministry work is a probability, and that strictly depends on what the Master wants. What is not a probability is waiting at the feet of the Master. The only thing about the waiting, however, is that heaven desires that it is in the will of the individual to wait.

Now then, let's analyze one more passage along this line to see if the course is more important than the ministry.

> *I have fought a good fight, I have finished my course, I have kept the faith: henceforth there is laid up for me a crown of righteousness, which the Lord, the righteous judge, shall give me at that day: and not to me only, but unto all them also that love his appearing.*
>
> —2 Timothy 4:7–8

Now then, this passage is from the book of Second Timothy. This was the last letter Paul wrote to his spiritual son, Timothy. He was at the end of his days. In this passage, he was telling Timothy that it was time for him to depart. Look at how he put it. He said he had finished his course. Did you notice that? Notice also that in order for him to finish his course in the University of God, he had to fight. (What we shall fight against will be discussed in a later part of this book.) Also notice that he mentioned nothing about his actual ministry. Meanwhile, this guy had evangelized the whole of Asia and a great part of Europe as it was in his days. Yet when he was ready to depart this world, he mentioned nothing about that amazing ministry. Now then, look at the reward, or certificate, that would be given to him at his graduation from the University of God: a crown of righteousness. Why is that so? Notice also the person issuing the certificate: Jesus Christ, who is the Righteous Judge. That means to me that Paul learned so much from the University of God that he became exactly like his Teacher—righteous. As far as heaven is concerned, this is the more important part of the two.

God's Plan

Heaven is tired of having great evangelists who are fornicators. Heaven is frustrated when its finest teachers of the Word are thieves and backbiters. There is no benefit for heaven when its best miracle workers have children from multiple women in different countries they travel to for the work of the ministry. Heaven would much rather prefer a bench warmer who is the best graduating student from the University of God than a minster who has toured the world but still has secret sins. Heaven would prefer someone excommunicated from the Church but who is now a living Bible that his neighbors and coworkers can read to find Jesus, to someone who is at the helm of affairs in the Church but who badly represents the Kingdom. Heaven would prefer a pastor with few congregations but who is doing well in the University of God to someone who has thousands of people in his congregation but points people to hell.

4

The Call to Holiness

The Valley of Dry Bones

The design of God for His people is for them to take the journey from the mountain of salvation down to the valley of dry bones. Unless that journey is taken, it will not be God's good pleasure to use the fellow in the area of ministry. We shall explore how to take our journey from the mountain of salvation to the valley of dry bones in a later part of this book. For now, let's talk about the matter of holiness. Many times we hear preachers say it is impossible to live a holy life. Many Christians have been brought up to believe that as long as we live in this body, we will always be under the power of sin. Hence, it is excusable for the finest of us to sin. This is far from what the Scriptures say about the matter. Sometime ago, I taught a group of young people, using Scriptures upon Scriptures, that it is possible to be in this flesh and live above sin. Though you might not be there yet, if you aim for it, you can get it. After a few weeks, another teacher came in to teach that same group in my absence. They happened to talk about holiness. The teacher began to show them from Scriptures why it is impossible to live a holy life while we are here in this flesh. Thank God a good foundation had been laid for those students. Their spirits could not absolve such teaching, so the class for that day became a debate session rather than a teaching session. That's how it's supposed to be. If you think it is impossible, then you cannot attain it. But if you believe it is possible, then it will be attainable for you.

Now then, before we look at how God administers His curriculum in the University of God, let's elaborate more on the issue of holiness. Is it heaven's intention for us to live a holy life while in this flesh? Let's look at a passage of Scripture to see the position of God regarding this question.

> *For I am the L*ORD *that bringeth you up out of the land of Egypt, to be your God: ye shall therefore be holy, for I am holy.*
>
> —Leviticus 11:45

Here, God is instructing the Israelites what His utmost desire is. His greatest desire is that they be holy. He clearly stated the reason for His desire. And the reason is simple—because He is holy. Now, there are a few things to consider from this desire. First, this is addressed to people whom we consider "Old Testament believers." This means they have a lesser advantage compared to New Testament believers. Yet, that did not change the desire of God for His people. It is clear from this passage that God will give no allowance to anyone who claims to be His. The only acceptable lifestyle for His people is a lifestyle of holiness. The reason for this desire makes it even more impossible to live anything short of a holy life. God clearly stated in that passage that the reason He expects His people to live a holy life is because He Himself is holy.

The Call to Holiness

If it is impossible for God to live an unholy life, then it is impossible for God to tolerate an unholy life. Someone might say, "Oh, the standard of holiness God expects from us is low." I would say to look at that passage again. It is as if God knew that a question such as this would arise. He compared the manner of holiness He expects from His people to the kind of holiness He Himself has. For example, it is as if someone says to a group of people, wear a white shirt today, for I am wearing white too. He is not saying to wear gray, neither is he saying to wear off-white. He is saying to wear white so that we all will be wearing the same color. That's exactly what God is saying here. He makes the standard for what holiness should be. We must hold to His own standard of holiness because that is what He has. That's another way you can say the passage. Let's consider another passage that will shed more light on this topic:

> *And ye shall be holy unto me: for I the Lord am holy, and have severed you from other people, that ye should be mine.*
>
> —Leviticus 20:26

See how the above passage is framed. God seems to be talking about the same thing in the same book. That's how important it is to God for His people to live a holy life. Now then, in this passage, God explains further why His people cannot afford to live anything short of a holy life. Notice the first reason He gives: "for I the Lord am holy." Meaning, "I am your leader, leading the way. I am holy, therefore you must be holy." In this particular passage, this seems to be the least important reason why they must live a holy life. The other reason seems to be more important to God. The second reason given in the above passage is that we must live a holy life because He has severed us from other people. Notice the word used in that part. The word "severed" is from the Hebrew word *badal*, which means "to divide, to make a distinction, difference, to withdraw from." What could that mean in relation to the topic under discussion? Notice that this word was not used to depict a gentle action. It was a forceful action. God didn't just softly separate His people. God forcefully removed His people from others. Why is that so? Because the lifestyle of the other people was not pleasing to God. God had to forcefully separate His people from the bad eggs so they would stop being corrupted. Now then, why should we think that, after all these efforts at removing His people from decay, He would permit anything short of holiness in their lives? If He will excuse sin, then there would have been no point in separating His people. Why go through the effort only for the people to continue to live the exact same lives they lived when they were in Egypt? It is clear to all in the above passage that God didn't separate His people to live however they wanted to live. He separated His people in order that they may live a holy life. And He dictates the standard of that holiness.

The above two reasons are good enough reasons to point us to the fact that the greatest desire of God for His people is for them to live a holy life. But God didn't stop at those two reasons. He gave a third reason to seal it up: "that you should be Mine." The reason for the holy life is for them to be His. That speaks volumes. That means His bringing them out of Egypt did not automatically mean they belonged to God. Destroying the greatest economy on earth at that time for the sake of this people was not a good reason for them to be called the people of God. Burying the strongest army on earth in the Red Sea without firing a single shot was not a good reason to show that the people belonged to God. Doing what has never been done before by making the whole congregation of about three million people walk on dry land in the midst of the sea was not a good reason to show that they were His people. The only reason good enough for God to consider them His people is for

The Call to Holiness

them to live a holy life. Can you see how important this matter is to God? Mind you, we are still talking about the Old Testament saints. If God requires nothing short of holiness from people we consider *less* privileged when compared to us, then I think it would be unscriptural and unreasonable for us today to expect God to understand that we are in this Body and therefore He should not expect much from us. The Scripture is clear that God is the same throughout all generations. The God who emphasizes holiness in the lives of the first people He brought out of sin has not changed. He will continue to emphasize holiness all through the generations as long as the earth remains. Let's take a look at one more passage from the Old Testament.

Thou shalt be perfect with the LORD *thy God.*

—Deuteronomy 18:13

This statement was made by Moses to the children of Israel as part of his departing speech shortly before he died. He made a profound statement, moving the matter to another level. In this passage, God, through Moses, went even beyond His demand for holiness. He went further to demand *perfection*. Perfection is a higher level of holiness. This statement was made forty years after the children of Israel had been "severed" from other people. This was enough time for God to give up on His desire for holiness from His people. Over these forty years, they had broken God's heart several times with their sins. Those were also reasons for God to have given up on His desire for His people to be holy. He had brought over three million people out from Egypt, and He demanded holiness from them, but they all perished due to their sins. Only two out of that crowd (apart from the children who had been under the age of twenty; we are not sure what percentage of the three million were children) would enter the Promise Land. That was more than enough reason for God to have lowered His standard for this new set. Two out of three million is 0.00007 percent (assuming the entire three million were above the age of twenty). That was a good reason for any reasonable leader to lower his standard so he could at least admit more people into his organization. That seems not to be what is happening here, however. Instead of reducing the standard to accommodate more people, God *increased* the standard. Does that mean heaven could be more concerned with quality than quantity? Does that mean heaven could be more concerned with us bearing fruit than with us just being part of the vineyard? Could it be that heaven does not mind if there is only one tree bearing fruit in the garden than having thousands of trees that have no fruit or bear bad fruit? In the above passage, heaven went beyond demanding holiness from the Old Testament believers. God demanded perfection. The word "perfect" in the above passage comes from the Hebrew word *tamiym*, which means "without blemish, without spot, undefiled." This seems an impossible task for people who are not able to keep up with the first level, yet that did not deter God from raising His standard. Can you see how important this matter is to God? It is clear from these Scriptures that God demands holiness from His people. It is also clear that anyone who teaches anything less is not speaking the mind of God. Herein lies a way to call out people who are from the devil or people who are not speaking on God's behalf.

Just in case someone says the principles of the Old Testament have passed, the God of the New Testament has reformed the standard. Let's see how that statement will hold as we look at God's standard in the New Testament for His children. But before we do, let's clear the elephant in the room—the matter of the death and resurrection of our Lord Jesus Christ and the matter of grace. Now then, someone might say, "Oh, you've got it all mixed up. The Old Testament saints were not living under grace. But *we* are living under grace. The death of Jesus Christ has covered us. The grace of God speaks for us. When God looks at us, He doesn't actually see us—He sees Christ in us. So, we can go on living our lives however we want because Jesus has already paid the price. Jesus has made the difference for us." Concerning the matter of grace, someone may say grace now covers up our sins. I am not sure which passage of the Bible gives them such assurance, but let's look at first, why Christ came, and then what grace is.

Why Did Jesus Come?

We can see from the Old Testament passages discussed above that God will not compromise His standard for us. All through the generations of the Old Testament saints, we can see God hammering on the topic of holiness. At a time, He had to flush the entire nation of Israel out of their land due to their unrepentant nature. He allowed suffering and pain to teach them to come back each time they wandered away from holiness. So, He decided once and for all to help the situation of humanity because He saw that it was impossible for man to keep all the laws. Hence, there are two things (apart from the many purposes He achieved with the coming of Jesus) He needed to take care of with Jesus regarding the problem of sin. First, we are all guilty of breaking the law of God. Every human on earth is born that way. Therefore, Jesus came to pay the penalty for our sin. Let's consider a few Scriptures along this line:

> *But of the tree of the knowledge of good and evil, thou shalt not eat of it: for in the day that thou eatest thereof thou shalt surely die.*
>
> —Genesis 2:17

Preparing for the Coming Glory

The soul that sinneth, it shall die. The son shall not bear the iniquity of the father, neither shall the father bear the iniquity of the son: the righteousness of the righteous shall be upon him, and the wickedness of the wicked shall be upon him.

—Ezekiel 18:20

For the wages of sin is death; but the gift of God is eternal life through Jesus Christ our Lord.

—Romans 6:23

From all of the above passages, first, we can see that all three Scriptures above are trying to communicate the same thing to us. It doesn't matter whether they are from the Old or New Testament, they speak the same language. Why wouldn't they? The entire Bible was written by one author, the Holy Spirit, using the pen of many men over a span of about 3,500 years. In the mouth of two or three witnesses every word is established, and here we have three witnesses. Between these three witnesses, at least a thousand years has passed. Hence, time did not cause the message or the tone of the truth to change. Truth remains the same regardless of how much time has passed. We can, therefore, see that the position of God is clear on the punishment of sin. Sin brings death, and righteousness brings life—the equation is as simple as that. Look at how God described Himself to Moses when Moses asked to know His ways:

And the LORD passed by before him, and proclaimed, The LORD, The LORD God, merciful and gracious, longsuffering, and abundant in goodness and truth, keeping mercy for thousands, forgiving iniquity and transgression and sin, and that will by no means clear the guilty; visiting the iniquity of the fathers upon the children, and upon the children's children, unto the third and to the fourth generation.

—Exodus 34:6–7

This above description is not just for Moses. It is for all who want to know Him and walk with Him. This, in summary, is the nature of God. This was not someone's opinion about God. This is God Himself telling us about Himself. Therefore, such a statement should not be ignored if we want to amount to anything with God.

Now, let's look at the portion of the above Scripture passage that relates to the matter of sin. It is clear from the above passage that God forgives sin. But there is something also very clear in the nature of God in that passage: "the guilty will by no means be cleared." That, to me, is a profound statement. If God says "by no means," it means there is nothing that individual can do to escape punishment as long as he is guilty of sin. This is the nature of God, as stated by God Himself. Though sin can be forgiven, it will never go unnoticed and unpunished. And just in case someone accuses us of building a doctrine from a single Scripture, let's look at another passage along that line:

The Lord is slow to anger, and great in power, and will not at all acquit the wicked: the Lord hath his way in the whirlwind and in the storm, and the clouds are the dust of his feet.

—Nahum 1:3

This is the prophet Nahum reporting to us, through the Spirit of prophecy, about the character of God regarding the issue of sin. Nahum lived over 1,500 years after Moses, yet they have the exact same thing to say concerning God. Look at the above passage. Even though God is slow to anger, it is impossible for Him to let the wicked go unpunished.

Look at how Nahum puts it: "not at all acquit the wicked." The word "acquit" comes from the Hebrew word *naqah*, which means "to clear" or "to free." That means that God will not in any way let the wicked go free. The guilty can never be cleared. Can you see that this is no different from what Moses recorded thousands of years before? Hence, it is insanity for us to think that God will be lenient with the issue of sin. It is clear that God treats sin worse than how we treat cancer. In order to be on the same page with God, we also have to treat sin like cancer. This nature of God as it relates to sin is in keeping with the three passages we considered earlier. Now then, this is one of the reasons why Christ came. None of us is without guilt. There is wickedness in the heart of every one of us. That means none of us should escape punishment. In order for us not to be punished, Jesus, who knew no sin, came to take our sins so our punishment could be laid on Him and His righteousness could be automatically imputed to us. Look at how Paul puts it in this passage:

> *For he hath made him to be sin for us, who knew no sin; that we might be made the righteousness of God in him.*
>
> —2 Corinthians 5:21

Hence, Jesus was made to be sin just because of us, so we can escape, because God cannot go back on His word. His nature clearly states that no guilty person will go unpunished. This is very clear so far. Now then, this is just half of the truth. We cannot just run with this truth and say it is the whole truth. There is another reason Jesus came as it relates to our topic of discussion. (Of course, you can agree with me that the coming of Jesus achieved many things for God.)

The second reason Jesus came was to help us deal with the issue of sin from the core. God is not only interested in dealing with our previous sins; He is also interested in taking care of our tendency to sin in the future. In discussing this, we shall look at it from the three phases. First, Jesus spent His whole life living a life of holiness according to the standard God requires. He was the only One who ever lived on earth who was able to stand tall in the face of the devil without falling for any of his gimmicks. He broke none of the laws of God in all His years on the earth. So, Jesus gave us, with His very life, a clear example of how to live the life God expects from us. Let us consider some Scriptures along this line.

> *Hereafter I will not talk much with you: for the prince of this world cometh, and hath nothing in me.*
>
> —John 14:30

The first thing to notice about this passage is that these words were spoken by Jesus Himself. The second thing to understand about this passage is the occasion in which it was said. It was not during a picnic; neither was it during a birthday party. It was not an opening speech for a sermon. These were the final words of Jesus to His disciples, spoken less than twenty-four hours before He was killed. Think about that. When a father is about to die, he often calls his children to give them his final instructions. Those instructions are usually more important than all the other instructions the father has given in all his years with his children. We see an example of this in the life of Jacob (Genesis 49:1). These last words of Jesus to His disciples were very important. Jesus said that the prince of this world had found nothing in Him. He didn't say the "prince of Jerusalem" or "the prince of Rome," for there are principalities in charge of certain territories. But rather, He called the devil the "prince of this world," meaning the boss himself—Satan—took it upon himself to search out Jesus, bringing his sophisticated scanning machine to detect sin. Such a scanner can even detect the intent to sin from miles away.

We are not even talking about sinning yet. Once the scanner smells an intention to sin, the prince of this world will reallocate his resources to achieve the downfall of that individual. In this situation, even the tiniest sin would have sufficed. The simple white lies we tell here and there would have been enough to derail God's plan for Jesus' work on the cross. The intentions to sin that no one sees would have been good enough as an allegation before the court of heaven. But even with the sophisticated scanning machine of the prince of this world, he found absolutely nothing to lay hold of concerning Jesus. That is what we call "perfection personified." This is the testimony of Jesus Himself. He gave us a practical example of how to live a holy life. Another Scripture along this line will help fulfill the law of two or three witnesses:

> *For we have not an high priest which cannot be touched with the feeling of our infirmities; but was in all points tempted like as we are, yet without sin.*
>
> —Hebrews 4:15

This passage is very profound. The tempter followed Jesus very closely throughout His lifetime. There is no manner of temptation common to man that was not tried on Jesus. The passage says that Jesus was tempted in all points. That means Jesus was tempted with riches, with women, with anger, with alcohol . . . you name it. Jesus was tempted with all kinds of sins—anything we can think or imagine. I am sure there are many temptations that He faced that we don't even know about. The devil must have gone back in time, checking through the archives of Jesus' bloodline to see the temptations that worked for men with great anointing. He tried women, because it had worked in the past for many in His bloodline, but Jesus overcame. He tried using the crowd to be His essence for doing the work of ministry, just like how he had succeeded with Saul, but Jesus did not commit Himself to men (John 2:24). He tried distracting Him from His purpose by pushing the people to forcefully make Him king, but Jesus overcame that too. He tried food. At least that had worked for Esau. But Jesus overcame. He went to and fro, searching the earthly bloodline of Jesus to see what made the men in His bloodline sin against God. Every sin in the bloodline was tried on Jesus—without success. In summary, every trick in the devil's book that had ever worked for any living being since the very first man, Adam, was tried on Jesus. But Jesus didn't fail, even in the minutest of the temptations. Think about that. Time and space will not permit us to explore this aspect of the life of Jesus, but it is incredible to realize.

The second phase was through the teaching. Not only did Jesus live the life, but He took it a step further to teach us the what and the how. Jesus taught us how to live the life. He spent all of His three-and-a-half-year ministry time teaching us the ways of the Kingdom and how to live a life that is pleasing to God. One of the most profound teachings of Jesus along this line is the Sermon on the Mount, recorded in the books of Matthew and Luke, though more elaborately in Matthew. Jesus, in the teachings of the Sermon on the Mount, clearly tells us His intention for spending those many hours to teach us. Let's look at the ultimate intention of Jesus for the Sermon in this single verse:

Be ye therefore perfect, even as your Father which is in heaven is perfect.

—Matthew 5:48

Now, let's do a mini-study on the above passage. Notice the first major word used in that verse is "therefore." As one of our fathers in the faith would say, whenever you see the word "therefore" in Scripture, you need to find out what it is *there for*. Now then, let's find out what that "therefore" is there for. If you go back to verse one of this same chapter 5, you will notice that a multitude had gathered around Jesus. When He saw the multitude, He opened His mouth and started to teach them. Verses 3 through 47 contain what He taught them when He opened His mouth. That was what led to the "therefore." The "therefore" in that passage is meant to tell the listeners the main purpose for all the teachings. Up until this point, Jesus had spent hours talking to them on how to live a life in such a way as to please God. Jesus brought that particular part of the sermon to a reasonable conclusion by saying, "The reason I took My time to elaborate on the right way for you to act in your daily encounters with other humans is so that you will be perfect." This is the reason for the "therefore." Now that we have learned this information, we need to understand what the "therefore" is pointing us toward. Now then, the second thing to note in the above verse is that Jesus is saying, "In the light of all I have said, if you can do exactly all I have taught you, you will be perfect." The key here is not that you have heard the word. The key to perfection is that you must *do* the word. Now then, the perfection expected here is not the perfection that men will see, the outward appearance, and say, "This is a holy man of God." The perfection being referred to here is the perfection that will make you like your Father in heaven. This has further increased the standard of this holiness. The standard is not measured against other men. It is measured against God. Here again, we can see God not relenting on His high standard of holiness.

The third phase in the second reason why Jesus came (as it relates to the topic of discussion) is that Jesus actually died and was raised from the dead to do two things. First, He is to live in us, and second, He is to intercede for us before the Father. How does this solve the issue of sin? It is clear from what we have discussed so far that Jesus is the only human who has passed through the face of the earth who did not break any of the laws of God. Now, this Jesus, who has lived a life completely pleasing to God, is now dwelling in you. The reason He is now dwelling in you (as it relates to this topic) is to be able to reproduce that sinless life in you. Let's confirm this from the Word of God.

> *And what agreement hath the temple of God with idols? for ye are the temple of the living God; as God hath said, I will dwell in them, and walk in them; and I will be their God, and they shall be my people.*
>
> —2 Corinthians 6:16

Notice what He said in the above passage: He will dwell in us. That's the first thing He said along that line. He is not just dwelling in you to just sit cool and feel cool. Notice the next statement: He will walk in us. The word "walk" here is from the Greek word *emperipateo*, which means "to be occupied, to go about." Can you see that? He is dwelling in us to walk in us. To walk here means to occupy, just like He told us to occupy (stay busy) until He comes back. He is going about in us for a clear purpose. The purpose He goes about in us is clearly stated in the passage. Look at it. In order to make us the people of God, He gets busy in us, reproducing His very life in us. The moment that life is reproduced in us, we automatically become the perfection God expects. This is exactly what He said in Matthew 5:48: "Be perfect as your Father." For us to be the people of God, we must attain perfection as God desires. That is the reason He is dwelling and walking in us. Now then, someone might say, "But the above passage says that God dwells in us, not Jesus." That's true. But God's dwelling in us is *through Christ*. Let me explain that a little more. When God says He will dwell among us, His intention is to do that through Jesus. For example, when God was to inform Israel about the coming Messiah, this is what He told the prophet Isaiah:

> *Therefore the Lord himself shall give you a sign; Behold, a virgin shall conceive, and bear a son, and shall call his name Immanuel.*
>
> —Isaiah 7:14

Did you notice the name of the Messiah there? Immanuel. What does that mean? It is from a Hebrew word that means "God with us." We know that that passage refers to Jesus being with us. Hence, God being with us takes place through Jesus. Let's look at another passage along this line:

> *Behold, I stand at the door, and knock: if any man hear my voice, and open the door, I will come in to him, and will sup with him, and he with me.*
>
> —Revelation 3:20

This is Jesus Himself telling us what He will do when we open the door of our heart to Him. Hence, when God says He plans to dwell in us, then He means He will do that through Christ.

Going back to the matter of God reproducing the life of Jesus in us, of course, we have to look at another passage so we can establish the Word:

> *Wherefore, my beloved, as ye have always obeyed, not as in my presence only, but now much more in my absence, work out*

The Call to Holiness

your own salvation with fear and trembling. For it is God which worketh in you both to will and to do of his good pleasure.

—Philippians 2:12–13

Our main focus in the above passage is on verse 13. Verse 12 talks about our role in the issue, but our focus is not on that at the moment. Let's focus on the role of God in this issue. Notice the role of God as described by the passage: "For It is God who works." Notice here that the passage mentions God doing the work. We have established previously that God does His work in us through Jesus Christ, who lives in us. Now then, the next question will be, what does Christ do in us? He works to achieve two things in our lives according to the passage. First, He works to will, and second, He works to do. The next logical question is, to will and to do what? That passage answers, "His good pleasure." So, let's start breaking it down from the last statement: His good pleasure. What does that mean? The word "pleasure" in the passage is from the Greek word *eudokia*, which means "satisfaction, delight, good will." Putting the phrase together, it means doing something to the full satisfaction or delight or goodwill of God. That's just part of the statement. Let's move to the next phrase: "to will and to do." "To will" is from the Greek word *thelo/ethelo*, which means "to have in mind, intend, to be resolved or determined, to purpose." "To do" is from the Greek word *energeo*, which means "to be operative, to be at work, to put forth power." Putting this second phrase together, we get something like this: to be resolved, determined, and to intend to get to work with power and enthusiasm.

To complete the equation, let's look at the first part of the passage, "for it is God which worketh." The word "worketh" is from the same root word as "to do" that we considered earlier. It means "to be at work, put forth power." Hence, putting the entire verse 13 together, we can see that God works with great power in us to bring our will to a place of strong determination where we can act to please God to the fullest. That is mind-blowing. This perfectly agrees with the other passages. This is how Jesus gets to reproduce His life in us. Jesus was the only Person who fully pleased God. He is the only Person whom God publicly proclaimed that He is well pleased with. He is the only Person in the history of humanity who got such a comment from God. And this comment did not come just once in the lifetime of Christ. It came twice. He was absolutely without sin all through His lifetime (just as we discussed earlier). Now, the above passage shows us how God can reproduce this life in us. First, through His great power, He will work through our mind and bring us to a place where we will not just agree, but we will decide and strongly determine to do His will. He doesn't stop there. He takes it a step further. He supplies His power, and the power supplied will empower us to do the will we have determined to accomplish.

We have looked at why Jesus came as it relates to our topic of discussion in a summarized version. From what we have considered so far, nowhere is it said that because Jesus paid the price, we no longer have to pay any price. Nowhere are we excused from pursuing holiness. Nowhere is it seen that God gave the New Testament saints some slack when it comes to the matter of sin. Rather, because much has been given to the New Testament saints, heaven requires much more from the New Testament Church.

Next, we shall consider briefly the matter of grace before we go into the main matter. Grace is not made available to cover up for our insufficiencies, as some suppose, but rather it is given to lift us above our insufficiencies. Grace is not given to make up for our weaknesses, but rather it is given to lift us above our weaknesses. That a lot of Christians still struggle with sin is not evidence that grace excuses sin. So, why has grace been made available to us? Let's consider two or three passages relating to this.

For sin shall not have dominion over you: for ye are not under the law, but under grace.

—Romans 6:14

The above passage is very simple. It starts with the word "for." The principle behind the word "for" in this Scripture is the same principle behind the word "therefore." Anytime you see any of those words in the Scriptures, you have to find out why they are there. Verse one of the same chapter gives us the main topic Paul is talking about:

What shall we say then? Shall we continue in sin, that grace may abound?

—Romans 6:1

We can see from this passage that the subject matter is about sin. From verse 1 through to verse 13, Paul was trying to tell us what Jesus did for us with regard to sin and what we need to do to overcome sin. It was in the light of this discussion that Paul says in verse 12 and 13 that therefore (because of the death and resurrection of our Lord Jesus Christ, which has given us the ability to be dead to sin and alive unto righteousness), we are not to permit sin in our space. Verse 14 then tells us why we must not permit sin in our space. That, in summary, is the reason for the "for" in verse 14. Now, with that understanding, let us tackle verse 14. It says that sin shall not have dominion over us. The three words—have-dominion-over—are all one word in the Greek, *kurieuo*, which means "to rule, be lord over or to exercise lordship over." Therefore, what that part of the Scripture is saying is that sin shall not exercise lordship over us. This means that as Christians, it is not possible for us to be helpless concerning the matter of sin if we are willing and obedient. The second half of the passage (verse 14) gives us the reason sin cannot exercise lordship over our lives—for we are not under the law, but under grace. The reason is simple. Because we are under grace. What does it mean to be under grace? It means grace is our master, and grace will teach us how to overcome sin. Grace is not given to cover up sin or weaknesses. Grace is given to teach us and empower us to overcome sin. Grace is more like a schoolmaster who teaches and empowers us to easily live above sin. Hence, putting all of this together, grace is given to us so we can exercise lordship over sin and not the other way around. But someone might say, despite the presence of the schoolmaster called grace, many Christians still struggle with sin. That's right. Just like everything with God, grace is a gentle person. He will never force you to take an action. He will only tell you what to do to exercise lordship over sin. It is your responsibility to carry out the instruction of grace. Carrying out the instruction is what will give you the edge over sin. The reason why many Christians still struggle with sin is not because they don't have access to grace. It is because they don't listen to the instruction of grace or allow grace to be their lord. If grace is not your lord, then automatically sin will be your lord. There is no vacuum in the Spirit, and there is no middle ground in the Spirit. If you are not on the side of God, automatically you have chosen to be on the side of the devil. There is no standing on the fence in the matters of the Spirit.

Now then, let us look at another passage that gives us an idea of the role of grace in the life of a Christian, lest we stand in danger of propagating a one-legged doctrine. We all know that a one-legged doctrine cannot stand the test of fire.

> *For the grace of God that bringeth salvation hath appeared to all men, teaching us that, denying ungodliness and worldly lusts, we should live soberly, righteously, and godly, in this present world.*
>
> —Titus 2:11–12

The above passage was written for our admonition. Take a look at the role grace plays in the life of a Christian in the above passage. The first role is that grace brings salvation. Notice that the salvation it brings is not only to Christians. The salvation it brings is for all men. But the moment you become a Christian; grace plays a different role in your life. Notice what grace does in verse 12. It teaches us. The word "teaching" in the above passage is from the Greek word *paideuo*, which means "to train up a child, an instructor, to chastise or to castigate with words." That's interesting. When we are going astray, away from the presence of God, yielding to the flesh, something within us expresses its displeasure, either by words or by stirring up an emotion that cannot be explained with words. That something is grace. According to the above passage, grace has two curricula included in its lecture to us. First, it teaches us to deny ungodliness, and second, it teaches us to live righteously. The above passage spells out how it does this. When it comes to living soberly, righteously, and in a godly manner, grace takes its time to train us up as a father would train a child or as a master would train his disciple. Another description for that aspect is to instruct. Grace gives us instruction as to what to do and when to do it in order to live a righteous life. On the other hand, when we begin to stray, grace begins to chastise. And sometimes it castigates in order to get us back on track.

Putting these last two passages together, we can see that they both speak the same thing regarding grace. In the mouth of two or three witnesses, every word is established.

Now then, going back to where we started from, the demand for holiness from God has not changed. If He demands perfection from the Old Testament saints, grace and the coming of Christ does not make Him demand less from the New Testament saints. If anything, grace and the coming of Christ would make Him raise the bar for the New Testament saints. If He demands perfection from the Old Testament saints, then He demands perfection raised-to-the-power-of-two from us, not less perfection. There is no single passage in the Bible, either in the Old or the New Testament, that tells us God has reduced His demand for perfection from the New Testament saints.

There is also another school of thought I wish to briefly address before moving into the demand of perfection in the New Testament. Some say there is nothing you can do to lose your status as a child of God. The doctrine then compares God to an earthly father who will never reject a child, no matter what he/she has done. The other side of the doctrine says that no kind of offense can make the DNA of the child change. No matter what the child does, the DNA of the father remains in the child. While that is true for human biology, that is not true for God. God is a spirit, and the matter of how DNA in the spirit works are different principles. In the DNA of God, there is no sin. No darkness at all exists in God (1 John 1:5). When you are born again, you take on the DNA of God. That DNA is light and completely devoid of darkness. This automatically makes you holy. As you grow in the Lord, the DNA expands and spreads all over your being, making you more and more filled with light and holiness. When sin comes in, it changes the configuration of the DNA, and it is no longer God's DNA. Such an individual dies the moment the DNA is misconfigured, though it takes time for the manifestation of the death to become physical. Hence, that doctrine is completely false and a fabrication from hell meant to keep people in sin. It may sound logical for humans, but it is not for God.

Holiness in the New Testament

Now then, let's examine some passages in the New Testament to see the demand of God from the New Testament saint regarding the matter of holiness.

> ... but as he which hath called you is holy, so be ye holy in all manner of conversation; because it is written, Be ye holy; for I am holy.
>
> —1 Peter 1:15–16

This is a good Scripture to start from. In this passage, we can see a link between the Old and New Testaments concerning the matter of holiness. Peter quoted directly from Leviticus 11:44. We can draw many conclusions from the above passage. First, the One who called us is holy. There is no compromise about the nature of God. And He is not just holy; His environment is also holy. Now then, notice that the verb used in that verse is "called." To call is to summon or to attract someone's attention. When you call someone, you expect the person to come toward you in response to your call, or at least respond to your call with a voice or body gesture. Hence, when God "calls," He is calling for you to approach Him. Fortunately, or unfortunately, God is not all that is holy; His dwelling is also holy. Hence, if you come to Him, you must be holy, for nothing unclean can approach His dwelling. Look again at how Peter phrased it: "As he which hath called you is holy, so be ye holy." Now, Peter went a step further by telling us the areas of our lives in which holiness is required. Peter said this is needed "in all manner of conversation." In order to understand the scope of the above statement, we must understand the meaning of "conversation," from the root word as it was used. The word "conversation" came from the Greek word *anastrophe*, which means "manner of life, conduct and behavior." We can easily deduce the scope to which Peter was referring from this definition. Peter was actually saying: Be ye holy in every area of your life, every area of your behavior, and every area of your conduct in life. This actually covers every part of our lives. Verse sixteen tells us that Peter was quoting from the Old Testament. That again demonstrates that the God we get to know in the Old Testament is the same God of the New Testament. He has not changed, and He will never change. And nothing can make Him demand less from us.

Let's take a look at a second Scripture to seal this up before going into deeper matters:

> *Nevertheless the foundation of God standeth sure, having this seal, The Lord knoweth them that are his. And, let every one that nameth the name of Christ depart from iniquity.*
>
> —2 Timothy 2:19

This passage is very profound. Let's try to break it down as simply as possible. The verse in focus starts with the word "nevertheless." In order for us to have a full understanding of this particular verse, we must know why that word is used. Paul started the chapter by telling Timothy what he needed to do in order to be a good soldier in the army of the Lord. But when Paul got to verse 15, the theme changed. Paul started talking about how to be an effective worker in the house of God, and how Timothy (and in extension, we) should be deeply conversant with the Word because false doctrine had swept into the Church, causing many to leave the faith. At this point, the word "nevertheless" appeared. This gives us a better perspective of what Paul was trying to achieve with verse 19 (our verse of interest). We can now discuss verse 19 in context and with a better understanding. Let's take it piece by piece. The first part says, "The foundation of God is sure." What could that mean? The word "foundation" here is from the Greek word *themelios*, which means "something put down, first principles of institution or system of truth." What that means is that concerning the institution called Christianity, the system of truth that forms the foundation of the institution (Christianity) is sure. The word "sure" comes from the Greek word *stereos*, which means "solid, stable, strong, firm, and immovable." That is, Paul was telling Timothy that the system of truth built into the foundation of the institution called Christianity is firm and immovable. That's phenomenal.

The next phrase says: "having this seal." There are a few questions to consider with regard to this second phrase. What is a seal? The word "seal" used here is from the Greek word *sphragis*, which means "signet, stamp." The "seal" used here is God's signet. A signet is a small type of seal, especially one set into a ring, which is used instead of or with a signature to give authentication to an official document. Putting the first two phrases we have considered together, Paul's statement therefore looks like this: The system of truth built into the foundation of the institution called Christianity is firm and immovable, and it has the authentication of the signet from God's ring. In order to find out what the inscription on the seal actually is, however, we must consider other phrases in this study verse. The next phrase is segmented into two parts, joined with the conjunction word "and," so we consider both together: "The Lord knows those that are his" and "Let everyone that nameth the name of Christ depart from iniquity." Those two phrases are the inscription on the signet of the greatest King. Let's look at two words in these two phrases that will bring a better understanding to the inscription. The word "nameth" comes from the Greek word *onomazo*, which means "to profess." The word "depart" is from the Greek word *aphistemi*, which means "to revolt." With these definitions in hand, the inscription on the signet therefore looks like this: "Let everyone who professes to be a follower of Christ revolt from sin." Those are strong words. Everyone means *everyone*. It is without exception. In conclusion, let us briefly explain what verse 19 means in light of what Paul was speaking of from verse 15. Paul was advising Timothy, and in extension, every single believer who is interested in being part of God's workforce, to study the Scriptures in such a way that God will certify them, because many people in the Church propagate false doctrine, and many people have been swept away by these false beliefs. Then, Paul went on further to say that even though all these false teachings and false doctrines were going on in the Church, the system of truth built into the foundation of the institution called Christianity—i.e., the Church—was firm and immovable; it had this signet from God's ring, and the inscription on the signet reads: "The Lord knows all those who truly belong to Him (from the mix multitude); let everyone who professes to be a follower of Christ revolt against sin." This could not be clearer. The position of God regarding sin and holiness is inscribed in the very foundation of the institution called Christianity. Sin is an abomination to God. If you wish to be part of the Body of Christ, you *must* depart from—and, indeed, revolt against—sin.

We can look at verse after verse of Scripture, and they will all tell us the same thing. The position of God concerning the matter of holiness is firm and unchangeable. If you want to be part of what God is doing,

The Call to Holiness

you have to fall in line. God can never fall in line with your ideology. You have to fall in line with His. It is the Kingdom of God, not your kingdom. He decides the rules, not you. Another thing we have to consider before getting into the crux of the matter is the fact that some people believe the Old Testament saints were instantly punished for their sins because Christ was not in the picture at that time, but we can be spared from the punishment of our sins because of the price Christ paid on the cross. That is very far from the truth. Every soul that sins shall die, the Word says—whether that person lived in Old or New Testament times. Let's consider some passages along that line:

For if we sin willfully after that we have received the knowledge of the truth, there remaineth no more sacrifice for sins, but a certain fearful looking for of judgment and fiery indignation, which shall devour the adversaries. He that despised Moses' law died without mercy under two or three witnesses: of how much sorer punishment, suppose ye, shall he be thought worthy, who hath trodden underfoot the Son of God, and hath counted the blood of the covenant, wherewith he was sanctified, an unholy thing, and hath done despite unto the Spirit of grace?

—Hebrews 10:26–29

This is a somewhat long passage, but I think it is worth the work of examining it. Let's see if we can learn something that relates to the matter we are discussing. Notice the first verse in the above passage. It says, "If we sin willfully after that we have received the knowledge of truth . . ." This is exactly what we are looking to address. The doctrine we are trying to debunk says that Christ has already paid the price for our sin, and thus we will not be punished for our sins because Christ has been punished already. The other part of this false doctrine says that the day we gave our lives to Christ, our past, present, and future sins were automatically forgiven. Hence, people who believe in this doctrine go on sinning because of this assumption. We can, therefore, conclude that such a fellow, who decides to go on sinning even though the power to live above sin is now available to him, can be said to be an individual who is willfully indulging in sin. The above passage says that to such a fellow, there is no more sacrifice that can be made for sin. This is because the sacrifice of Christ was never meant to permit us to keep sinning, but rather to set us free from sin so we can live a "sin-free" life. If the sacrifice of Christ had been meant to just enable us to continue in sin, there would really have been no need for Christ to come in the first place. His sacrifice was too great a price to pay for the nature of sin in humanity not to completely die. He could have just stayed in heaven and maintained His nature as God while we continued in our sin. He paid the price through a great sacrifice, and that sacrifice was meant to entirely destroy the nature of sin in humanity. The only way the sacrifice can bring deliverance to anyone is when such a person believes that the sacrifice is the only way to his deliverance. Hence, the first part of the above passage is saying that if this sacrifice is ignored, and if people who are supposed to know the power that this sacrifice provides (Christians) go on sinning willfully, then there is no more sacrifice to cover for such a lifestyle. That verse alone spells hopelessness for all who indulge in such. What that means is that because there is no further sacrifice to make up for their excesses, if they continue in those acts until transitioning away from this earth, then they will be separated from God eternally. That's a serious issue.

Let's look at verse 27 to see what else the Bible has to say concerning this matter. That verse brings even more terrifying news to such a fellow. If there is no further sacrifice available for such people, then what is available to them is only judgment and fiery indignation. This is a serious matter. Look at the conclusion of that verse. God sees such a fellow as siding with His adversaries. A good question to ask here is this: What kind of judgment will such a person face? Verses 28 and 29 give us a clue of the kind of judgment they will face. It says those in the Old Testament who did this kind of thing (that is, sinned after knowing the law, sinned willfully) died without mercy. Now, the right question follows in verse 29: What kind of punishment or judgment is right for the fellow of the New Testament who sins willfully? The concerning thing in verse 29 is the description given to such a fellow. A believer who still continues in sin after the sacrifice that Jesus made on the cross, according to verse 29, is guilty of the following crime: First, they have trodden underfoot the Son of God. That is a serious crime. That means they have had contempt for the Son of God; they have despised Christ. That also means they have rejected Christ with disdain. How much worse could this get? Think about it: That alone is a crime worthy of eternal damnation. The second crime such a fellow is guilty of is that he has literally called the blood of Jesus an unholy thing. What then could such a fellow say about his salvation, knowing that he can be saved only by the blood of Jesus? That person can therefore be said *not* to be a believer. The third accusation that heaven will bring against such a fellow is that he has done despised the Spirit of grace. That may seem a little difficult to understand. Hence, let's try to break the words down to get a better picture. The words "hath done despised" is from the Greek word *enubrizo*, which means "to insult." Hence, putting it together, this means that such a fellow has insulted the Spirit of grace when he indulges in sin willfully after understanding the sacrifice Jesus made on the cross. From our research on grace, we discovered that grace teaches us to live a godly life. It is therefore an insult to the Spirit of grace to say we can continue in sin because Christ has already paid the sacrifice for sin. Am I trying to say that no sin is permitted, regardless of your age in your walk with God? No, that's not what I am saying at all. As we grow in the Lord, we will definitely fall and stumble at times. For a righteous man can fall seven times, but he must rise again. It is okay when we stumble and fall on our way to perfection. God has made provision for such falls. Look at this passage:

> *If we confess our sins, he is faithful and just to forgive us our sins, and to cleanse us from all unrighteousness.*
>
> —1 John 1:9

That passage was written for Christians. When you sincerely repent before God and confess your sins, you will be forgiven. But this has to happen *on your way* to perfection. If you continue in sin while *deliberately* ignoring the voice of your conscience, when you *deliberately* sin because you think you can just go back and ask for forgiveness, when you don't care about living a holy life, when you fall into the same sin over and over again *without remorse* and with no desire to desperately cry out to God for help, when you make excuses for your shortcomings as you ignore the work of grace, when you strongly believe the false doctrine that permits you to make sin a lifestyle, then you fall under the category of those who *willfully sin*. The Christian life and sin are not compatible. You can't be a Christian and continue in sin. One has to give way for the other.

There are some who say you can never lose your salvation. That depends on what such people mean. Some say that no matter what you do, you can't lose your salvation. If that means you are still going to be called a Christian as long as you are alive, yes, I agree with you. There is still hope for you as long as you are alive. But when such a fellow dies in that state, he cannot go to be with God in heaven. So, the question is, what is the use of a salvation that does not give you eternal life? So, when someone says that no matter what you do, you cannot lose your salvation, that's just another trick of the devil to deceive you into continuing in sin. The position of God concerning sin is clear: If you are to be called by the name of the Lord, you must be as far away from sin as the north is from the south.

Let's take a look at one more Scripture along this line before we wrap up this part of our discussion:

> *The Son of man shall send forth his angels, and they shall gather out of his kingdom all things that offend, and them which do iniquity; and shall cast them into a furnace of fire: there shall be wailing and gnashing of teeth.*
>
> —Matthew 13:41–42

This passage was written when Jesus, the very One who paid the sacrifice for our sins, was teaching about the seven principles of the Kingdom of God. To understand the passage above, we need to give a little background to the chapter. Chapter 13 of the book of Matthew contains seven parables. All of these parables strictly refer to the matter of the Kingdom. This chapter actually gives a timeline of the story of the Kingdom, starting from the ministry of Jesus until the end of the age. You can understand this picture when you put the seven parables together. But that is not our focus right now. The passage above is the explanation Jesus gave for His second parable. What we should note is that Jesus said sin is an offense to heaven. There is no way sin can be packaged that will be acceptable to heaven. If Matthew wrote those words on his own, then we might have said there is a possibility that Jesus had something different to say. But this statement was made by the One who paid the sacrifice Himself. This is a clear indication that there is no doctrine anywhere, neither in the Old Testament nor in the

New Testament, anyone can use to give an excuse for sin to be acceptable. We shall explore the above passage deeper in a later part of this book. But we stop here for now on the matter of sin and move on to how to get to the valley of dry bones, from which God recruits His army generals.

5

The Making of the Champions

God's Generals

The valley of dry bones, as depicted by the prophet Ezekiel, is a place where heaven's champions are made. Better put, it is a place where God's generals are forged. It is designed to meet the full requirements for the man whom God would use. But before anyone gets to the valley of dry bones, that person must, of necessity, go through and graduate from the University of Heaven. Of course, the curriculum is different for everyone because of our individual differences. But it is designed in such a way as to make the greatness in us pop out under adequate pressure. It is designed to completely remove self, flesh and its works, and wordliness from us. This adequate pressure means that God will not permit the tiniest bit of pressure above what anyone can handle. The pressure that will be permitted is just exactly the right amount to achieve what is needed to be achieved in us. Let's explore the process involved in this curriculum for a better understanding.

In considering this, we shall explore Ezekiel 37:1–10 as our primary Scripture passage. Let's take it verse by verse and consider the process through which God takes His elect to pull the greatness out of them after removing self, flesh and worldliness.

> *The hand of the Lord was upon me, and carried me out in the spirit of the Lord, and set me down in the midst of the valley which was full of bones.*
>
> —Ezekiel 37:1

The first thing to note about this passage is that it was God Himself who set this up. He was telling the prophet how He planned to raise His army. God took the prophet to the valley, the place of the "almost finished product." The valley is the place where God forges His champions. The valley is the factory of God. The word "valley" here is from the Hebrew word *biqah*, which means "a split, a braking or cleaving of something in half." It also means "to break, to cut, or to divide something in half." This signifies that the valley is a place where God succeeds in breaking through to us. It is a place where heaven is able to completely split us to bring out the best that is hidden within. It is the only place where God can make a break in our lives, where God can break flesh, worldliness and self away. For example, when a seed is in the hand of a farmer, the seed is good for nothing until the farmer plants it. When the farmer plants the seed, the seed will still remain useless until it goes through certain processes. The first process is that the seed will die. After dying, the outer coat will split before the process of growth begins. There has to be a splitting away of the outer coat for the seed to produce. If there is no breaking away, there cannot be any growth. In the same way, God has to take us to the place of splitting before anything good can come out of us. Hence, a valley is a place of death. It is a place where the chaff has to be broken away from the grain so that the grain can be useful to the farmer. As long as you are still on the mountain of your pride, the self, your ability, your eloquence, etc., you cannot achieve any significant thing for the Lord.

The mountain is the place where you are full of yourself. It is where your own ability is what you think will suffice. It is a place where you depend on your own abilities and your own confidence. It is a place where you don't believe you need God, even though you are working for God. Many men of God work *for* God, but they do not work *with* God. They never pray to get a sermon from God; they pray for God's blessings on the sermon they dig out by themselves. They have the research tools at their reach and the intellectual ability to search a theological lexicon to deliver a great message. They are very strategic in their approach. They get direction for their life and ministry through their great intellectual and strategic planning skills. They have no time to wait upon God.

If God wants to be gracious to such a fellow, then God will orchestrate a journey for him to descend from that mountain into the valley. This journey into the valley can take a few months to several years, depending on the yielding ability of the fellow. But one thing is clear: God will not stop until the fellow gets to the valley.

The next thing to note about the above passage is that the valley is full of dry bones, not living men. This is a very important thing to note when dealing with God. In the factory of God, no flesh is needed. God cannot tolerate flesh in any form, shape, or size. In the valley, which represents the place where God raises up His generals, no flesh can remain in that place. Look at what Paul said concerning this matter:

Preparing for the Coming Glory

For ye see your calling, brethren, how that not many wise men after the flesh, not many mighty, not many noble, are called: but God hath chosen the foolish things of the world to confound the wise; and God hath chosen the weak things of the world to confound the things which are mighty; and base things of the world, and things which are despised, hath God chosen, yea, and things which are not, to bring to nought things that are: that no flesh should glory in his presence.

—1 Corinthians 1:26–29

Though the above passage is a little bit lengthy, we can quickly draw out the point we are trying to make. It would have been easier to concentrate on verse 29 alone, since it carries the substance of our point, but in order to avoid the danger of taking the passage out of context, it is better to look at it from verse 26. Here, Paul was trying to tell the church in Corinth the tenets of the calling they had in God. According to Paul in the above verses, God does not call the wise as long as their wisdom is of the flesh. God does not need the mighty in service of Him, as long as the mighty are operating with a bit of their flesh. God cannot use the noble as long as their flesh is involved. The bottom line of what Paul was trying to tell the Corinthian church—and in extension, us—is that no matter how gifted the individual is, as long as there is flesh involved, God has no need of such talent or skill or gift. The reason is simple. God will not permit the flesh to take responsibility for what He alone can do. God will not share His glory with any man. God will go to any lengths to ensure that before He pours out His raw power on anyone, that person must have arrived at the valley of dry bones, where no flesh exists. We shall look at the above passage deeper in a later part of this book.

The Making of the Champions

Now then, let's explore further, using life examples, the process through which God takes those who are willing. This process starts the moment we step our feet into the Kingdom. Everyone who steps into the Kingdom must be subjected to these conditions except he refuses to advance in the process. When someone is born again, he is more or less on the mountain—far away from the place God wants him to be. Yes, heaven is very happy that a soul has made it to the mountain of God from the pit of hell. Some might ask, "What do you mean by the 'pit of hell'? As long as that person is alive, he is not yet in hell." My answer would be that the position of heaven concerning unbelievers is different from the way we think. Anyone who has not accepted Christ is separated from God. Whether he is alive or dead, he is a citizen of hell, just like anyone who is a child of God is a citizen of heaven, whether dead or alive, because he is seated in heavenly places with Christ even while walking on the face of the earth. When a person is not born again, he is locked in the miry clay in the pit of hell, whether dead or alive. The only difference between the dead and the living is that there still is the hope of coming out of the miry clay for the living. The dead man has no hope. Hell will be his lot forever. Look at how the psalmist puts it:

He brought me up also out of an horrible pit, out of the miry clay, and set my feet upon a rock, and established my goings.

—Psalm 40:2

Notice that in the above passage, the miry clay is located in a horrible pit. When the person was brought up out of the pit, he was set upon a rock. So, when that fellow comes to Christ, he is brought up from the horrible pit of hell, filled with miry clay. When the fellow makes it to the top of the mountain (the rock), his body is still heavily padded with the sticky, miry clay. Though the fellow is no longer in the pit, the miry clay that had gotten stuck to his body will not let go until something is done about it. Now then, the mountain, where we find ourselves the moment we give our lives to Christ, is the mountain of pride. We are full of pride and selfishness. The spirit is a new creature quite alright, but the soul is still full of self and pride. The worldliness that such an individual has known for all the years he has been in the world before coming to Christ is still locked in the soul. This is the point where we meet the first bottleneck of distraction. Of course, hell is not happy that it has lost a soul. It will do everything possible to return that soul to hell. If it cannot return the soul to hell, it will do everything possible to prevent the soul from advancing into the valley of dry bones. One of the tricks the enemy uses at this point is to take advantage of the zeal for God that is locked into the soul. The zeal that consumes such a soul should push the person to seek to know more of God and increase his love for God. But the devil will redirect this zeal to seeking approval from the "church elders" by having that one join the workforce without first taking the necessary time to grow. Unfortunately, the majority of today's churches do not have eternity as their focus. They do everything except raise up an army for the Lord. Money, power, and fame have become the primary focus.

Ideally, the time when a fellow is still trying to clear off the clay stuck on the soul and body is not the time to be enrolled in the workforce of a local church. Apart from the darkness that remains on the soul, Mr. Flesh is still very much alive. It is God's responsibility to bring us out of the miry clay, because no matter how hard we try, no one can come out of the miry clay through self-effort. But it *is* our responsibility to do something about our soul, Mr. Flesh, and the world, which will relentlessly come after us. A common mistake that most of us make is to enroll in the workforce of the Church right away—to be in the choir, to become an usher, to volunteer in a myriad of ways. At a time when the individual should be gaining nourishment on mother's milk, the individual is instead battling to meet the requirements of the local church. This is especially bad when the local church authorities do not have eternity in focus. It is the devil's way of distracting us from what truly matters. Look at how Jesus puts it:

> *For Moses said, Honour thy father and thy mother; and, Whoso curseth father or mother, let him die the death: but ye say, If a man shall say to his father or mother, It is Corban, that is to say, a gift, by whatsoever thou mightest be profited by me; he shall be free. And ye suffer him no more to do ought for his father or his mother; making the word of God of none effect through your tradition, which ye have delivered: and many such like things do ye.*
>
> —Mark 7:10–13

In the above passage, the Church at the time of Jesus had full access to the Word of God. However, in addition to the Word of God that had been handed down by Moses, they had their own doctrines that they forced the congregations to follow. In fact, they laid greater emphasis on their own traditions than on the ways of God. They didn't mind if the new convert broke the law of God in an attempt to fulfill their own doctrines. By so doing, Jesus said, they made the Word of God of no effect. This is a serious matter because that same spirit that prevented those people from obeying the laws of God is still in the Church today. Now then, after few months or years of working very hard at fulfilling the doctrine of the denomination and pleasing the elders of the local church, the new convert receives the good hand of fellowship because he has been properly schooled in the doctrine of the denomination (rather than in the ways of God). With such approval of the elders comes trust and promotion, from departmental membership to departmental leadership. This fellow has experienced portfolio growth without spiritual growth. The spirit is born again quite alright, but the soul and the flesh are still very much untouched. The fellow will just keep rolling around the mountain in circles without venturing into the valley of dry bones below. That is what Jesus called the tradition of the church elders. The fact that such fellow is a worker in the local church brings satisfaction to both the fellow and the church elders. Though this act is interpreted as spiritual growth, as far as heaven is concerned, the fellow is a disaster waiting to happen. Some even grow in their portfolios to become pastors, evangelists, apostles, or general overseers in the Church. But their souls never experience the salvation that will lead to conformity to the image of Christ. This is usually where the Body of Christ gets its bad name. Many don't want to associate with Christians because they see that we are no different from the world. This is the window through which worldliness crawls into godliness. Worldliness still remains comfortable in the Church even after many years of 100 percent attendance.

Another obstacle the devil puts in the way of a Christian to prevent him from embarking on the journey to the valley of dry bones is the issue of natural ability. It is possible that an individual may have natural talent, perfect voice to sing, the ability to speak publicly, excellent leadership qualities, good team spirit, etc. Such abilities could be misinterpreted by the local church leaders as God's gifting to their local assembly through that person, and it is then misused in the name of bringing growth to the assembly. Over time, such a fellow with leadership skills, for example, will be placed in a position of leadership. Someone might ask, where else should we use our natural abilities other than in the house of God? But we have already established the fact that your ability is useless to heaven unless you make it to the valley of dry bones. The major problem with that setting is that the new convert eventually grows to become exactly like the elders who brought him up. The soul is not renewed, and Mr. Flesh is still very much in charge of that fellow. That person cannot be trusted with heaven's treasure. If he will make it to heaven at all at the end of his life, it will be by the skin of the teeth and God's mercy.

The next question is, does this mean that new converts should not volunteer to work in the church? The answer is simple. We shall explore two examples from the New Testament Church (which applies more to us today) to see how converts are recruited into the workforce of the Body.

> *Then the twelve called the multitude of the disciples unto them, and said, It is not reason that we should leave the word of God, and serve tables. Wherefore, brethren, look ye out among you seven men of honest report, full of the Holy Ghost and wisdom, whom we may appoint over this business. But we will give ourselves continually to prayer, and to the ministry of the word.*
>
> —Acts 6:2-4

This is a very good place from which to start our discussion. The passage above gives a picture of the problem the newly founded Church had at its inception. The Church was barely ten years old. At that time, the twelve apostles were running the affairs of the Church, but their numbers were increasing exponentially, and so more hands were needed to take care of the administrative aspects of the organization. The Twelve were overwhelmed with the needs of service and their other spiritual assignments, and it was creating obvious lapses that were then generating conflict in the Body. So, many began to complain, and their complaints reached the ears of the Twelve. So they came up with a Holy Spirit–inspired solution. Let's explore the solution from the passage above. Notice the first thing they did in the above passage. They called the disciples unto them. They didn't call the entire congregation, and neither did they call any new converts into the meeting. They called the multitude of the disciples. The next question is, who was considered a disciple? The word "disciple" is from the Greek word *mathetes*, which means "a learner, or a pupil." The next question is, what was this particular group of disciples learning, and from whom were they learning it? The answer is obvious. They were learning from the Twelve everything Christ had taught the Twelve when He was on the earth. In essence, they would eventually become as spiritually mature as the Twelve if they followed the instructions of the Twelve. So, within the Church as a set, there were many subsets. New converts, disciples, apostles, evangelists, and prophets are subsets within the set called the Church. Now then, the Twelve commissioned these learners to be the ones to choose the first official workforce of the Church, as stated in the Bible. The Twelve clearly declared to them the subset from which they should pick these workers and the qualifications needed of the workers. Let's look at it in verse three. The place from which they must choose the workers was from among them, meaning the disciples. Not anyone who wished to volunteer, nor any new convert, nor anyone from the congregation could simply become part of the workforce immediately. This was very specific. The person(s) chosen for the workforce must come from among the group of the disciples. Within the disciples, there was another subset from which the workers must be chosen. Look at it in verse three above. First, they had to be men of honest report. That means the people around them, who had known them for years, must have been able to bear witness to their good behavior. The testimony of people concerning them had to be good. The characters who produced this honest report could not only be generated by teaching from the discipleship classes; it would be generated from the day-to-day dealings they had with the people around them. The next qualification was that the disciple must be full of the Holy Spirit and wisdom. Notice that character certification came even before spiritual certification. This is so because God is more interested in the fruit a person produces than the gifts a person exhibits. So then, we can see from the above passage that it is not acceptable for a new convert to immediately join the workforce of a local church. The new convert must first enroll into the life discipleship class of the Holy Spirit under the tutelage of a human teacher before venturing into the workforce. In order not to build this doctrine on one passage, let's look at another passage to seal this up.

> *Likewise must the deacons be grave, not doubletongued, not given to much wine, not greedy of filthy lucre; holding the mystery of the faith in a pure conscience. And let these also first be proved; then let them use the office of a deacon, being found blameless.*
>
> —1 Timothy 3:8–10

This passage was extracted from the letter Paul wrote to Timothy, who was the pastor of the church in Ephesus. Paul was not there when the Twelve gave the criteria for selecting people into the local church's workforce. In fact, he was not even born again at that time. This letter was written about twenty years after the event in Acts 6. But yet, the criteria for joining the local church's workforce was not brought low. Rather, it had intensified over the years. Look at how Paul put it in the above letter. This was the same role the apostles had given the first qualification for in Acts 6, but here Paul adds even more points to the initial qualification given by the apostles. First, he says they must be grave. The word "grave" comes from the Greek word *semnos*, which means "honest." That actually covers for the only character criteria the apostles gave in Acts 6. Apart from the "honest report," Paul went further by giving more character criteria, as if to make it even more difficult to get into the workforce. The person must not be double-tongued, they must not be a drunkard, and they must not be greedy of filthy lucre. Notice verse 10. Even if they meet all the criteria listed, they must also be proven first to see if they truly had substance before they could be considered. One might expect this criteria to be less stringent, but instead the apostle seems to make it more difficult. This is the nature of the Church concerning its workforce. We will not gain any good results unless we follow the precepts left by our forefathers.

Now then, let's go back to the ideal. When someone steps into the Kingdom through the door of salvation, the fellow must decide to seek God with the zeal that is locked in his soul. As earlier stated, he is still a raw fellow, filled with self and pride. The soul is still the old self that needs urgent renewal. The fellow must sit at the feet of Christ until pride and the self is destroyed. What the local church can do for such fellow at this time is to put him under the tutelage of a well-trusted elder who will disciple him for a period of time until this fellow is able to stand firm in the faith. See how Jesus Himself puts it in this passage:

> *And he goeth up into a mountain, and calleth unto him whom he would: and they came unto him. And he ordained twelve, that they should be with him, and that he might send them forth to preach.*
>
> —Mark 3:13–14

The Making of the Champions

Notice how it is put in the above passage. Jesus was on the mountain, and He called the followers unto Himself. Where did He call them from? They were not on the mountain when He called them. For Him to call them unto Himself means they were not on the mountain. They must have been below the mountain. Hence, they were pulled out of the horrible pit of miry clay. But Jesus did not then immediately put them to work. He didn't immediately send them out to preach. He called them so that they should be with Him. Notice the verb that is used in that statement: "should." That means the ideal that heaven expects of you at this point is for you to simply be with Him. However, it is a matter of choice. The choice is on your part, not on heaven's part. Heaven is making it compulsory for you to seat at His feet; however, it is not in heaven's character to impose its will on you. Then, after seating at His feet, when He is satisfied, He will decide which role to assign to you. Notice that this second part is optional on heaven's part. The feet of Jesus is where the journey to the valley of dry bones should begin.

Now then, the early disciples had the privilege of seating at the feet of Christ. But Jesus stayed with them for only three and a half years. And the process must continue so that the disciples of today can be of the same quality as the disciples of old. Hence, when Jesus was leaving, He promised to send another Comforter. The words "another Comforter" mean He would send a Person of the same caliber as Jesus. At this point, even though the responsibility to take off the garment of miry clay fell mostly on the fellow himself, heaven has designed a help for him. The next step for heaven in the new convert's journey to the valley of dry bones is to introduce him to the ministry of the Holy Spirit. The Holy Spirit is the agency through which heaven will tutor the fellow until he becomes the dry bones that heaven can use. The Holy Spirit is introduced to the new believer through the vehicle of baptism. Notice that the human vehicle God will use to achieve His purpose in the life of the new convert is not mentioned. This is because the Holy Spirit must be the One to supervise the growth of this convert. The role of the Church in the journey of this new convert is to provide the necessary resources and attach a mature elder to be the human face through which the Holy Spirit can work. The Holy Spirit will work through the elder to provide navigation to the new convert on how to get to the valley of dry bones.

Now then, let's talk briefly about baptism, to clear up some doubt before moving on. There are three major baptisms that are required in order for anyone to advance in the Kingdom of God: water baptism, Holy Spirit baptism, and baptism with fire. Water baptism is required as soon as anyone steps into the Kingdom through the door of salvation. The essence of water baptism is to break the power of sin over the life of the believer. A believer who is well tutored before undergoing water baptism will be able to tap into the benefit of this, as heaven has designed it to be. Sin will no longer be a compulsion to such a believer. Rather, he will have the ability to make the choice whether to sin or not to sin. The choice not to sin should naturally occur to such a believer because he loves God. Water baptism is also a public demonstration of the fact that the fellow is now on the side of Jesus and not the enemy.

The Holy Spirit baptism makes available the fullness of the Spirit to the believer. Let's spend a little more time here to dispel the false doctrines around this particular baptism. The benefits of being baptized in the Holy Spirit are tremendous. However, there is a bottleneck at this point. This bottleneck is an ancient roadblock that has prevented many people from advancing with God further in this area. Many doctrines have deemphasized the baptism of the Holy Spirit. It has prevented many from being immersed, or baptized, in the Holy Spirit. Though this is not our major area of focus, let's try to briefly address this bottleneck before moving

The Making of the Champions

on. There is a doctrine out there that says the Holy Spirit is involved in the work of salvation, and *that's* the Holy Spirit baptism, that there is no need for a separate additional experience. That's partly true and partly false. There is nothing as dangerous knowing only half the truth in Christendom. The first part of that doctrine is true, but the second part is completely false. It is true that the Holy Spirit is the Person involved in the work of salvation. But apart from the work of salvation, the Holy Spirit also champions Holy Spirit baptism, and this is a separate experience from salvation. Let's search the Scriptures to see if the born-again experience is a separate experience from Holy Spirit baptism:

> *Now when they heard this, they were pricked in their heart, and said unto Peter and to the rest of the apostles, Men and brethren, what shall we do? Then Peter said unto them, Repent, and be baptized every one of you in the name of Jesus Christ for the remission of sins, and ye shall receive the gift of the Holy Ghost.*
>
> —Acts 2:37–38

Let's give a little background to the above passage. After the resurrection of our Lord Jesus, He stayed on the earth for another forty days, teaching the disciples more details about matters of the Kingdom. He concluded by telling them to wait in Jerusalem for the baptism of the Holy Spirit. This baptism would empower them to do the work they had been called to do for the Kingdom. So, the disciples went to Jerusalem, gathered together in an upper room, and continually prayed and fasted. On the fiftieth day after the resurrection of Jesus, the Day of Pentecost fully came, and God fulfilled His promise by sending the Holy Spirit to them. They were all baptized and spoke in tongues—the only physical evidence that they had been baptized in the Holy Spirit. When the people around them saw this event, they gave it all kinds of names, because they had never seen such an occurrence before. Some said the disciples were drunk, and others said they were simply babbling nonsense. But then Peter stood and preached to them, telling them the story of the plan of salvation that heaven had furnished for all humanity.

Those who listened to the message were convicted, and they asked Peter what they must do to be saved. Look at the response of Peter in verse 38. The first thing Peter asked them to do was to repent. That's the first thing every sinner must do when they want to turn to Jesus. After salvation, the next natural thing to do when you arrive in the Kingdom is to undergo water baptism. Let's see if that was the advice Peter gave. Look at the second part of verse 38. The next thing Peter advised was for them to be baptized in the name of Jesus! Everyone will agree that this instruction refers to water baptism. But then, there was a *third* experience Peter mentioned in the same passage—the gift of the Holy Spirit. That is what we refer to as Holy Spirit baptism. Notice that it is a completely separate experience from being born again. If it is the same experience, Peter would not have separated them. Someone might say, "But it was not recorded that they spoke in tongues." Let's look at another example to show the two experiences, as well as show evidence of them speaking in tongues:

> *And it came to pass, that, while Apollos was at Corinth, Paul having passed through the upper coasts came to Ephesus: and finding certain disciples, he said unto them, Have ye received the Holy Ghost since ye believed? And they said unto him, We have not so much as heard whether there be any Holy Ghost. And he said unto them, Unto what then were ye baptized? And they said, Unto John's baptism. Then said Paul, John verily baptized with the baptism of repentance, saying unto the people, that they should believe on him which should come after him, that*

The Making of the Champions

is, on Christ Jesus. When they heard this, they were baptized in the name of the Lord Jesus. And when Paul had laid his hands upon them, the Holy Ghost came on them; and they spake with tongues, and prophesied.

—Acts 19:1-6

Now then, consider the above passage. Paul traveled to Ephesus during one of his ministry journeys, and he met some men who claimed to be disciples of Jesus. Paul saw some characteristics of repentance in them, but he also noticed they didn't speak in tongues. So, he asked if they were baptized in the Holy Spirit. Unfortunately, they had never heard about the Holy Spirit. Hence, they were surprised when Paul asked about this experience. Apparently they had only experienced John's baptism. John had preached repentance, and many people, including Jesus, went to be baptized in the Jordan River—water baptism—by John. These twelve were part of those who had been baptized during the evangelistic outreach of John. After their baptism, they traveled back to Ephesus and continued in their new way of life. They apparently hadn't even heard about the death and resurrection of the Lord Jesus Christ. So, when Paul met them, they only knew about the baptism of John. Paul then preached to them about Jesus, for it seems they had never even heard about Jesus. They listened to the message of Paul and decided to be born again. Notice what happened to them after they were born again in the last part of verse 5. They were then baptized in the name of the Lord. The same phrase is used for "water baptism" in Acts 2 that we considered earlier. Hence, the first two steps into the Kingdom were fulfilled—being born again and experiencing water baptism. The next natural step into the Kingdom is the baptism of the Holy Spirit. See what happened in verse 6 of the above passage. Paul laid his hand on them, and the Holy Spirit came upon them. What happened next? They all spoke in tongues. Here we see clear evidence of all three experiences, as well as the evidence that these men were baptized in the Holy Spirit and spoke in tongues. Therefore, we can see from the above two passages that we have considered so far concerning this issue, that even though the Holy Spirit is responsible for all the steps we take in our journey into the Kingdom, the born-again experience and Holy Spirit baptism are two separate experiences. Every Christian who wishes to advance in the Kingdom must have both of these experiences. The Spirit of God is very gentle. He will never force you to go beyond the point you wish to go. Many doctrines have prevented many from advancing in the Kingdom.

Let's return to our progression into the Kingdom of God. After water baptism, then the individual becomes baptized in the Holy Spirit. Like we said earlier, this is not the time to enroll in the workforce of the local assembly. This is the time to sit at the feet of the Master. The Master will use the Person of the Holy Spirit to carry the fellow through. The lessons come in the form of real-life events. That's the only way to conform us to the image of God. What matters to God is that we arrive at the predetermined destination (for those who are willing). The valley is the place where God has predestined all His children to go. The valley is actually the true mystery behind the predestination mentioned in Roman 8:28–30. There are doctrines that suggest that predestination means that God has already selected those who will make it to heaven. That is so far from the truth. If that is true, then John 3:16 has to be a lie. Jesus said that God gave His only Son to the entire world, not to a select few. Now let's explore Romans 8:28–29 a bit:

> *And we know that all things work together for good to them that love God, to them who are the called according to his purpose. For whom he did foreknow, he also did predestinate to be conformed*

to the image of his Son, that he might be the firstborn among many brethren.

In this passage, Paul gave us an idea of the qualities a man needs to possess in order to descend into the valley. All who wish to take this walk with God into the valley must love God. This is very important element in the journey. The road sometimes can be rough. If there is no genuine love for God, the enemy can easily convince us that God is the enemy. The enemy can do a mind-bending trick to make us attribute our difficulties along the way to God. For example, Joseph had a dream that he would one day be a leader or even a king. But then he found himself a slave in the house of a stranger. As if that were not bad enough, a few years later, he ended up in prison for a crime he did not commit. The devil could easily have played a trick on his mind to make him feel like God was the architect of his problems. But a deep love for God will give us an edge in such situations that the enemy might want to take advantage of.

The next quality that is required to taking this walk with God, according to the passage in consideration, is that those who are called are called according to purpose. This quality does not in any way suggest that God called only a few. Every single person who walks into the Kingdom through the door of salvation is called. Your response to His call determines whether you will be chosen.

For many are called, but few are chosen.

—Matthew 22:14

Consider the above passage. That particular verse is the concluding part of a parable that Jesus told the people during one of His teaching sessions. In that particular parable, everyone was called, but only few responded to the call. Hence, when Paul wrote about those who were chosen in the passage just before this, he was not talking about a select few whom God Himself chose. He was talking about those, out of the many who were called, who responded to the call. Putting everything together in Romans 8, we can see that those who are born again are those who have responded to the call of God. God predestined that everyone who is born again must end up in the valley.

The word "predestine" comes from the Greek word *proorizo*, which means "to predetermine, to decide beforehand, or to appoint beforehand." It is important to note that what God chose beforehand was not the people themselves; it was the office or the destination, just as we discussed earlier. What this means is that God determined before any of us came into the picture that whoever accepts Christ must end up in the valley. Unfortunately, many Christians die without taking one step away from the mountain, while some die on their way to the valley. Regardless of the position any Christian takes, whether to descend or not to descend (no matter the doctrine such a Christian is using to support his actions), it must be clear that the predetermined plan of God for all those who come to Him is the valley.

Another thing to note in the Romans 8 passage above is that Paul states the end product of those who arrive at the valley. Notice what Roman 8:29 says: the end product of predestination is conformity to the image of His Son (Jesus). What does that mean? Let us give a little explanation here. For example, a liquid doesn't have a shape of its own. It usually takes on the shape of the container in which it finds itself. God's expectation for us is that by the time He is done with us, we can be poured into the Container called Jesus, such that when we walk in the street, it is actually Christ who is walking in the street. Hence, we can reproduce the exact works that Christ produced when He was here on the earth. This is especially important in these last days, because the only hope of the world is Christ living in us. The words "conformed to" in Roman 8:29 comes from the Greek word *summorphos*, which means "to have the same form as another." What that means is that the actual intention of God for us when we step into the Kingdom is that by the time we get to the valley, which is our predestined destination, through the situations and circumstances that God permits, we will look exactly like Jesus. Then, at the end of the age, when Jesus is judging the world, He will say to us, "Oh wow, this guy looks exactly like Me." But if a believer doesn't go through the process, then at the end of the age, Christ will ask such fellow a strange question: "Who is this? He doesn't look like Me at all. I don't know him." Therefore, the lower we descend in our journey into the valley, the more like Jesus we will look.

6

The Wilderness Experience

The way the Holy Spirit administers this curriculum can be better explained when we study the lives of the men who have gone before us. Let's take a case study for a better understanding. Moses was destined to deliver Israel from captivity. Heaven deliberately arranged for him to grow up in Pharaoh's palace to ensure the slavery mentality did not affect his esteem, amidst other reasons. He was cultured in the highest form of learning available in his day. He was a war general and a city builder; he was brought up in the palace and was even propped up to potentially be the next pharaoh. At the peak of his career, however, he had an encounter with the Holy Spirit, and he became what the New Testament Christians would call "born again." Look at his experience in the passage below:

> *By faith Moses, when he was come to years, refused to be called the son of Pharaoh's daughter; choosing rather to suffer affliction with the people of God, than to enjoy the pleasures of sin for a season; esteeming the reproach of Christ greater riches than*

the treasures in Egypt: for he had respect unto the recompence of the reward.

—Hebrews 11:24–26

Consider the above passage. It started by saying, "By faith Moses, when he was come to years . . ." We cannot tell how old he was when this happened, but we know he must have been above the age of thirty. This is because in the Jewish culture, a male child was considered a son or a legal representative of his parent or a man at the age of thirty. Hence, we can safely say that Moses was above the age of thirty. Then, the passage in verse 24 tells us that Moses made a decision. He refused to be called the son of Pharaoh's daughter at that time. This was a very serious decision. What it meant was that he refused his right to authority, his right to the throne, and his right to greatness. A good question we need to ask at this point is. How did Moses come to this conclusion? The passage doesn't leave us in darkness concerning why Moses made that decision. Verse 24 starts by saying, "By faith . . ." That means that Moses came to this conclusion by faith. That is still a bit vague. What does it mean to come to a conclusion or to make a life-changing decision *by faith*? What is the definition of *faith* to start with?

Now faith is the substance of things hoped for, the evidence of things not seen.

—Hebrews 11:1

According to the above passage, faith is a substance and an evidence. The substance or evidence is the Word that God gives concerning the situation. We do not know what God told Moses, but we can clearly tell that whatever God told him must have included the fact that he was a Jew and that he had been brought into the palace for such a time as this—to

The Wilderness Experience

deliver the Israelites from slavery. Hence his decision in verse 25. He knew he belonged to the Jewish community, and he saw their sufferings and realized that the palace was not where he belonged. Notice that in verse 26, the substance he received also included the treasures kept in heaven for him if he would pursue his destiny—Christ's greater riches. Hence, it is clear that this man, Moses, was now born again and on his way to being used by the Almighty to accomplish a specific purpose.

> *And it came to pass in those days, when Moses was grown, that he went out unto his brethren, and looked on their burdens: and he spied an Egyptian smiting an Hebrew, one of his brethren. And he looked this way and that way, and when he saw that there was no man, he slew the Egyptian, and hid him in the sand.*
>
> —Exodus 2:11-12

Unfortunately, at this point in his walk with God, Moses made the mistake many of us make. He thought he could accomplish God's purpose through human strength and accomplishment. Humanly speaking, Moses was a highly accomplished and distinguished young man. No man was more qualified for the job than he. But God cannot use any iota of our flesh. It stinks before Him. No matter your accomplishments, they are useless to heaven. You have to descend to that valley, where every accomplishment is stripped off so that God's glory can burst forth. Moses stepped out in the flesh, hoping to achieve God's purpose with his human qualifications. He stepped out one day with his shoulders high, to check out how his people were faring. There he saw an Egyptian dealing roughly with a Jew. He thought to himself, *God has told me I am their deliverer I can start right now!* With the power of his own might, he knocked down the Egyptian. By so doing, he assumed that the Israelites would immediately accept him as their savior. What he didn't realize is that no matter how good a preacher is, no one will listen to his message until God certifies such a fellow. God did the exact same thing for Jesus; He will do it for all of us, without exception.

Moses felt accomplished. One Egyptian had been displaced on just day one of his efforts. He was highly motivated, and so he stepped out again the next day.

> *And when he went out the second day, behold, two men of the Hebrews strove together: and he said to him that did the wrong, Wherefore smitest thou thy fellow? And he said, Who made thee a prince and a judge over us? Intendest thou to kill me, as thou killedst the Egyptian? And Moses feared, and said, Surely this thing is known.*
>
> —Exodus 2:13–14

Unfortunately for him, heaven had not yet approved him; hence the people he was sent to deliver would not accept him. The question was asked of him: "Who made you a judge over us?" One would think that the Israelites would have been tired of their bondage and be happy to have a deliverer. But they wouldn't have Moses rule over them because he had come in his own name. Come to look at it, how many Egyptians would Moses have killed before the Israelites could be set free? Can you see how limited the arm of flesh is? As far as heaven is concerned, the flesh can do nothing that will please heaven. Moses met with disappointment and resentment on all fronts. The people he had thought he was sent to deliver rejected him. At the very time he was supposed to be the next leader of the most powerful nation on earth, a bounty was placed on his head by Pharaoh. He was rejected on all fronts. He had to abandon the mission of rescuing his people. God

The Wilderness Experience

sentenced him to forty years in the University of God. His flesh was so ingrained that it would take forty years to "flesh" it out. Working in the flesh not only set Moses back forty years, it also set back the agenda of God for the nation of Israel by thirty years. Consider these two passages:

And he said unto Abram, know of a surety that thy seed shall be a stranger in a land that is not theirs's, and shall serve them; and they shall afflict them four hundred years.

—Genesis 15:13

Now the sojourning of the children of Israel, who dwelt in Egypt, was four hundred and thirty years.

—Exodus 12:40

In the first passage, God revealed to His friend, who was also a prophet —Abraham—that his descendants would stay in Egypt for four hundred years. However, in the second passage, when the prophecy came to pass, they actually stayed in Egypt for four hundred and thirty years. The next question is, What went wrong? Why did the prophecy not come to pass exactly as heaven had predicted? I will give my observed opinion of what I believe must have gone wrong. This is not a doctrine, neither is it cast in stone. This is just what I believe is the cause of this shift in the number of years, from my own experience and study of the Scriptures:

When Moses was of age (Hebrews 11:24), the Holy Spirit began to stir the spirit of Moses up to prepare him for his assignment. This stirring was meant to push him into the place of prayer. In the place of prayer and obedience, the Holy Spirit would then begin to "un-flesh" all the flesh that would get in His way. This process usually takes a long time.

Preparing for the Coming Glory

It takes an average of ten years of consistency in the place of prayer and in the place of obedience to the bidding of the Holy Spirit to completely remove the flesh from a man and get that man ready to be used of God (although I strongly believe that God may accelerate that time frame in these last days to prepare His army for the coming battle). That's not to say that God cannot use a man at any point in time of his walk with God. But there is a time in our walk with God when heaven certifies someone as a son. At that time, the relationship between the man and God becomes a covenant relationship. God is then bound to take care of the affairs of that man, while the man is "condemned" to seek only the interest of God. That is a glorious condemnation. Heaven bestows a kind of glory on the person, because heaven knows that wherever he goes, he will do exactly what Jesus would have done if He were physically present. That is the point in time to which I am referring. It takes an average of ten years of consistently remaining in the place of prayer and obedience to get a man to that point.

The next question will be, how did I come to determine this average to be ten years? First, this timeline is just what I have observed from men (both in the Scriptures and in our time) who have followed God and become great tools for the Kingdom. You may have a different observation. That's fine. This is just my own opinion. Let's briefly consider two examples from the Scriptures to verify this claim.

Abraham was seventy-five years old when God called him (Genesis 12:1-4). This call of God did not translate into a covenant until ten years had passed. Even with all the great plans and promises God had for Abraham, God did not make a covenant with him until after ten years had passed (Genesis 15:1-9; 16:1-3). The covenant is the sign that God could now call this fellow a son. That is the point of glorious condemnation for the man.

The Wilderness Experience

The second example is the disciples of Jesus. After learning directly from the Master for almost four years, they were then baptized in the Holy Spirit to prepare them for the power and glory that comes with the glorious condemnation. Yet they did not see their first recorded miracle until after about ten years into their journey with God. Hence, the journey between the Upper Room experience to the beautiful gate experience took about six years (Acts 2–3).

Now then, back to the man Moses. According to the Scriptures, this stirring began when Moses was forty years of age:

> *And when he was full forty years old, it came into his heart to visit his brethren the children of Israel. And seeing one of them suffer wrong, he defended him, and avenged him that was oppressed, and smote the Egyptian: For he supposed his brethren would have understood how that God by his hand would deliver them: but they understood not.*
>
> —Acts 7:23–25

Unfortunately, when Moses felt the stirring of the Spirit, instead of turning to the Holy Spirit in the place of prayer, he pursued the desire of his heart in his own strength, hoping to capitalize on his accomplishments and position as a member of Pharaoh's household. This truncated the program of the Holy Spirit to bring him into a place of glorious condemnation—the valley of the dry bones. If my theory is right, then the journey to the valley of dry bones should have taken Moses ten years. But instead, he was redirected to the wilderness, to be restructured into the image of Christ. That process took forty years. Hence, doing the math, if we subtract the ten years Moses *should* have used to journey to the valley of dry bones, from the forty years he spent in the wilderness of preparation, then we have the additional thirty years the children of Israel spent in the place of bondage—because of the error of one man. The process that was supposed to take ten years became complicated by the interference of the flesh and human wisdom. Moses was then forcefully driven into the school of adversary, which took an additional thirty years (forty years in total for Moses, and an extra thirty years for the deliverance of the people of Israel).

Back to the issue at hand. The error of Moses not only cost him forty years in the wilderness, but it also cost the Israelites an extra thirty years in the house of bondage. We can clearly see how God can use life events, situations, and circumstances to work out His glory in our lives. In order to descend to the valley of dry bones, the believer must abandon his own will and adopt the will of the Father as the sole plan for his life. Consider the passage below:

> *Not every one that saith unto me, Lord, Lord, shall enter into the kingdom of heaven; but he that doeth the will of my Father which is in heaven.*
>
> —Matthew 7:21

Notice what Jesus says in the above passage. There is no unbeliever who will call Jesus Lord here on the earth. Hence, this statement was addressed to all those who are in the Kingdom. That is the first thing to note about this passage. Then He went on to say further, before you can enter the Kingdom, you have to be ready to abandon your own will and take on the will of the Father. Remember, according to John 3:3, being born again only gives you the opportunity of seeing the benefits of the Kingdom. You cannot partake in the inheritance of the Kingdom unless you decide to actually enter. The word "will" in the above passage is from the Greek word *thelema*, which means "determination, purpose, decree, or choice." This has exactly the same meaning as the word "predestination" in Romans 8:29, which we considered earlier. The word "predestine" actually means "to predetermine." Doing God's will is the same as following the path assigned to you, which will take you to the very bottom of the valley of dry bones.

The Man Reuel

In order to understand how God schooled Moses, we must understudy the man Reuel, Moses' father-in-law. Many preachers have called this man an unbeliever. But when we take a closer look at this man, I beg to differ. He is not an unbeliever. Come with me on the journey of discovering who this me really is. The first-time any real spotlight came on him took place in Exodus 2:16. Let's go there:

Now the priest of Midian had seven daughters: and they came and drew water, and filled the troughs to water their father's flock.

Reuel is first introduced to us as a priest. It would likely have been easier to just us his name. Why use four words to describe a man when you could have used just five letters, in a book that is highly summarized and has no space for excess? The Bible is a book that has no space for meaningless words. There is much in the history of humanity that was cut out because it is of no use to our spiritual growth or knowledge of God. This same book used four words to introduce a man when just one word could have easily been used. The phrase used to introduce him is "the priest of Midian." He was introduced with his office rather than his name, even though that was a longer route for the writer to take. That speaks something about him. The first thing we learn about him is that he was a priest. A priest was a go-between, or an intercessor,

Preparing for the Coming Glory

between man and God. Such a person was necessary because of the holiness of God. His holiness means that God is totally separate from fallen man and, in a real sense, unapproachable. This means that anyone in the land of Midian who wanted to know about God had to contact Reuel. He was the only go-to in the land of Midian, or at least the most important go-to man, when it came to the oracle of God. Notice the word "the" in front of his address, meaning he was *the* priest. All other priests might be "a" priest, but he was "the" priest. Another thing is that he was not just a priest over his own household. He was the priest of Midian. Now, the great question many may ask is: Was he a priest of *God* or a priest of an idol, a god with a small *g*? Let's go on. We shall find out if he is the priest of God or the priest of a false god.

The next time Reuel is mentioned, he is not called by his office. He is called by his name. In the Bible, a person's name defines his destiny or purpose. For example, when Abram began his journey with God, his name was Abram. Abram is not a bad name. It actually means "exalted father." That is not a bad name. It actually spoke of his potential fatherhood. But God had to change his name in order to redirect his destiny. It became "Abraham," which means "father of a multitude." This is where God was taking him to. Eventually, thousands of years after that redirection, he became the father of many nations. The same thing took place with Jacob, who became Israel. We could go on and on with other examples to show how important a name is to the destiny of a person, but let's move on. Going back to this priest, it is good to know what his name actually is. Let us see what the Bible calls him.

> *And when they came to Reuel their father, he said, How is it that ye are come so soon to day?*
>
> —Exodus 2:18

The Wilderness Experience

Notice how his name is introduced in this verse. This passage could have easily read, "and their father, the priest," instead of giving his name. But heaven ensured that his name was included in the equation, just one verse away from when he had been introduced as the priest. So, let's consider the name "Reuel" and see if it gives any insight into what kind of person this man was and which kind of priest he was.

The name "Reuel" is from a Hebrew word that means "the friend of God." This tells us a lot about the kind of person he was. From what we have gathered so far, we can tell one or two things about this man. First, he was the main priest in the region of Midian. That does not really tell us what kind of spirit supervised the altar he was priest over. But when we look at the next clue given, we can tell the kind of spirit that was supervising the altar he was presiding over. His name means "the friend of God," not "a friend of God." That means that everyone in the community knew him as *the* friend of God. Hence, we can clearly say without much doubt that he is a priest of the Most High God. And he was not just the priest; he was the friend of God. Now then, they called him the friend of God. This means that every other friend was just "a" friend, but this was "the" friend of God. Everyone knew him not just as the priest of the area, but as "the" friend of God. In addition, there is another name this man was called. Let us check another verse of Scripture to see whether that will relate to what we are considering.

> *When Jethro, the priest of Midian, Moses' father in law, heard of all that God had done for Moses, and for Israel his people, and that the Lord had brought Israel out of Egypt.*
>
> —Exodus 18:1

It is clear from this description that the person in-question is Reuel. Notice the title, "the priest of Midian," and the phrase "father-in-law"

Preparing for the Coming Glory

again in the above passage. The only thing different about this description is that another name is introduced for the father-in-law of Moses. Hence, we can confidently say that Moses' father-in-law also went by the name "Jethro." The name "Jethro" means "His abundance" in Hebrew. I believe the word "His" in that name is referring to God. Hence, from the short research we have done so far, we can confidently say that the man Jethro is the main priest of the Almighty God in Midian. He was not just a priest by profession; he was the friend of God who bore the oracles of God. He knew God intimately, and he played the role of a go-between for everyone in the region of Midian who wanted to communicate with God. Although Moses found himself by chance in the house of this man, everything had been orchestrated by God. With this understanding, we can now go back to Moses' journey down into the valley of dry bones.

There are two types of announcements in the school of heaven. The first announcement is done for the hearing of the people around the fellow whom God wants to use. This announcement alerts people to the fact that this person has the calling of God upon his life. It distinguishes this individual from others. This announcement creates a series of events that will push the individual into the wilderness. The second announcement is heralded in heaven. The people of the earth will only see the effect of this second announcement. They will not hear the call of the trumpet. This announcement is given to the spiritual world. It is made to say that God is satisfied with the training of this individual and he is now a graduate of the University of God. He can now be gainfully employed by the conglomerate of heaven. When I say "announcement," I don't mean that someone will take a microphone and announce to the public or to the assembly that a certain person has received the call of God. In actual fact, there is mostly nothing like that. What I mean

The Wilderness Experience

is that, usually, when God has His hand on someone (which can be anyone and everyone), there is something special about that fellow that allows the people around him to know that God has put something in him. He may even be the least person in the fellowship at that time. But those who can observe will see the mark of God on his life.

Now back to our man, Moses. He must have been complaining, as many of us do. He had been totally fine before he became a "Christian." His problems all started when he heard from God. Moses was the overseer of the entire land of Egypt. He dictated the course of events, which buildings and which cities should be developed, how the resources of the empire should be allocated, what nations to attack or not to attack, what nations to plant a garrison in, among many other decisions. All eyes were on him to be the next pharaoh. Then the word of the Lord came to him, for the Bible says that by faith (by the word of God), he realized that he didn't belong to the throne of Egypt. The Bible didn't say what that word was. But if we are to guess, it would have been along this line: "I have seen My people's suffering. I have brought you to the palace for this purpose, to set My people free from their bondage." This is usually the first problem many of us encounter. Heaven has announced its intention in using us for a mission that God wants to accomplish. This is not the time to start planning out what to do and how to accomplish it ourselves. Usually, the mission that heaven announces is greater than anyone can do on their own. There was no way Moses could have accomplished the mission heaven had announced in his own ability. If heaven announces its intention to a man, it is not because it wants the man to carry it out right away. It is because heaven expects the man to start seeking God for direction on how to accomplish the mission—in God's methods and timing.

Preparing for the Coming Glory

But just like many of us, Moses went about it in his own way. He started to make the move because he had heard from God, thinking it was the right thing to do. This is a common lecture the University of God must start with. Heaven expects us to take only one action. When heaven announces its intention to someone, because the intention is usually far bigger than the person can achieve by himself, heaven expects such a fellow to proclaim a personal quarantine period during which time the individual will be locked out of the world. Moses did not pass that particular "five-unit course." And so heaven had to orchestrate a series of events through a natural course that would force him to register and take the wilderness course. This is usually a longer route to take.

Moses knew the plan of God for his life quite alright, but he never thought he needed to consult God on how to go about it. He never asked God for the map that showed the step-by-step journey he must take to get to the destination heaven has designed for him. He went about it in his own way. After his first achievement, he felt a sense of pride, a sense of real accomplishment. He must have whispered to himself, "I have just started my ministry!" He did not realize that anything done in our own understanding is considered "nothing" by heaven. The plan to that understanding might be elaborate; many professors of theology and the brightest minds around could have come together to design the path the ministry should have taken. But if God is not the sole Designer of that path, the laborers have labored in vain. Look at how Jesus puts it here:

> *I am the vine, ye are the branches: He that abideth in me, and I in him, the same bringeth forth much fruit: for without me ye can do nothing.*
>
> —John 15:5

The Wilderness Experience

Notice the last phrase in the above passage. Without Him we can do *nothing*. It doesn't say we cannot do anything without Him. Those are two different statements. The second means you cannot lift a finger to carry or do anything without Him. The first means you can do whatever you want, but no matter the empire you build, if you build it without Jesus, it will amount to nothing in the eyes of heaven. In the case of Moses, he achieved so much by himself to the extent that he was willing to kill, and in actual fact, he killed someone for the course of his mission. As far as he was concerned, he had proven to heaven that he was worthy and fit for the job. But he was disappointed at the response of heaven. The people he thought would naturally accept him because he was clearly fighting for their release denied him to his face:

> *And when he went out the second day, behold, two men of the Hebrews strove together: and he said to him that did the wrong, Wherefore smitest thou thy fellow? And he said, Who made thee a prince and a judge over us? Intendest thou to kill me, as thou killedst the Egyptian? And Moses feared, and said, Surely this thing is known.*
>
> —Exodus 2:13-14

The next natural course will be, "Since you guys don't want to accept me as your savior, let me just go back and continue to enjoy my time in the palace." But now Moses was stuck. He could not go back to the palace to continue on his path to becoming the next pharaoh, as the palace now saw him as a traitor; neither could he stay with the Hebrews because they had rejected his leadership. He had no choice other than to take the course heaven had prescribed for him—the wilderness experience. Heaven considered him too full of the self and the flesh to be used just yet. He had to be "de-fleshed."

This seems to be a pattern with God—after the announcement comes the wilderness experience. There are two types of wilderness experiences. The first is when a fellow follows the right path prescribed by the Holy Spirit. The traveling is usually done in a straight line, and it is a shorter route—as it is said, the shortest way to a point is through a straight line. But the second is the one the fellow is forced to follow because he has refused to follow the path prescribed by the Holy Spirit. It is usually a rerouting. Hence, it is not a straight line. This makes for a longer course. The bottom line is, both paths will lead to the destination heaven has designed. But one is more strenuous and long, while the other is shorter and less strenuous. The rerouting in the second wilderness experience can occur several times. Humans are typically unstable. Only a very few remain on a prescribed path until the end. Every once in a while, someone might wander away from the path. This wandering leads to further rerouting back onto the path. Each wandering away and rerouting back to the path makes the journey even longer. Hence, a journey of forty days can become a journey of forty years, depending on the number of times of wandering away and rerouting. Strict obedience to the instruction of the "GPS" is the key to a shorter wilderness journey.

The Case of Joseph

Let's consider the case of Joseph. Heaven made its first announcement to Joseph through a strange dream he had one night. He was so excited about this dream that he couldn't wait to share it with his brethren:

> *And he said unto them, Hear, I pray you, this dream which I have dreamed: For, behold, we were binding sheaves in the*

field, and, lo, my sheaf arose, and also stood upright; and, behold, your sheaves stood round about, and made obeisance to my sheaf.

—Genesis 37:6–7

His first error was that he took a microphone after gathering the assembly and made the announcement public. This was supposed to be classified information. Notice the arrogance with which he spoke to his elder brothers. The announcement was clear to all: "This guy is going to rule over us." Joseph didn't stop there. He taunted them with the announcement daily. Then he had another dream. He did not hesitate to tell it to the world again. This time, the sphere of his leadership had been extended in the dream. Look at how the Bible puts it:

And he dreamed yet another dream, and told it his brethren, and said, Behold, I have dreamed a dream more; and, behold, the sun and the moon and the eleven stars made obeisance to me. And he told it to his father, and to his brethren: and his father rebuked him, and said unto him, What is this dream that thou hast dreamed? Shall I and thy mother and thy brethren indeed come to bow down ourselves to thee to the earth?

—Genesis 37:9–10

The announcement again was clear. Joseph was a born leader. God had ordained it. But there was a problem. The Joseph at that moment was a Joseph who was full of himself, full of pride and his own personal agenda. This Joseph had a relationship with God quite alright, but this Joseph was still on the mountain where he'd met God. This Joseph was no good for heaven. This Joseph was actually appalling to heaven. Heaven could not use this Joseph because there would be no glory to heaven. If heaven bestowed any ability on this Joseph, it would be for his personal consumption. "I . . . I . . . I" would be at the beginning of every statement this Joseph made. In order for this Joseph to become the Joseph who would accomplish the purposes of heaven, he had to be sentenced to a life in the wilderness. Heaven must decide to push him down the mountain of salvation into the valley of dry bones. And that is what heaven did. The court in heaven sat to judge, and the judgment came out against him. He was found guilty and sentenced to multiple years in the wilderness. The specific number of years that he would spend in the wilderness would depend on how fast he could learn. So it was written, and so it was done!

Seconds turned into minutes, minutes turned into hours, hours turned into days. The devil saw an easy prey in Joseph—he had released the secret of his destiny, after all—but heaven saw an opportunity. That faithful day, a day Jacob, his father, would live to regret but heaven would live to rejoice, Joseph was sent to check on his brethren. He went to the place where they usually camped, but he did not find them. He searched and searched, but they were nowhere to be found. There were no cell phones in those days, or he could have called them to ask. There was no way to find out where they had gone. But heaven was intentional about its program for Joseph. The case had already been concluded. Joseph had already been sentenced. A man had been planted around the brothers when they were making the decision to relocate. The man was a man of no importance on earth. No one cared about him. His name was not even known. But heaven approved of him, for he was a messenger of heaven:

> *And a certain man found him, and, behold, he was wandering in the field: and the man asked him, saying, What seekest thou? And he said, I seek my brethren: tell me, I pray thee, where they*

The Wilderness Experience

feed their flocks. And the man said, They are departed hence; for I heard them say, Let us go to Dothan. And Joseph went after his brethren, and found them in Dothan.

—Genesis 37:15–17

Notice how this man was introduced in the above passage: "a certain man." He was not known by the system of the world, but he was divinely planted by heaven to lead Joseph into the wilderness, where he would be stripped of self, pride, and the flesh. He was positioned in a place where he could become the hand that heaven could use to push Joseph down the mountain of pride and into the valley of dry bones. Many a man has been planted on our paths in life to push us down from our great mountain to a place where God can confidently bestow His grace and power upon us. We saw the same take place with Moses. A slave man was planted when he was busy displaying his ignorance; he thought he could deliver Israel with his position and power. The man was sure to tell him that he had been there when Moses was murdering the Egyptian. He was also sure to tell Moses that he could not kill him the same way he'd killed the Egyptian. This man was also nameless, but he was known by heaven. Many a time God plants men on our path to bring us into the place of our wilderness experience. But we sometimes see these men as enemies and attack them mercilessly.

That fateful day, Joseph went to seek his brethren in the location described by "the certain man." He still had his garment of pride on, the garment that gave him an edge over all those around him. He was the most favored of the clan of Israel, the soon-coming king. From afar, the colors of the coat of pride glittered in the eyes of his brethren. The devil quickly saw an open door, built on envy and hatred:

> *For where envying and strife is, there is confusion and every evil work.*
>
> —James 3:16

The enemy is like a roaring lion, going up and down seeking whom he may devour. He saw a wide-open door in Joseph's brothers, and he took it. He only knew that Joseph would be a leader of some sort. He also knew that Joseph's future position would threaten his own purpose on the earth, but he didn't know the details of what, how, and when this will unfold. So, the devil's final verdict to his demons was to finish the guy before he ever got near the corridors of power. Hence, while Joseph could only be identified by his coat of many colors, his case was concluded:

> *And when they saw him afar off, even before he came near unto them, they conspired against him to slay him.*
>
> —Genesis 37:18

Nine of the ten brothers of Joseph were seated together when the colors of Joseph's coat first glittered on the horizon, and the devil entered their midst to convince them to take him out. The Spirit of the Lord quickly looked among the nine to find someone He could influence with a contrary idea, but He found none. Nine of them concluded to waste the young man so that his destiny would not see the light of the day. But heaven intercepted the plans of the devil and his demons. Heaven found a vessel in an unlikely person. He had already been listed in the "bad" book of Israel. An eternal curse had already been placed on him. He had been stripped of his position of leadership and reduced to perpetual failure and struggle. He was busy doing other things away

The Wilderness Experience

from the nine when the Spirit of God intercepted his thoughts: *Go quickly to your brethren and hear what they are up to*:

> *And Reuben heard it, and he delivered him out of their hands; and said, Let us not kill him. And Reuben said unto them, Shed no blood, but cast him into this pit that is in the wilderness, and lay no hand upon him; that he might rid him out of their hands, to deliver him to his father again.*
>
> —Genesis 37:21–22

As soon as Reuben delivered his message, he went back to his business, leaving the nine others to carry out his instruction. Finally, Joseph made it to where his brethren were, still very full of himself. As soon as he arrived, he started "dishing" out instructions to his brethren as if he had already ascended the throne. But to his amazement, he was first stripped of his coat and then tied up. The first level of his flesh was stripped off of him. He could not, in his wildest imagination, believe that they would ever do this to him. While he was struggling just to survive, the nine decided to ignore the advice of Reuben. They were filled with indignation for Joseph and just wanted to finish him off. But heaven called unto Reuben again to go and check on the brethren to see what they were up to with the young man. He came and saw them maltreating the young man, and he immediately knew they still had the intention of killing him. He quickly weighed into the situation, putting himself between the nine and the one, dragging Joseph out of their claws. He appealed to their emotions. This was their blood, he said, and he has already been stripped of his most treasured possession, the coat. He has now been knocked down from the horse of his pride; he is already struggling for survival. For a proud man to beg for mercy with tears is a suggestion of how low he has come. For the first time, the

Preparing for the Coming Glory

ten saw the anguish of Joseph's soul and had pity on him. But the devil still had a foot in the heart of the nine that was difficult to get rid of, and heaven was not yet satisfied with the result. Yes, he had finally been enrolled in the school of the wilderness, but he still had to attend the lectures and sit and pass the exams.

> *And they said one to another, We are verily guilty concerning our brother, in that we saw the anguish of his soul, when he besought us, and we would not hear; therefore is this distress come upon us. And Reuben answered them, saying, Spake I not unto you, saying, Do not sin against the child; and ye would not hear? Therefore, behold, also his blood is required.*
>
> —Genesis 42:21–22

So, the one prevailed over the nine through the power of the Holy Spirit, and Joseph was put into his first prison. The first deal was done. He had finally been enrolled into the school of the wilderness, even though it was not intentional. He was now at the edge of the mountain, and only a strand of thread was keeping him from falling, and he was holding tightly to that thread. Heaven had achieved something. Next, Joseph had to start attending classes. Heaven had to cut off the thread to make the fall begin. The job of Reuben was done. Heaven needed to set another series of events in motion that would force Joseph to start attending lectures, events that would cut the thread and send him descending the mountain. Just then, the Ishmaelites came into sight. While the ten saw the anguish of Joseph's soul when he was begging for his life, the Spirit of God was able to break through the stronghold of the demons in the heart of Judah. He became sober when he realized the fact that he had just consented to killing his own brother. While

The Wilderness Experience

the struggling and the tussle had been going on, the blocks that had built the stronghold in his heart were being dismantled, block by block, until none was left. Jacob finally came to the conclusion that it was not worth murdering his own brother. Heaven found another ally in him. The tussle finally ended. The nine confined Joseph to his first prison and decided to celebrate it by eating and drinking. While they sat to eat and drink, heaven unfolded its second series of events. Judah was made to lift up his eyes from the sumptuous meal, and he saw a train of businessmen coming their way. Instantly, a bright idea was dropped into his mind by the inspiration of the Almighty:

> *And they sat down to eat bread: and they lifted up their eyes and looked, and, behold, a company of Ishmeelites came from Gilead with their camels bearing spicery and balm and myrrh, going to carry it down to Egypt. And Judah said unto his brethren, What profit is it if we slay our brother, and conceal his blood? Come, and let us sell him to the Ishmeelites, and let not our hand be upon him; for he is our brother and our flesh. And his brethren were content.*
>
> —Genesis 37:25–27

Jacob made the suggestion, and the eight gave him their ears. He prevailed over them. When the train finally reached their location, the deal was already concluded in the spirit—Joseph's application had been accepted, and he was admitted into the school of the wilderness experience. Again, the Master, who is highly skilled at de-fleshing His generals, had prevailed over brother Joseph. And phew! He went down the cliff of the mountain. He actually rolled down, not even climbed down. Each roll removed a layer of his flesh.

The Master in the Wilderness

Let's consider God's master template so we can know exactly what we are expected to do when the initial announcement is made. In Matthew 3:

> *And Jesus, when he was baptized, went up straightway out of the water: and, lo, the heavens were opened unto him, and he saw the Spirit of God descending like a dove, and lighting upon him: And lo a voice from heaven, saying, This is my beloved Son, in whom I am well pleased.*
>
> —verses 16–17

Here, heaven has clearly announced its satisfaction with Jesus. When Jesus was baptized, He was not the only person at the venue. Look at what the Bible says concerning the ministry of John:

> *Then went out to him Jerusalem, and all Judæa, and all the region round about Jordan, and were baptized of him in Jordan, confessing their sins.*
>
> —3:5–6

Notice all the places where people came from to listen to what John had to say and to be baptized by him. The Scripture didn't say that some from Judea came to John. It says that they came from *all* Judea. All the places mentioned above were major cities in the time of John. So, you can imagine the number of people who came to John on daily basis. When Jesus came to be baptized, He was not the only person there. As usual, the service was jam-packed. And John had already made the announcement that he was not the Messiah. He had also clearly stated

The Wilderness Experience

in one of his meetings that God had given him a clue of who it was who would come after him. Look at how he put it in the below passage:

John answered them, saying, I baptize with water: but there standeth one among you, whom ye know not; He it is, who coming after me is preferred before me, whose shoe's latchet I am not worthy to unloose.

And John bare record, saying, I saw the Spirit descending from heaven like a dove, and it abode upon him. And I knew him not: but he that sent me to baptize with water, the same said unto me, Upon whom thou shalt see the Spirit descending, and remaining on him, the same is he which baptizeth with the Holy Ghost. And I saw, and bare record that this is the Son of God.

—John 1:26–27, 32–34

Thousands of people come to John on a daily basis. John himself did not know who the Messiah was, although he knew the Messiah was the Son of God. He knew that Christ was the One for whom the whole of Israel had been waiting. But he didn't know Him yet, even though they were cousins. The Holy Spirit whispered to him, giving him a sign to look out for. On that particular day, thousands of people had attended John's evangelistic crusade. Jesus happened to be one of them. After many days of looking for the sign the Holy Spirit was to give him, John finally saw the One upon whom the Holy Spirit had descended and remained. In the days of his ministry before Jesus came, he must have seen many upon whom the Spirit had descended, but it had always lifted after some time. However, when John saw Jesus, the Spirit descended and remained, as long as John continued to wait. So, he confirmed that this was the Son of God they had all been waiting for, for so long. After the message for that day was given, it was finally

Preparing for the Coming Glory

time for willing people to be baptized, and as John was baptizing many, he saw Jesus on the line. Jesus had also come to be baptized! John was shocked. When it was finally Jesus' turn, John protested. How could he, a mere man, baptize the very Son of God?

> *Then cometh Jesus from Galilee to Jordan unto John, to be baptized of him. But John forbad him, saying, I have need to be baptized of thee, and comest thou to me? And Jesus answering said unto him, Suffer it to be so now: for thus it becometh us to fulfil all righteousness. Then he suffered him.*
>
> —Matthew 3:13-15

This conversation happened in the full glare of the thousands of people who had attended the service. Now then, one must understand that at this time in the land of Israel and among all Jews scattered all over the world, everyone was expecting the Messiah to show up at any moment. In fact, according to Josephus (a Jewish writer at that time), at least thirty people had already shown up claiming to be the Messiah. Hence, the word *Messiah* was not far from the lips of the average Jew. John was considered a great prophet by everyone—from the ordinary people in the street to the king in the palace. When someone of the caliber of John announced, in the full glare of the crowd, that you were greater than he, you automatically and immediately became a superstar. Jesus didn't need any other form of advertisement to start His ministry. In fact, after this announcement, two of John's disciples followed Jesus home that very day. Think about that: Many eyes were on Jesus. All He needed to do was to organize a crusade. He wouldn't even need to do much advertisement before the venue would be packed.

But Jesus did something strange that day. Instead of immediately securing the largest venue in town to start His own evangelistic crusade,

The Wilderness Experience

He yielded Himself to the leading of the Holy Spirit. And the Holy Spirit drove Him in the opposite direction:

Then was Jesus led up of the Spirit into the wilderness to be tempted of the devil.

—Matthew 4:1

And Jesus being full of the Holy Ghost returned from Jordan, and was led by the Spirit into the wilderness.

—Luke 4:1

It was the Spirit who called for the wilderness experience. After the announcement, of a necessity, must come the wilderness experience. If not, the ministry will be taken over by the enemy for his own pleasure. It will not serve the purpose of God. The announcement differs from person to person.

Unlike the last two characters we considered, heaven didn't have to orchestrate a series of events to push Jesus into the wilderness. Jesus was not lifted by the announcement that came from the mouth of the then–most authentic prophet (mouthpiece) of God. If Jesus were to act in the flesh, He would have started His ministry in the strength of the announcement. He wouldn't need much advertisement. Instantly, two main disciples of the already-established prophet followed Jesus home immediately after the announcement. You can imagine how much of the crowd He would have pulled if a flyer came out stating that the prophet John had endorsed His crusade. Yes, it would have been successful, as many of the crowd who followed John would have attended His meeting, but heaven would have considered it as nothing, for it would have been born out of flesh. No, our Master showed us the way to go. He had to put His own personal ambition aside to seek the will of God.

Now then, neither did heaven say, "Oh, it's Jesus, so we don't need to roll Him down the mountain. He is not in the category of men who must be de-fleshed." Yes, that is correct. But heaven was also trying to show us a template. Every course that should be taken in the University of Heaven in order for you to be approved by heaven was taken and passed by Jesus. Look at it here:

For we have not an high priest which cannot be touched with the feeling of our infirmities; but was in all points tempted like as we are, yet without sin.

—Hebrews 4:15

Notice how the above passage puts it. Look at the statement, "but in all points." This clearly means that every test available in the University of Heaven that was designed to bring man down into the valley of God was taken and passed by Jesus. The word "tempted" is from the Greek word *peirazo*, which means "to test, endeavor, discipline." You can see that this actually refers to the course. When someone wants to ask for your field of profession in another way, he says, "What is your discipline?" Hence, from that passage, it is clear to us that Jesus passed all the courses in the University of Heaven.

If Jesus, being the very Son of God, was mandated to take these five-unit "must-pass" courses before He could be enrolled to the force of heaven, no one who wants to amount to anything in the army of God will escape it.

7

The Isolation

Another prerequisite course that must be taken in the University of Heaven is the course of isolation. As long as we remain among the crowd, where our John-the-Baptist has declared us to be the Messiah, we will never be useful in the hands of heaven. We are known as champions in that setting; we are the natural go-to whenever there is a problem. Our confidence is in our own ability. Sometimes heaven requires that we vacate the current location and go to a strange location where we are not known, a new area that we know nothing about, just to create a true trust and dependence on God. But sometimes heaven makes you stay in the *same* location, in the *same* crowd, but yet it isolates you from the crowd. That is usually more difficult to bear, as the people who have known you to be a champion now look at you as a failure, a hypocrite among others. Usually, men don't voluntarily isolate themselves like the Master did. We are usually forced into isolation. And the easiest way to force such isolation is to create problems that will make those very people who were shouting, "Hosanna in the highest" when they saw you, to begin to shout, "Crucify him; he deserves to die!" You can understand how much easier it would be to be isolated "from the crowd" that to be isolated "in the crowd."

I give two life examples to further explain the difference between being "isolated from the crowd" and being "isolated in the crowd" before we move back to the characters we have been examining.

Many years ago, when I was working in a particular ministry, I dedicated my life to the work of the Lord in the ministry, and over the years I grew into a position of authority in that ministry. I became a local champion representing the ministry in different states of the country. I had attended some classes in the University of Heaven, and I had started descending the mountain of pride down into the valley of dry bones. But heaven needed to achieve the second purpose by calling for isolation from the world that I knew—the world that defined me, the world that brought me fulfillment and joy, the world that cried "hosanna" whenever I drove through Jerusalem on my donkey. Many spread their cloaks on the floor when I walked in. I had moved from the God of the work to the work of the God. I was a superhero, busily saving souls from corner to corner. The judgment sat against me. And it was agreed that I must take the next course in the University of Heaven. The decree was made, and so it was written, so it would be done. Heaven brought a precious jewel before me, a jewel that would bring promotion, but it came with a price. "What is the price?" I asked. When heaven told me the price, I didn't realize how great a price it would be. In my natural ability to obey my Master, I signed the contract without knowing its full cost. That single decision cut me off from everyone I knew and loved in that world. The very mouths that had shouted "hosanna" when I walked in started to shout, "Crucify him!" The very hands that had spread their cloaks on the floor when I walked past were the very hands that participated in cutting me off. No matter how hard I tried to get back to them, it

The Isolation

always backfired. I was forced to isolate myself. The good thing was that I relocated to another setting. Hence, my isolation was away from the crowd. Someone who could have gotten anything done just by making a phone call became someone who would chase and chase and still get nothing done. I use to take pride in the fact that I knew people in almost every important location in the country. But every single person, every single link, was cut off by that singular contract heaven had asked me to sign. They all turned against me in one accord. No matter how much explanation I gave, it always fell on deaf ears. I was forced to isolate.

The second example is an example of isolation *in* the crowd. I knew of a man of God who was already going down the mountain. But heaven needed to make him take this course of isolation. He was doing well in the fellowship where he was serving. No one took Bible study more seriously than he did. He was given the office of "teacher" by the Lord. But the situation became so bad that soon all the fellowship members had gravitated toward his teachings while neglecting the other leaders in the fellowship, and envy soon set in. The others then collaborated with a woman to say he had slept with her. Imagine the kind of isolation that would have brought! This man had also signed a contract with heaven not to say anything about the situation to anyone. Hence, it was difficult to know the truth. He remained in the crowd, but the event caused the same people who had cried "hosanna" when he taught the Bible study to begin to shout, "Crucify him!" To this day, many still don't know the truth about the matter. You can imagine all kinds of names he would have been called. You can trust church folks to bring a high level of persecution—such suffering in the hands of religious fellows is usually unprecedented.

This is the nature of heaven—when a layer of flesh is removed from a person, that person becomes more useful to heaven than he used to be. This affords heaven the opportunity of getting through more easily to the person in order to bring God's agenda to life. As heaven continues to use this fellow, it gets to the point that heaven needs even more access to the person because the assignment has increased and the range of reach has become wider. Then heaven will need to push the fellow farther down the mountain to remove more layers of the flesh so the fellow can then be even more useful to heaven. See how Jesus put it in John 15:

> *Every branch in me that beareth not fruit he taketh away: and every branch that beareth fruit, he purgeth it, that it may bring forth more fruit.*
>
> —John 15:2

Notice what Jesus said in that passage about the Vice Chancellor of the University. The Head Teacher Himself will ensure the purging so you can bear more fruit. The word "purge" in the above passage is from the Greek word *kathairo*, which means "to cleanse, to prune (from filth, impurity)." Notice who is to be purged. Not the fellow who is not bearing fruit (the one who refused to go down the mountain despite the efforts of heaven); it is the one who is bearing fruit (who has already taken the first step down the mountain)

Let's return to our man Moses.

Moses was known as a man mighty in speech. Highly skilled in it. A nation builder. Dining with the men who ruled over nations. Egypt at that time was the power nation of the world, and Moses was at the helm of its affairs. His refusal to voluntarily take the course of the University of Heaven forced him into isolation. Luckily for him, he was isolated away from the crowd. He was still wearing his regalia of pride when he appeared in the land of isolation:

The Isolation

And when they came to Reuel their father, he said, How is it that ye are come so soon to day? And they said, An Egyptian delivered us out of the hand of the shepherds, and also drew water enough for us, and watered the flock.

—Exodus 2:18-19

He was not recognized by his language. He was recognized by his regalia. A man who never worked alone. He'd had the strongest army on earth at his command, but now he was alone in the most obscure place. He could not access his glory. There was no one to cry hosanna when he walked in the room at this place. All they saw in him was an ordinary Egyptian. They didn't even know his name. They didn't know his abilities. None of his works came with him. There was no record of his greatness in the archive of the land of isolation. He had been completely stripped of this layer of flesh. Now the ambition to save a people had come to a natural end. He had come to the end of the road with his own plan. He was now completely isolated from the people he was supposed to deliver. And he remained in isolation until he satisfied the examiners.

In his isolation, one of the things that died was his pride. Moses was in the middle of nowhere. He could only find rest by a local well. A man who had recently sat on one of the highest thrones on earth was now found seated by a well.

Now when Pharaoh heard this thing, he sought to slay Moses. But Moses fled from the face of Pharaoh, and dwelt in the land of Midian: and he sat down by a well.

—Exodus 2:15

Preparing for the Coming Glory

A particular wing had been broken. His pride could no longer fly. He was condemned to find rest by a well. But heaven was not satisfied yet.

So, based on the decree of the Watcher, our brother Moses started his descent into the valley of dry bones by being driven from the place and position where he thought he'd had the power to deliver his people. Now a king-to-be, the most intelligent and outspoken leader in the most powerful nation on earth, found himself sitting by a well.

The unsatisfied Examiner decided to conduct a midterm exam. Was the wing of pride completely broken? How much of the self did he still have? Let us see how well he would do on this midterm exam. Again, he saw what he considered to be unfair treatment of helpless people. While seated at the well, he saw what he considered injustice. Powerful men had colonized the well because they felt they could not be challenged. No one knew how much pain these ladies had endured for years at the hands of these men.

> *Now the priest of Midian had seven daughters: and they came and drew water, and filled the troughs to water their father's flock. And the shepherds came and drove them away: but Moses stood up and helped them, and watered their flock.*
>
> —Exodus 2:16–17

Notice how the above passage was framed. The ladies came to the well first. While they were trying to draw water from the well, the men came. The men were used to oppressing these women. They took their time to feed their sheep and fill their containers. After they were done with all they needed to do, then they would permit the ladies to have access to the well. We cannot tell why Moses chose to find rest near this well, out of all the public places in the land of Median. But one thing is

The Isolation

clear: the Watcher who orchestrated his move out of the land of Egypt must have a hand in the place where Moses found rest. Another fact we can tell from the passage is that the ladies were used to this injustice. This is what they faced regularly. They were so used to this oppression that they didn't even need argue or contest the situation with the shepherds. They just stood still and waited until the men had used the facility to their satisfaction. This is what was meant for the public, for everyone to have an equal right to the facility. But these men refused the women this right. The men usually took their time when using the well, so much so that by the time they were done, the day was far spent. Look at what their father said the day they came home early:

And when they came to Reuel their father, he said, How is it that ye are come so soon to day?

—Exodus 2:18

The father was also so used to this oppression that he didn't expect the women to return home until the moon was out. Even as a very important man in the society, a priest, he couldn't seem to do anything about the situation. Let's go back to our brother who had found a resting place by this very well. When Moses saw the injustice and oppression, it reminded him of the oppression his people faced at the hand of the most powerful nation on earth. His instinct to deliver came into play again. He arose with his strength to deliver the oppressed. And again, he succeeded. The script was marked. He failed the midterm. Heaven concluded that he still had a lot to learn. There was still a beast inside him that kept the beast outside of him alive. A huge part of his self-ambition still existed. Heaven could not work with that. It would give no glory to God. Heaven had to come up with another "de-fleshing" situation that would completely skim the flesh out from the bone as

Preparing for the Coming Glory

Moses rolled down the mountain. The Assessors sat again to decide the next course of action. The verdict was to roll him farther down the mountain. The verdict was stamped by the Watcher. So it was written, and so it would be done.

The ladies left the scene of action with only a thank-you. Although they had never seen Moses before, they were sure he was a stranger, and they were just lucky to have him around that day. They concluded the victory would not last. So, they left without much appreciation. Moses experienced another blow to his ego. How were they any different from the Israelites he had been trying to save? The voice of that young slave echoed uncontrollably in his mind:

And he said, Who made thee a prince and a judge over us? Intendest thou to kill me, as thou killedst the Egyptian?

—Exodus 2:14

Were these women any different? He could not familiarize himself with the ladies. They seem oblivious; they seemed to take his gesture of kindness for granted. Again, Moses reached the end of the road. Depression set in. The same fear he had experienced when he'd thought he was doing the Israelite a favor came back again. Though he had no place to lay his head, he could not make such a demand from the ladies. Though he had not eaten any decent meal in many days and there was no hope of eating one anytime soon, yet he could not make a request from the people he had just saved. He watched in despair and frustration as they took their troughs and, leading their father's sheep, walked away. What a failure he was. His ego was further broken. In Egypt, the road was so blocked that he could not stay with the Israelites and he could not go back to the palace where he'd come from. Now the same situation plagued him: He could not go to the shepherds for shelter

The Isolation

and food, and yet he could not follow the ladies he had just delivered. This was another huge blow to his pride. When looking at the course of isolation from the Master's point of view, we shall shed some more light on some of these failures of Moses.

While he was busy dealing with his fears and loneliness, the Curriculum Designers were now ready for the next set of classes he needed to take. Heaven ministered to the priest to invite this strange man into his household. Heaven had prescribed a mentorship class for him through one of their finest in the land:

And when they came to Reuel their father, he said, How is it that ye are come so soon to day? And they said, An Egyptian delivered us out of the hand of the shepherds, and also drew water enough for us, and watered the flock. And he said unto his daughters, And where is he? why is it that ye have left the man? call him, that he may eat bread.

—Exodus 2:18–20

The man Reuel could not fathom how it was possible for the women not to at least offer to give the strange man some bread. He could not fathom why they had left him in the street to spend the night. He quickly gave the order for the man to be brought back to his home. We cannot tell who went back to the well to get Moses. We cannot tell whether the priest himself went with one or all of the ladies to fetch Moses. What we can tell is that Moses was brought back to the house. With a little conversation and 11interview with Moses, the priest came to the conclusion that the man Moses was a wanderer. He had no place to lay his head, and he had no hope of a refreshing meal for days to come. The man explained to Moses how humble his abode was. He had no son to care for him. His few sheep were left in the hands of his daughters, who suffered oppression daily at the hands of the male shepherds. He had no other source of income other than milk, meat, and cotton from the sheep. He had a little room he could afford to spare for Moses, however. The story was humiliating. Even the Israelites who were supposedly slaves in Egypt could give better offers. At the least, they had good meals and lived in the best city of the land. The only issue was the labor they are forced to do. But after much consideration, Moses had no choice. He accepted Reuel's offer and was further subjected to "humiliation." He had been sentenced to leading sheep in the wilderness. If you look at this situation deeply, you will see how humiliating it would have been for Moses to be leading sheep. Let's see how the Scripture puts it:

> *And Moses was content to dwell with the man: and he gave Moses Zipporah his daughter.*
>
> —Exodus 2:21

The above passage says that Moses was content to dwell with Reuel. Let's analyze that passage. First, the word "content" comes from the Hebrew word *yaw-al*, which means "to yield or to agree to through the idea of mental weakness." Let us take a deeper look at this. Someone who had recently lived in the White House was now being subjected to living in the house of a shepherd. Someone whose opinion must have been sought before any building project could be undertaken in the kingdom was now following after "smelly" sheep. Moses was a master planner, a great war general, mighty in words and in deed, and he was now following after sheep in a remote village in the wilderness. Nothing could have humiliated a man of his caliber more than this. He was forced to start descending down into the valley from the mountain of self and pride. The flesh was being taken out of him piece by piece. The

The Isolation

world as he knew it was being turned upside down and inside out. This was exactly what heaven wanted. Look at this passage:

Though he were a Son, yet learned he obedience by the things which he suffered.

—Hebrews 5:8

If Jesus was made to suffer in order to learn obedience, none of us will escape going down into the valley of God. As you go down into the valley step by step, steadily but as slowly as you can tolerate, heaven will begin to "un-flesh" you until you reach to the bottom of the valley, using real-life situations and experiences. Back to Ezekiel 37:1: by the time you get to the bottom of the valley, you will be completely fleshed out. Notice what the prophet saw in the valley: bones. And not just bones, but very dry bones. Everything that makes you who you are would have fallen out on the way down into the valley. The bones cannot be recognized in the midst of other bones except through DNA testing. The fellow is completely stripped of his personal identity and pride. Notice what the prophet says in verse 2:

And caused me to pass by them round about: and, behold, there were very many in the open valley; and, lo, they were very dry.

—Ezekiel 37:2

The journey to the valley will milk out all the fluid so there will be no possibility of the flesh rising again. By the time the fellow gets to the valley, he will be unrecognizable. He is dry and completely powerless. Ambition and self-will are completely dead, with no possibility of rising again. There is no marrow left to keep the bone alive. The bone dies a permanent death. The journey down into the valley dealt a blow of death to all the faculties of the flesh of the individual. Heaven steadily rocked the world of Moses until he became a useable vessel. The Moses we once knew was the one who was calling the shots in the then-most-powerful nation in the world, but now he found himself in the house of "the" priest, following after sheep.

The Man Joseph in Isolation

Joseph was now taken out of the way. The brothers had come up with a way to inform their father:

And they took Joseph's coat, and killed a kid of the goats, and dipped the coat in the blood; And they sent the coat of many colours, and they brought it to their father; and said, This have we found: know now whether it be thy son's coat or no. And he knew it, and said, It is my son's coat; an evil beast hath devoured him; Joseph is without doubt rent in pieces.

—Genesis 37:31–33

There was no hope of ever getting Joseph back. His fate was sealed. Joseph was isolated from the place where his flesh had been king. Heaven had arranged a hand to push him down from the mountain. It was a freefall—rolling down without any hope of ever stopping until he reached the valley. He was brought to Egypt, where no man knew of his dream. He was far away from where he had been known as "the soon-coming king," to a place where he was seen as a newly purchased slave:

And the Midianites sold him into Egypt unto Potiphar, an officer of Pharaoh's, and captain of the guard.

—Genesis 37:36

The Isolation

Heaven had dealt a huge blow to the top layer of brother Joseph's flesh. In this new place, the thought of ever becoming a king eroded completely from his memory. Being a slave in those days was like a death trap. It was like a house that had an entrance, but no exit. Many who started as slaves died as slaves. Joseph seems to have reached his end point. Dreams of becoming king met their natural end. Even when they came, he completely ignored them. No hope was left of ever recovering. Joseph settled in his heart that this was likely his final destination. There was no one to complain to. No one could bring justice. He decided to live his life one day at a time.

At this point, what was most important to heaven was that he had been isolated from the place where his flesh had gloried. Now he had no other choice but to turn to God. No ability to hold on to, no coat to flaunt, no body of people to rule over. Rather, he was now the slave, the one being ruled over, the one being looked down upon. Like everyone experiences who has a genuine relationship with God, the place of isolation is a place that forces a man to cry out unto God. That is the idea of the isolation—so that you can spend time with the Holy Spirit. In the place of prayer and fasting, the Holy Spirit will begin to shape you. Just like impurities are taken out of gold to refine it, the Holy Spirit, in the face of isolation, began to take out those impurities. No more gathering around the fire at supper with the Israelites. That had been Joseph's favorite place. After dinner, Jacob would tell the clan stories about their ancestors. At this time Joseph would glow with pride: "Hear me well, guys, I had a dream . . ." The grandchildren would wish to one day be like Joseph. The mothers wished Joseph was theirs. He was already ruling as king long before the fulfilment of the dream. But here, in isolation, no one knew about the dream, and in fact, no one cared if he ever had any dream at all. He was a slave. A slave was bought for profit. He must profit his master by working. He had no time of his own. The master could call at any time. One verse summarizes his isolation and condemnation:

> *And the Midianites sold him into Egypt unto Potiphar, an officer of Pharaoh's, and captain of the guard.*
>
> —Genesis 37:36

Joseph was left with no choice other than to seek God. There was no coming out of this until the Master was satisfied. This was a place where a man would be forced to abandon his ambition. Until that ambition was abandoned, the fellow could not be used. When personal ambition and agenda are forgotten because there is no hope of ever achieving it oneself, then heaven kicks in. So that when you begin to achieve it, it will be clear to you that this was not done by your own power. You had been given the opportunity to try, but you failed. The failure was orchestrated to be without any hope of recovery. There was no hope of recovery for Joseph. He completely abandoned his mission to rule and picked up another project—the project of the Holy Spirit. He spent time praying and fasting. Lots of hours that should have been spent talking away with his brethren were now spent in the presence of God. One thing isolation affords you is ample time to spend with God. This is the time God takes advantage of to shape you. We will address more of the curriculum designed for Joseph and Moses in the place of isolation when we talk about the Master Himself coming into the place of Isolation.

8

The School of Waiting

Jesus is the Standard that God expects from all of us. When God brings a man into His fold (through the door of salvation), His expectation for that man is clear from the start. He has no plans to expect less, and He will never expect less. He has an SI unit of measurement (an SI unit is the international system of units the whole world accepts and follows as a standard of measurement), and He measures every man against Christ. The more you yield, the more like Christ you will become. In actual sense, you don't become like Christ; Christ fills the container called *you*. Christ fills the container in such a way that when heaven looks at you, they no longer see you, but they see Christ. That was why Paul said in Galatians 2:20:

I am crucified with Christ: nevertheless I live; yet not I, but Christ liveth in me: and the life which I now live in the flesh I live by the faith of the Son of God, who loved me, and gave himself for me.

Notice what he says in the second phrase: "Not I but Christ lives in me." Can you see that? The more you go down the mountain, the more

Preparing for the Coming Glory

Christ takes over your faculties—until you get to the floor of the valley. In the valley, you have the fullness of Christ. Let's look at God's intention for man from the beginning:

> *And God said, Let us make man in our image, after our likeness: and let them have dominion over the fish of the sea, and over the fowl of the air, and over the cattle, and over all the earth, and over every creeping thing that creepeth upon the earth.*
>
> —Genesis 1:26

Notice the first part of that passage. At the board meeting held before man was created, it was concluded that the man must be created in the likeness of God. When the finished product came out of the factory, the likeness was so identical that no one could tell the difference between God and man. "This is a mini-God!" the angels exclaimed. Hence, God's initial standard for man was Adam. But Adam fell and no longer lived up to the standard. God had to prepare another standard. That is where Jesus came in.

All of the above was said to point us to the fact that if we are to understand God's expectation for every point of our lives, we must look to Jesus, who is the SI unit of man. When the announcement came about the most-awaited man of the century, from the very mouth of the most revered prophet of the century, the Master did exactly what heaven expected every man in that situation to do: isolate. Look at it:

> *Then was Jesus led up of the Spirit into the wilderness to be tempted of the devil. And when he had fasted forty days and forty nights, he was afterward an hungred.*
>
> —Matthew 4:1–2

The School of Waiting

Let's take a deeper look at the above passage so we can see exactly what Jesus did and understand what heaven expects us to do in situations like this. Notice the word that starts the chapter. It is an unusual word. Who starts the chapter of a book with the word "then"? That tells us that the next words will be a continuation of events described in the previous chapter. Now then, before this chapter, the events that have occurred took a span of at least three days (even up to a month—we cannot exactly tell). The Bible didn't specify how long the event before chapter 4 lasted, but we are sure that it was not immediately after the announcement that Jesus had gone into isolation. Let's attempt to give a rough sequence of events here for the purpose of understanding the steps the Master took to pass His own exams in the University of God.

First, the great prophet, Prophet John, the Baptizer, became an international prophet, and people from all over the region went to him for prayers, for baptism, and to know the mind of God for the moment. After many months of ministry (we don't know how long for sure), it was time to answer the-most-asked-question of his time: Are you the Messiah? He rightly told them he was not. But he made it clear that the Messiah was far greater than him, and he talked about it every day he preached. Who could be greater than John the Baptizer? Everyone was looking forward to seeing someone whose shoe latchet the greatest prophet at the time was not qualified to loose. All of a sudden, one day, an unsuspecting young man attended John's service, and boom, His cover was blown. Before thousands of people, John confirmed that this was the One they had been waiting for. Not just in one service, but in at least two different days and probably in more than two services. You can imagine how far that would have spread. The message of John went as far as Ephesus in his time. One can

Preparing for the Coming Glory

only imagine how far the announcement went. The news would have spread far and wide. In those days, there was no media or Facebook posts to disseminate information like we have today. Information only moved as people traveled from place to place. Every Jewish man who lived anywhere in the world was mandated to visit Jerusalem for a feast in the Temple three times each year. John's ministry spanned one of those feasts. Many Jewish men from other countries would have traveled down to Jerusalem to worship. They would have heard about the new prophet in town talking about repentance and the soon-coming Messiah. And they would have taken this message back home to their family members and other people who loved the Jews. Hence, the message of the unveiling of the Messiah would have gone far and wide.

Now then, Jesus went into action. His first action was to seek the face of God for what to do. People were already singing His praises. Disciples were leaving their masters to follow Him. Men were leaving their professions to follow Him. Parents were happy to release their hope of future survival to follow Jesus. All these things happened just based on the announcement of the great prophet. It takes discipline and deep understanding not to immediately start ministry work. After all, you are the long-awaited Messiah, so why wait? Why seek direction when God's representative on earth has announced you? But not the Master. There was tremendous pressure for Him to perform, both internally and externally: "Messiah, what are You going to do today? Where are You going to preach today? Won't You perform a miracle for me?" Even His mother contributed to the pressure:

And when they wanted wine, the mother of Jesus saith unto him, They have no wine. Jesus saith unto her, Woman, what have I to

The School of Waiting

do with thee? Mine hour is not yet come. His mother saith unto the servants, Whatsoever he saith unto you, do it.

—John 2:3–5

Notice that by the time of this event, the wedding at Cana, John the Baptizer had already announced Him. He even had called disciples to Himself, and these disciples went with Him to the wedding. His mother had been told many prophecies about Him long before He was born. While Jesus was still a baby, many great prophets had given her words for the Child that she kept very dear to her heart. Now that the prophet John had finally proclaimed the release of the Messiah, she expected Him to immediately start showing the people why God had brought Him to this place. Everyone was expecting Him to do something to show that He was truly the Messiah. We know the accuser would not be the last in this venture. In fact, from what we know of the accuser, it is when the internal pressure fails to achieve the ultimate goal of the accuser that the external pressures kick in. The accuser would have pushed Jesus several times to do one or two things just to prove to people around Him that truly, as the greatest prophet had announced, He was the Messiah. But Jesus refused to fall for it. The accuser used far and near people—even people who were dear to His heart, yet He resisted the temptation of acting outside of God's timing. We don't know how long He stayed after John's baptism before starting His ministry. It was maybe a few days to a week. One thing we know for sure is that He didn't move a finger ahead of God. He prayed. When He received no response from heaven, He was also being tested for we know that He learned obedience by what He suffered.

Was there haste in His soul to act just like Moses and Joseph did? Was He in a hurry to showcase His anointing just like Joseph did? Did He want to act outside of God's will and suffer His work to become nothingness before heaven? Would He listen to the cry and call of the people, like King Saul did, because the people who were waiting for him to show himself as king started to scatter when they noticed he wouldn't act. Or would He wait until God was ready to move? All these and many more considerations were being observed by the Examiners in the University of Heaven. What is that haste in your soul? The haste to be and to do, the haste that prevents you from spending time in the presence of God until you get your direction. Here, the Master did something phenomenal. Despite His God-nature, He waited. He dealt with the haste in His soul. He spent time in the presence of God at night, and He went about His work in the day. He studied the Scriptures to the extent that He could quote any passage of the Torah off hand. He didn't immediately quit His job after the announcement, like Moses had abandoned his post to go and start helping the slaves. At work, the accuser would use people around Him to stir up the haste locked in His human soul: "Is that not the One whom John called the Messiah? He's a *carpenter*? I saw Him read the Torah last Sabbath." There would have been all kinds of side talk, front talk, and back talk. Yet, our Example did only one thing: wait. Several hours He spent in the place of prayer, yet no response from heaven. But still He waited. Some of His followers might have assumed this Messiah was not going anywhere. They might even have left Him. Such will go and spread false news about Him. And the devil would make sure He heard such. Yet He still waited. One of the goals of the school of waiting is to remove the haste that is locked in the human soul.

There are two important types of haste that God usually seeks to deal with using the tool of waiting. (God cannot be confined to a formula. There are usually very many things we don't know about that God can use one tool to achieve in the life of a man. But for the sake

The School of Waiting

of our discussion, let's stick to these two.) The first haste is the haste of getting into the limelight. Everyone wants to make it in record time. The motivational speakers will tell you that if you have not achieved such and such by the age of thirty, you are a failure. That does not hold true with God. While Joseph became the prime minister of Egypt at the age of thirty, Moses didn't get to the office of his destiny until the age of eighty. While David ascended the throne at the age of thirty, Aaron did not enter the office of a priest until the age of eighty-three. While Mary gave birth to her firstborn Miracle Child before the age of twenty, Sarah did not give birth to her firstborn miracle child until the age of ninety. Nothing can confine the timing of God to the timing of man. Until God is satisfied with the fellow's growth and development, He will not move forward with the person. Age is just a number with heaven. Anyone who wants to become something in the hands of the Almighty must learn to put the haste of becoming something at a record age aside and walk in the timing of God for his life. It is this haste that makes men dabble in what they should not touch, so they can make it at a record age. In the place of waiting, God will make sure such haste dies a natural death. A prolonged silence from God in the place of waiting will go a long way toward reorienting anyone who wants to become something in the hand of the Almighty. Many of the fellow's mates will become something at a certain age. But he will just watch the years pass him by, and as far as the world is concerned, he is wasting away. But when God is ready for that fellow, all the years that seem to have been wasted in the wilderness of waiting will be restored in multiple fold. The people who seem to have gone ahead of him will suddenly see him in front of them. What a mighty God we serve!

The second haste that God seeks to deal with in the place of waiting is the haste that prevents men from tarrying in the presence of God.

Preparing for the Coming Glory

When one is newly born again, before one is called, heaven has already provided the answer. While he is still trying to find a comfortable position to kneel, the answer to the unspoken prayer has already come. But as one grows older in his walk with God, God deliberately begins to withhold answers to prayer. If that is not done, many a Christian will become a microwave Christian. Two minutes in the presence of God and out they go. It is in the Presence that we are shaped. The fire and the light from the presence of God is what shapes us into what heaven has designed us to be. The longer gold spends in fire, the purer it becomes. But if we run from His presence, then it will be difficult to remove the impurities from our being. Hence, heaven must create a reason to make us tarry in the presence of the Almighty. Again, we must understand that God is the Father of all spirits, the God of all flesh, the Creator of all things. You should never expect Him to respond in your own time. He will respond in His own time. Someone can go for a palm-reading and get an immediate response. That is because the spirit being inquired of is a servant-spirit. It is a created spirit. Ideally, such a spirit should be under the authority of man, not the other way around. They respond quickly in order to give people incentive to keep coming back so they can be lured into bondage. Not so with God. Everyone who must inquire of the Lord, especially for personal direction, must learn to wait. It is in the place of waiting that one will have an encounter with the Father of spirits. It is in the place of waiting that one will have an encounter with the Word.

Somebody might say, "Oh So and So is a prophet, and the other fellow is an apostle. They see angels as easily as they see humans. Hence, they can easily know the mind of God without waiting." That is not a true statement, and it is unbiblical. Everyone must wait on God at some point, no matter who the person is. The only advantage some have over

The School of Waiting

others is that they have learned and perfected the art of waiting. Yet this doesn't exclude them from waiting. They still have to wait. The visions and messages they get is related to their office and is for the purpose of the ministry. If they have to inquire of the Lord for personal issues and even ministry work, they have to wait like every other person does. Let's look at some biblical examples for a better understanding:

> *And the Lord said unto Moses, Come up to me into the mount, and be there: and I will give thee tables of stone, and a law, and commandments which I have written; that thou mayest teach them. And Moses went up into the mount, and a cloud covered the mount. And the glory of the Lord abode upon mount Sinai, and the cloud covered it six days: and the seventh day he called unto Moses out of the midst of the cloud.*
>
> —Exodus 24:12, 15–16

For the purpose of our discussion, verses 13 and 14 were skipped here. Now let's analyze what we have above. In verse 12, God called Moses to come up to meet with Him. Moses did not initiate the call. It was God who invaded his space and demanded a meeting. God told Moses the meeting venue, but He didn't give the meeting time. Moses went to the venue, and that's when the waiting started. It must be noted that he didn't just go there to seat, sleep, or relax until God called him. He was still and in reverence, body, soul, and spirit, waiting for the Father to call. This also included worship, meditation, and the study of the Word (and, for the New Testament believer, speaking in tongues). He did that for the whole of day one. God did not show up. He did the same thing one day two, and still there was no trace of God. He did the same thing on day three, and there was not even a voice from God. Many would have decided that enough is enough. God won't show up.

Preparing for the Coming Glory

But not Moses. He went another twenty-four hours. God still did not show up. It was not until the seventh day that God showed up. It took seven days of waiting before a Man with the caliber of Moses could meet with God. God will not change because of anyone. He is the same yesterday, today, and forever.

Another example can be seen in the life of Jeremiah:

Then all the captains of the forces, and Johanan the son of Kareah, and Jezaniah the son of Hoshaiah, and all the people from the least even unto the greatest, came near, and said unto Jeremiah the prophet, Let, we beseech thee, our supplication be accepted before thee, and pray for us unto the Lord *thy God, even for all this remnant; (for we are left but a few of many, as thine eyes do behold us:) that the* Lord *thy God may shew us the way wherein we may walk, and the thing that we may do. And it came to pass after ten days, that the word of the* Lord *came unto Jeremiah.*

—Jeremiah 42:1–3, 7

Consider the above passage. Let's give a little background to the passage for a better understanding. This event happened at the time when Babylon had finally conquered Israel after repeated calls from God for repentance fell on deaf ears. Nebuchadnezzar took captive most of the important people in all fields of life and left the nonentities and a few intelligent people to form a Babylonian-controlled government over the state of Israel. Jeremiah the prophet was given the choice to stay in Jerusalem or to go with the captives because he was highly respected by the chief general of Babylon's army. Some of the generals of the Israelite army who had escaped from the battlefield and the remnant left back decided to enquire of the Lord whether they should stay back in Jerusalem and help the newly formed government to succeed or escape to Egypt (which was still a superpower at that time) so they could be protected from Babylon. The reason why this enquiry was proposed was because an invader had destroyed the governor that Nebuchadnezzar set up in Israel. For fear of retaliation from the emperor, Israel needed to know the mind of God concerning which way to go. Jeremiah was one of the greatest prophets known in Israel. He was sent by these remnants to inquire of the Lord as to which direction to go—whether to stay or to run to Egypt. Now, back to the passage above. Jeremiah went to God to inquire of the Lord. Jeremiah was no ordinary prophet. He was a major prophet in Israel. But it took him ten solid days of waiting on the Lord before he could know the mind of God regarding the issue.

Hence, in the place of waiting, patience is required. One thing is very sure: God will definitely show up. But the date and time is determined by Him, not by the person in waiting. God is a jealous God. He wants to be sure you have no other options left. Humans naturally, unconsciously, at the backs of their minds, like to have options. *If this does not happen at such and such a time,* we think, *I will move on to such and such an option.* This phenomenon is natural with man. In actual fact, it is called *planning*. But it is not so with God. If a man wants to deal with God, he must be ready to make God his only option. No planning to go to other options just in case God fails to show up. Because the surest way to make God *not* show up is to prepare for what to do in case He doesn't show up. If you must come to God, you must eliminate all other options. The next natural question is, am I saying that because we are Christians we should not plan? No. That's not what I am saying, for he who fails to plan is already planning to fail. What I am saying is that when you come to God, you cannot have a plan. Wait on God in the place of isolation until He shows up. When He shows up, He will tell you what He hopes to achieve with your life. That thing He tells you becomes a goal. You can now plan around the goal to achieve God's purpose for your life. You don't plan before you get a goal from God because if you do, it means you are planning on a goal you have set for yourself.

Another goal God seeks to achieve with the school of waiting is to test whether one has a personal ambition. Until that personal ambition dies a natural death, heaven will not proceed with the fellow. God may call someone to be a great evangelist. Though the person yields to the call, initially with good intentions, along the line, the person might begin to use the grace that heaven bestows for the call for his own personal use. For example, a man who is called to bring the Gospel to a city will be equipped with grace for the job. This grace has the ability to pull people to him. The purpose of the pull is so he can achieve God's purpose by bringing the Gospel to them in its purest form possible. But a man who has a personal agenda can easily abuse such grace. When the grace pulls people, then the man may build an empire for himself. He becomes an emperor who ensures that no man lifts a finger without his permission and approval. He begins to lord things over the people as if he were their lord and savior. He forces them, with his actions, to think that outside of him they cannot make it in life. God may have restructured some lives through his ministry. God may have turned a hopeless situation in someone's life around through his ministry. All these are people who must owe their lives to him. They will be reminded daily of how, if not for his ministry, their lives would have no meaning. If anyone breaks away from the tyranny, the person becomes a victim of his anger. Such anger will be unleashed with the full force of the empire and all that is loyal to the empire. The empire is built around himself

The School of Waiting

and his family. When it is time for him to die, he will not seek the face of God for his successor. Why should he? After all, he built the empire for and by himself. Look at how Jesus puts it in this passage:

> *Who then is a faithful and wise servant, whom his lord hath made ruler over his household, to give them meat in due season? Blessed is that servant, whom his lord when he cometh shall find so doing. Verily I say unto you, That he shall make him ruler over all his goods. But and if that evil servant shall say in his heart, My lord delayeth his coming; and shall begin to smite his fellowservants, and to eat and drink with the drunken.*
>
> —Matthew 24:45–49

Consider the above passage. Notice what Jesus said in verse 45. The Lord made the servant the ruler over His household. The household originally belongs to the Lord. He decided to make the servant ruler over the household. The word "household" is from the Greek word *therapeia*, which means "attendance or collectively domestics." Hence it is talking about a family, a people. The people the fellow uses to build his empire are the people the grace for the position brought. They belong to the One who bestows the grace, and not to the servant who is to oversee the household. He must treat the household as the Master prescribed and not for his own purpose. Notice what Jesus said concerning servants who use the grace upon them to build an empire for themselves. He started by saying, "And if," not, "And when." The words "And if" mean it's not an expectation of heaven for anyone to use the resources of heaven to build his own empire. While the words "And when" suggest that heaven expects everyone who is bestowed with the grace to use the resources for personal gains and ambition, it will only be a matter of time. The fact that the words "And if" are used in the above passage rather than "And when" suggests that it is not the expectation of heaven for anyone to use the resources of heaven to build an empire for himself. According to the above passage, there are three main characters displayed by those who use heaven's resources to build an empire in their own name.

The first is to smite. The word "smite" is from the Greek word *tupto*, which means "to thump, pummel, to disquiet one's conscience." Look at that. The aim of this action is to beat the subject into a shape or form that he (the emperor) wants. With words or fists or any tool that is available to them, they beat God's people into the shape or form they have designed for them. Hence, servants conform to the image of the fellow and not to the image of God. The reason God made him an overseer was to teach the people to conform to the image of God. But because he was using the resources of God to build his own empire, the Holy Spirit could not be a part of that. Hence, the Holy Spirit would not convict anyone to willingly conform. Therefore, this leader would use natural forces to smite the followers into the shapes and sizes he has envisioned for them. This will make them conform to his own image. These are products that will not pass the quality control scrutiny of heaven. There is no part of it that conforms to the image of God, but rather all of it conforms to the image of the leader (who has already derailed from the path of God). Anyone who finds himself in such assembly should move quickly to where they can be shaped in the image of God. There is no time for any form of solidarity. We are in the last few seconds of the end times. Look at what happened to Adam when he fell:

> *This is the book of the generations of Adam. In the day that God created man, in the likeness of God made he him; male and female created he them; and blessed them, and called their name Adam, in the day when they were created. And Adam lived an*

The School of Waiting

hundred and thirty years, and begat a son in his own likeness, after his image; and called his name Seth.

—Genesis 5:1–3

See how clearly it is portrayed in the above passage. When God created Adam, God created him in the image of God. His shape and form were in the image of God. He behaved exactly like God, and therefore he had the characteristics and abilities of God. He was given the charge by heaven to reproduce men after the likeness in which he was created. This is the same charge given to all who will pass through the corridors of salvation, who have graduated into the administrative offices of the Messiah (prophets, teachers, pastors, etc.). But before Adam could begin the assignment he was given, he sinned and fell short of the glory and grace bestowed upon him. He became a shadow of what God expected him to be. The man who was to rule over the entire creation was now subject to the creature. Sickness and diseases were not supposed to be part of the picture, but that became commonplace after the Fall. This fallen man, who was now a shadow of the expectation of heaven, did not go back to the factory so that God could restore his lost glory. He went his way and decided to fulfill the assignment in his own way. Look at what verse 3 said about the product that came out of the factory he was building. The first product that came out was Seth. The product was built after the fallen Adam's image and not the original God-image he'd had when he was created. We know the rest of the story. As the factory built products down the line of time, it grew further and further away from the original product, so much so that God had to shut down the factory to rebuild another. This is because each product kept building another product after its own image rather than changing the factory setting back to the original one that God had created.

Preparing for the Coming Glory

So, this fellow who was asked to rule over God's household started to build an empire for himself by changing the original factory settings that heaven had committed to him. Hence, products that came out of the factory were then after his own image—very far from the intention of heaven for giving the grace to pull the people.

The second character was that he began to eat. The word "eat" is from the Greek word *esthio*, which means "to devour, to consume." Because heaven was not happy with the product coming out of the factory, the supply of funds would be limited. But this fellow was bent on building his empire in such a way that would wow the onlookers. He must begin to convert the stones that God intended to use to build his temple into bread for his personal consumption. Look at how such a temptation came to the Master:

> *When he had fasted forty days and forty nights, he was afterward an hungred. And when the tempter came to him, he said, If thou be the Son of God, command that these stones be made bread. But he answered and said, It is written, Man shall not live by bread alone, but by every word that proceedeth out of the mouth of God.*
>
> —Matthew 4:2–4

Notice verse 2 of the above passage. Jesus was obviously hungry, as He had been without food for days. The tempter didn't bring food to quench His hunger. The tempter pointed to the stones. These stones were humans that God intended to use to build His Temple. God brought these stones to the Man of God to beat them into heaven's desired shape so they could fit into different parts of the building that heaven has designed. Look at how Peter puts it:

The School of Waiting

You also, as lively stones, are built up a spiritual house, an holy priesthood, to offer up spiritual sacrifices, acceptable to God by Jesus Christ.

—1 Peter 2:5

We are all lively stones. God is the Architect of His own building. He made us to be different forms of precious stones. But these stones have ragged edges that will not make them fit into the building when the Constructor is laying the blocks. We have to be beaten into the right shape and size in order for the Builder to easily lay the block in a fitting way that will not jeopardize the integrity of the building. It is these stones, in their raw form, that are brought to the Man of God to beat into the shapes and sizes that God has designed. (God is the Architect of the building; hence, He is the only One who knows the shapes and sizes of stones that will fit specific places in the building.) In the face of hunger, the enemy takes advantage of the legitimate need to push the Man of God to convert the stones brought to Him into bread. The tempter did it to Jesus. We are definitely not going to be spared. Notice the response of Jesus to the devil. It was not within His power to convert God's stones to bread. God would decide with His Word what He planned to do with the stones. It is the same Word that God would also use to satisfy His (Jesus') legitimate needs. But the man who wants to build his own empire sees the stones as bread because the devil made him to see them as bread. He freely converts them to bread because he has the power to do so. And he begins to use this bread to satisfy his hunger rather than using the stones to build the Temple of God. Note that what the devil uses is a legitimate need. Oh, it's the pastor's birthday—everyone must donate. Doesn't your pastor deserve a new car? Such statements should not be heard in the Church, especially if they are pushed by the pastor. Is it wrong to bless the pastor? The answer is

Preparing for the Coming Glory

no. Pastors can and should be blessed. However, because he is the one responsible for the salvation and deliverance of the people, that does not give him one iota of the right to demand any form of favor from the people. He doesn't even have the right to expect anything from them. His expectations and demands must be directed toward the Lord and not the people. Only Jesus can demand anything from the people because they are all His. I remember the case of a man of God whose members contributed money to buy him a new car. They presented the car to him in a grand style during the service. But the man of God rejected it fiercely. It was not an SUV. His mates in ministry were all using SUVs. Why would his church members belittle him by buying him just a car, and not the more prestigious SUV? What a matter! When serving God in the capacity of a pastor or an apostle or an evangelist, or in whatever capacity, it must be of note that people who hold such offices are not employed by men. They are employed by God. Their members are not in any form or shape obligated to pay their salaries. Only God can. When one begins to milk money out of the members using any form of celebration (be it a birthday, a wedding anniversary, Christmas, etc.), it is seen by heaven as converting stones into bread. Our God is faithful and just. If He employs them, He will definitely take care of them, far beyond how the world does

Another aspect of note that brings sorrow to heaven is the misappropriation of God's funds. Many people affiliated with the ministry give their sweat to it because they love God. This is done with the hope that the man at the helm of affairs will appropriate the funds the way heaven expects. But we have seen many a fellow who turns such funds into his own personal funds. Without fear, they put their hands deeply into God's money to fund their excesses and personal ambition. They satisfy their gluttonous nature using offerings and tithes donated to further the purpose of the Kingdom. They go on expensive vacations with money put under their care and meet their own personal, luxurious desires at the expense of the Kingdom. Am I saying a man of God should not be taken care of by the ministry he oversees? The answer is no. A man of God can be paid from the purse of the ministry. But a man of God has no right to touch the money of the ministry that is apart from his salary. He has no right to borrow money from the ministry. The ministry's money is not an emergency fund to touch when in need. It is the life (blood) of men bestowed upon him for the furtherance of the purposes of the Kingdom. Let's take a look at a Scripture or two to see how heaven looks at such matters:

> *Also before they burnt the fat, the priest's servant came, and said to the man that sacrificed, Give flesh to roast for the priest; for he will not have sodden flesh of thee, but raw. And if any man said unto him, Let them not fail to burn the fat presently, and then take as much as thy soul desireth; then he would answer him, Nay; but thou shalt give it me now: and if not, I will take it by force. Wherefore the sin of the young men was very great before the Lord: for men abhorred the offering of the Lord.*
>
> —1 Samuel 2:15–17

The above passage is about the two sons of Eli. Their father, who was a good priest before God, was in his old age at the time of the above passage. He had trained his children in the work of priesthood. So, it was time for him to retire and let his children run the show. But the boys were bad boys and had no respect for God and the offering of His people. The priests were to take a portion of every animal brought for sacrifice in the Temple. But before they were allowed to take any portion, they must first allow the fellow to offer his sacrifice to God. After then, they could take any portion they wanted to take. But these young men would not allow them to offer their sacrifices because they wanted the meat raw. What is most disheartening was the attitude it created in the minds of the people. Look at the end of verse 17. Men who originally loved God and freely sacrificed to God, because of their love for God, started to hate to offer anything to God. That's exactly what happens today. We have many people who have come out to say how detestable it is to pay tithes and offerings to the Church. Many have stopped paying tithes because of the erroneous perception that all pastors are alike, that they will live large on the people's offerings. The worst is how God sees it. Look at the beginning of verse 17. The passage doesn't say it is a sin before God. It doesn't say it is a great sin before God. It says it is a *very great* sin before God. That is exactly how God sees it. It is a show of love to God for someone to willingly give his hard-earned money (which is equivalent to his blood) to the furtherance of the course of the Gospel. When such a fellow stops giving because the man at the helm of affairs has greedily lived a luxurious life with the funds given to the ministry, then heaven sees it as a *very great sin*.

Let's take another passage to see how much God detests this act:

Wherefore kick ye at my sacrifice and at mine offering, which I have commanded in my habitation; and honourest thy sons above me, to make yourselves fat with the chiefest of all the offerings of Israel my people?

—1 Samuel 2:29

Now then, God sent a prophet to Eli to tell him how heaven saw what his sons were doing. Look at what God said concerning the way they handled His offering. The first word we should pay attention to in the above passage is the word "kick." It is from the Hebrew word

The School of Waiting

bawat, which means to trample down. That is serious. That means that when one begins to handle the ministry funds as he would his personal funds, he is trampling down on God's money, trampling down on human blood and souls. The second issue God raised here was the issue of honor. It conveys honor to God to treat the money of the ministry with fear and trembling. Every dime sowed into the ministry is done so by the blood of the men who love God. The best any man at the helm of affairs of such funds can do is to honor God by using the money for the right purpose—the furtherance of the course of the Kingdom. The next issue God brought up in the above passage is the issue of making themselves fat with the best of all the offerings of God's people. I heard of a man of God who goes to the accountant after the service while they are counting the tithes and offerings for that day. He asks them to separate the money into different denominations and different currencies. After the separation is done, he takes the ones with the highest denomination of the best currency and walks away. This is what he does after every service. That's exactly what God is pointing out here with the above passage. These men make themselves fat with *the "chiefest"* of God's offering. They live in luxury at the expense of the ministry.

Heaven has not left us in darkness as to how to handle such matters. Let's take a look at how a man who feared God handled God's offering:

And David longed, and said, Oh that one would give me drink of the water of the well of Bethlehem, that is at the gate! And the three brake through the host of the Philistines, and drew water out of the well of Bethlehem, that was by the gate, and took it, and brought it to David: but David would not drink of it, but poured it out to the Lord. *And said, My God forbid it me, that I should do this thing: shall I drink the blood of these men that have put their lives in jeopardy? for with the jeopardy of their*

> *lives they brought it. Therefore he would not drink it. These things did these three mightiest.*

> —1 Chronicles 11:17–19

That is a very solemn passage. David longed to drink water from a particular well in Bethlehem. At that time, the Philistines had a garrison in Bethlehem. No Israelite was permitted in that area, let alone a soldier. But three men went of their own accord, broke through the defense of the military men stationed at the location of the well, and brought water for David's pleasure. That is how men who love God wake up every day—they drive thousands of miles in jeopardy of their own lives to bring their blood sacrifice to God as a show of their love for Him. It would not be out of place for David to have drunk this water. But this man, David, understood the power of sacrifice. He knew that it would not go down well for him to drink the water for it would amount to the drinking of blood. Blood should be poured out before God as a show of love. It must not be drunk by men. These men were offering themselves in place of goats and rams. It was a sacrifice too big for any man to take upon himself. It was solely meant for God.

A man who wants to build the empire of God will also be hungry just like we see in the case of Jesus. But this hunger will be filled with the desire to build God's empire. Look at how the Master frames it:

> *Blessed are they which do hunger and thirst after righteousness: for they shall be filled.*

> —Matthew 5:6

You see that? Jesus was hungry for sure. But His hunger was directed toward righteousness, toward a right standing with God, toward carrying out the exact desire of heaven as it is systematically prescribed.

The School of Waiting

When one reads the passage in consideration (Matthew 4) further down, one discovers that Jesus was not only filled by heaven with more grace and power to fulfill the commission, but His physical hunger was also quenched by supernatural means.

The third character of a fellow who uses the resources of heaven to build his own empire is drunkenness. The word "drunken" in the passage (Matthew 24:49) comes from the Greek word *methuo*, which means "intoxication," metaphorically speaking of one who has shed blood or murdered profusely. Notice again how Jesus put it in the passage. He didn't say, "This fellow is drunk." He said, "This fellow went to drink with those who are drunken." Hence, he sorted the men who were building big things in the world and began to compare himself with them. So and so has thirty branches all over the nation; we must have thirty-five. All were intoxicated with the desire to outdo each other. And in the process of doing so, many of the stones were converted to bread and being trampled to death. That was why Paul made a remarkable statement in one of his teachings:

> *For we dare not make ourselves of the number, or compare ourselves with some that commend themselves: but they measuring themselves by themselves, and comparing themselves among themselves, are not wise.*
>
> —2 Corinthians 10:12

Consider the above passage. Paul said he dared not compare himself with others. Why? He had a blueprint from the Master he was following. That blueprint was unique to him. God had a blueprint for every single person who walks through the corridor of salvation. No two blueprints are the same. In fact, no two blueprint have similarities. Heaven is just that sophisticated. No matter the billions of people who will walk through that corridor, they all will have unique blueprints that cannot be copied. When a man decides to abandon the blueprint that heaven gave to him and build another blueprint for himself, he has to measure it against something. When heaven builds its own blueprint, it is measured against God's desire and standard. But this fellow could not build his own blueprint with the uniqueness of God's intention for he did not know anything about the original plan, neither had he ever seen the architectural plans of heaven. In order to build a viable blueprint, he must measure it against something. The only way to do that is to begin to compare himself with other successful ministries around him. Notice how Paul put it in the above passage. He could have said they compared themselves with themselves. That would have conveyed a meaning. But he said they compare themselves *among* themselves. This gives further explanation to what Jesus said in Mathew 24:49. The fellow has to go to the drunk to join them to drink. He cannot drink by himself. It is while they are all being intoxicated with personal ambition that they begin to compare themselves among themselves.

Heaven will usually wait until one's personal ambition dies a terrible death before heaven will proceed with its agenda for that fellow. Moses had a personal ambition: to be the deliverer of Israel, a macho-man, mighty in word, a powerful negotiator. He had the skill to topple nations and territories. His ambition was to show the Israelites that just as he delivered Egypt from their enemies, he could also deliver the nation Israel from Egypt. Heaven immediately stepped aside. Heaven waited, and waited, and waited. The ambition still lived. Heaven continued to wait. Heaven could not afford to let Moses redesign the factory setting so the product would be made in the image of Moses. It took heaven forty years of waiting before it could achieve its goal with Moses. One thing we must know about God is that He is in a timeless zone. His time

The School of Waiting

is not like our time. Heaven doesn't have a problem waiting. As long as that personal ambition is still within the fellow, heaven will not apply its resources to help the fellow. When that fellow gives up his personal ambition, then heaven will now unfold its own ambition. The Master was not spared from this. Heaven waited to see, just like it did with the first Adam, whether or not He would betray the trust given to Him. Would heaven regret bestowing its ambition on Him, only for Him to shelve it aside for His own personal ambition? Heaven must wait to see. He must pass the test of waiting. If Jesus had a personal ambition, He would have started the process of building His own empire. Heaven must be sure He had no such agenda. When heaven was satisfied that there was no such agenda in the mind of Christ, heaven then moved Him on to the next level.

Another agenda that must die in the place of waiting is the hand of Uzzah. The hand of Uzzah is the hand of man. Some believe that the work of God has to be helped with human ability in order for it to prosper. Sometimes it seems God is too slow for our human pace. Hence, man must apply the hand of Uzzah in order to bring the purposes of God to pass. Let's look at this man, Uzzah, in order to understand fully what it means to include the hand of Uzzah in the work of God:

> *And when they came to Nachon's threshingfloor, Uzzah put forth his hand to the ark of God, and took hold of it; for the oxen shook it. And the anger of the L*ORD *was kindled against Uzzah; and God smote him there for his error; and there he died by the ark of God.*
>
> —2 Samuel 6:6–7

To give a little background to this story, David the king, with great zeal for the Lord, decided to bring the Ark of God into the city of David.

Preparing for the Coming Glory

Zeal for the Lord is good, but zeal without knowledge can have very dangerous consequences. God was specific in the method by which the ark must be moved. A clear prescription was given back in the time of Moses on how the Ark must be transported when necessary:

> *And thou shalt make staves of shittim wood, and overlay them with gold. And thou shalt put the staves into the rings by the sides of the ark, that the ark may be borne with them.*
>
> —Exodus 25:13–14

> *And when Aaron and his sons have made an end of covering the sanctuary, and all the vessels of the sanctuary, as the camp is to set forward; after that, the sons of Kohath shall come to bear it: but they shall not touch any holy thing, lest they die. These things are the burden of the sons of Kohath in the tabernacle of the congregation.*
>
> —Numbers 4:15

Consider the above two passages. The Ark was built with four rings by its four top corners. Two rods made of shittim woods (a specific kind of wood) should be inserted into the rings in such a way that one rod would be held at each end by two rings. This would make it possible for four men to carry the Ark holding the ends of the rod from all sides. God was also very specific on who could carry the Ark. Out of the twelve tribes of Israel, only the Levites were permitted to transport it. Even among the Levites, only the sons of Kohath were allowed to carry the Ark, and even they had specific instructions on how to carry it. Whatever they did, they must not touch the Ark. That is why the shittim rods were placed there. They could only carry the Ark through the rods.

The School of Waiting

David and his advisors did not check the Scriptures for direction. There was a priest at that time who knew the ways of the Lord, but they did not bother to engage the services of this priest concerning the transportation of the Ark. They went with zeal, fired up by their passion for God. Now then, back to our man, Uzzah. He was the son of Abinadab. The Ark had been in his family's house since it had been recovered from the hands of the Philistines during the days of Samuel. Abinadab was not a priest, and neither was Uzzah. That was deviation number one. The next problem is that the ark had been set upon a new cart. Though that may have seemed prestigious in the eyes of man, it was disgusting in the eyes of God. The final straw that broke the camel's back was the man Uzzah. The word "Uzzah" comes from a Hebrew word that means "strength." The man Uzzah had lived with the Ark for many years in his home, and so he had become over-familiar with the Ark. There was no record that God had blessed his family because the Ark was in their house. It might interest you to know that when the Ark first got to the house of Abinadab, many years before the event at Nachon's threshing floor, it was not Uzzah who was put in charge of it:

> *And the men of Kirjathjearim came, and fetched up the ark of the* Lord, *and brought it into the house of Abinadab in the hill, and sanctified Eleazar his son to keep the ark of the* Lord.
>
> —1 Samuel 7:1

Notice the name of the man who was sanctified to keep the Ark when the Ark first arrived at the house of Abinadab: Eleazar. So why was he not the one to bear the Ark when David was transporting the Ark from their house? What happened to Eleazar? Why was he not even mentioned among the two sons of Abinadab when David was moving the Ark? It is possible that he had not followed the precepts of God and

Preparing for the Coming Glory

had been destroyed. The Ark had brought a curse to the family rather than blessing. This was exactly the problem the Philistines had had. Eleazar was no more, and now Uzzah was dead as well.

However, this same Ark stayed in the house of Obed-Edom for only three months, and the people around him went to report to the king that God had blessed the household of Obed-Edom because of the Ark. It will also interest you to know that just like Abinadab, Obed-Edom was not a priest. But yet, he was blessed beyond measure for keeping the Ark of God. The blessing was not reported by anyone from the household of Obed-Edom. It was actually reported by people who were not part of the household but who saw what God was doing in the household. We can only imagine how massive the blessing was to have called the attention of the people around them. One should wonder why the same Ark, which had not lost its potency, stayed in Abinadab's house for many years, and yet no blessing was recorded. Uzzah had become used to accomplishing God's work with human efforts. Everything they did for the Ark at his house was based on their own prescriptions, their own accomplishments. They might have built a special hut for the Ark in their sitting room, furnished the floor with rugs from Lebanon and linens from Assyria. All such attempts are the use of human efforts to accomplish God's purpose. No wonder God was not pleased with them. On the other hand, when the Ark visited Obed-Edom, the first thing the man did was to ask, in reverence, what to do, when to do it, and how to do it. The next thing he did was to ask for strength to do what is demanded of him. No wonder the blessing came through the floodgates of heaven so much that he could not contain it.

As usual, the character, Uzzah, was brought up with the understanding that God could not possibly accomplish His purposes by Himself. He needed the strength of man to do that. The oxen shook, and the Ark was shaken with it. For a moment, it looked like the Ark was going to fall. The natural instinct built into Uzzah kicked in. It would have been a shame for the Ark to fall off the cart. It is obvious that in this situation, God Himself cannot hold back the Ark from falling. Even if God were to act, He wouldn't be able to act fast enough to halt the fall of the Ark. The ministry must not be put to shame at this point. Any form of delay was dangerous. It must be okay to "help" God accomplish His goals once in a while. The world doesn't need to see what we do. That's what we do in behind the scenes. And so Uzzah stretched forth his hand to help God with his own strength to prevent the Ark from falling. He was instantly electrocuted and fell to the ground, dead. Everywhere the strength of man is engaged to accomplish the purposes of God, heaven always strikes that hand. Moses tried to accomplish God's purposes with his own strength by taking on the Egyptians one by one. Even though it was a step toward accomplishing God's purpose, he was struck down. God will not permit the fingerprints of mortal men on His work. Only the signature of God can be permitted to be on His product. No man is permitted to take any ounce of glory for the product of God. A good way to prolong your stay in the place of waiting is to place your fingerprint on the work that only God can accomplish. God will not permit man to share His glory under any circumstance. If God tells a man he will be a great leader, the man doesn't need to do anything in the natural realm to accomplish it. There is no need for politicking, no need for gimmicks to help God, for that will be counted as the hand of Uzzah, and that hand will be cut off without mercy.

How Heaven Expects Us to Treat the Hand of Uzzah

This is a very serious matter for everyone who wants to become something in the hand of the Creator. We must learn to let God

Preparing for the Coming Glory

accomplish what only He can accomplish, and we must learn to do only what heaven has prescribed for us to do. A good example of what to do with the hand of Uzzah can be learned from the life of David. At about the age of seventeen, David was anointed to be the king of Israel by one of the most powerful prophets in the entire history of Israel. It was said about this prophet that God ensured that none of his words fell to the ground unfulfilled:

> *And Samuel grew, and the* Lord *was with him, and did let none of his words fall to the ground.*
>
> —1 Samuel 3:19

That means that anything Samuel said becomes a law. It must be fulfilled. This same prophet came to the city where young David and his family lived. In the full glare of the elders of that city, he anointed David as king—while Saul was still on the throne. That bred envy, and David eventually became a fugitive. Many years passed; the word of Samuel seemed to have fallen to the ground. The prophet Samuel died without seeing the word come to pass, yet David still believed it would come to pass. Then it was time for heaven to present the hand of Uzzah to David and see if he would pass the test. There could not be two kings on the throne of a nation at the same time. In order for another to be king, the incumbent had to die a natural death or he had to be killed. As long as Saul was alive, David could never be king of Israel. All the people around David who wanted a position in his cabinet were praying and wishing for the death of Saul, but he only kept getting stronger. So, one day, God opened the curtain to see what was in the heart of David:

> *And he came to the sheepcotes by the way, where was a cave; and Saul went in to cover his feet: and David and his men remained in the sides of the cave. And the men of David said unto him,*

The School of Waiting

*Behold the day of which the L*ORD *said unto thee, Behold, I will deliver thine enemy into thine hand, that thou mayest do to him as it shall seem good unto thee. Then David arose, and cut off the skirt of Saul's robe privily.*

—1 Samuel 24:3-4

Consider the above passage. *God* brought Saul to David. I don't know how someone could be so engrossed in the business of "number two" that he wouldn't know that somebody was coming up behind him! But God made Saul unaware in order to see what was in the heart of David. The hand of Uzzah surfaced. His followers told him how much they had prayed for this moment. His time had finally come. "Go and accomplish God's purpose with your strength," his friends said. In fact, they interpreted the event as the orchestration of God and backed it up with Scripture. As far as they were concerned, there was obviously no other way Saul was meant to die other than through the hand of David on that day. Hurriedly, David went there. He saw the man, oblivious that his life was about to be taken from him. David unsheathed his sword, ready to cut off Saul's head with one strike as he did with Goliath. Then, in a split second, he had a change of mind. Instead, he cut a piece off the hem of Saul's garment and crept away with it. Later, when in the place of communion with God, the Spirit of God convicted him of sin. If he could cut off the hem of the garment of God's anointed, what would he do the next time? The head was not far from the garment. What would be the guarantee that he wouldn't cut off Saul's head next time? The followers of David were disappointed. A man highly skilled with the blade and with stones, and David could only get a piece of cloth from his archenemy? If the hand of Uzzah could not find expression in the life of David, it could find expression in the lives of the men of David. They all pulled out their swords, ready to go and attack the army of Saul

Preparing for the Coming Glory

with the sole purpose of killing him. Thank God, David had a quick communion with the Holy Spirit:

> *And he said unto his men, The LORD forbid that I should do this thing unto my master, the LORD's anointed, to stretch forth mine hand against him, seeing he is the anointed of the LORD. So David stayed his servants with these words, and suffered them not to rise against Saul. But Saul rose up out of the cave, and went on his way.*
>
> —1 Samuel 24:6–7

He was able to hold back the hand of Uzzah. On the other hand, God was also disappointed, though for a different reason. God was saying that a man with a great relationship with God could build enough hatred in his heart to cut the hem of the garment of God's anointed in the bid of accomplishing God's purpose. And if so, what would he do next time? Heaven was not satisfied with his performance in the exam. He had to retake the exam. The examination committee of the University of Heaven sat and concluded that David must sit for the same exam again. Heaven must be sure that the hand of Uzzah had no place in the heart of David or even around David. Another opportunity was given:

> *So David and Abishai came to the people by night: and, behold, Saul lay sleeping within the trench, and his spear stuck in the ground at his bolster: but Abner and the people lay round about him. Then said Abishai to David, God hath delivered thine enemy into thine hand this day: now therefore let me smite him, I pray thee, with the spear even to the earth at once, and I will not smite him the second time. And David said to Abishai, Destroy him not: for who can stretch forth his hand against the LORD's anointed, and be guiltless? David said furthermore, As the LORD*

The School of Waiting

*liveth, the L*ORD *shall smite him; or his day shall come to die; or he shall descend into battle, and perish. The L*ORD *forbid that I should stretch forth mine hand against the L*ORD*'s anointed: but, I pray thee, take thou now the spear that is at his bolster, and the cruse of water, and let us go. So David took the spear and the cruse of water from Saul's bolster; and they gat them away, and no man saw it, nor knew it, neither awaked: for they were all asleep; because a deep sleep from the L*ORD *was fallen upon them.*

—1 Samuel 26:7–12

Consider the above passage. No one should be in doubt that this was an orchestration by God Himself. Once again, the curtain was opened. The committee of the University of Heaven sat to observe. What would David do now? God Himself brought a deep sleep upon an entire army. That was a very strange phenomenon. Now then, David went down to observe Saul and his army, accompanied by one of his trusted generals. Upon getting there, the hand of Uzzah surfaced from the outside. There was absolute silence in heaven and on earth. Would David take the hand? Would he try to accomplish God's purpose with his own human strength? Would he put his signature side by side with God's signature on God's product? The committee waited. The presenter of the hand of Uzzah did so in such a way that it appeared to be God who was presenting it. Deep understanding and discernment were required at this point. This was the day the Lord has made. David, you should rejoice and be glad in it. David had learned his lesson. He refused to take the hand of Uzzah. He rejected the generous offer. Though God had anointed him king over Israel, there was still a king on the throne, and that king had also been anointed before he got to the throne. It was not David's place to judge whether or not an anointed fellow was out of sync with God. His place was to honor God. He had been given many lectures through the Scriptures and with daily communion with the Holy Spirit. He now knew how dangerous it was to lay a hand on the anointed of God. Yet, David believed that, as was prophesied by Samuel, one day he would ascend the throne of the land of Israel. But only the hand of God would accomplish it. He not only engraved that on his spirit, but he also verbalized it at the slightest provocation. Notice what David said in verse 10. It was only the hand of God that could accomplish the mission of God. By so doing, David had completely eliminated any hatred locked in his heart for Saul—so much so that when Saul died and David was told of it, he mourned for him as a son would mourn for a father.

The examination committee sat again. Discussion ensued. The conclusion was easy to reach. David had satisfied the Examiner. The decision was made. David would always reject the hand of Uzzah. After that, heaven began its orchestrations that would bring David to the throne.

I remember an incident that happened many years ago. A very good friend of mine was in a relationship with a fellow Christian lady. Over time the Lord made him understand that the lady was not the destiny helper He had for him. This happened when he was in a platonic relationship with his true destiny helper. He was now in a fix. What should he do? He came to me to ask my advice. How could he break up with a person and date another when both were mutual friends? The Holy Spirit dropped in my heart what to say to him: You cannot kill your Saul because God has promised your David that he will be king. Wait for God to take Saul out of the picture so your David can ascend the throne by the hand of God. But my advice seemed stupid. In the matter of love, waiting is a luxury. He went ahead and applied the hand of Uzzah. The result was devastating.

The School of Waiting

Let's consider the matter in the life of our faith forefather, Abraham. When Abraham was called by God, the condition of the calling was centered on being the father of many nations:

Now the LORD had said unto Abram, Get thee out of thy country, and from thy kindred, and from thy father's house, unto a land that I will shew thee: and I will make of thee a great nation, and I will bless thee, and make thy name great; and thou shalt be a blessing.

—Genesis 12:1–2

It goes without saying that Abraham must have at least one child from his only wife in order for God to keep His part of the deal. At first, it was easy enough to believe, even though Abraham was seventy-five and his only wife was sixty-five years old. They faithfully executed the instructions of God. They separated themselves from their known world and registered in the University of Heaven to take the course of patience.

Days turned into weeks, and weeks into months, and months into years. There was no trace of any sign of God ever fulfilling His promise. Not even a miscarriage was in the picture. The tempter presented the hand of Uzzah to Abraham:

Now Sarai Abram's wife bare him no children: and she had an handmaid, an Egyptian, whose name was Hagar. And Sarai said unto Abram, behold now, the LORD hath restrained me from bearing: I pray thee, go in unto my maid; it may be that I may obtain children by her. And Abram hearkened to the voice of Sarai. And Sarai Abram's wife took Hagar her maid the Egyptian, after Abram had dwelt ten years in the land of Canaan, and gave her to her husband Abram to be his wife. And

Preparing for the Coming Glory

he went in unto Hagar, and she conceived: and when she saw that she had conceived, her mistress was despised in her eyes.

—Genesis 16:1–4

Notice the above passage. After ten years of taking the curriculum of patience, the test of the hand of Uzzah surfaced. See how the chapter started. Sarai bare Abraham no children. That was the bone of contention. They had prayed, fasted, and trusted, but they'd received nothing. In fact, a chapter before, Abraham even had a visitation from God. He made the same complaint to God. Sarah his wife had borne him no children. God reassured him with almost an oath that Sarah would conceive. But yet, Sarah was able to convince Abraham that it was clear that she was barren. The barrenness was not new to them. It had been there before God made the promise. It seemed to them that when God had made the promise, He did not realize that Sarah was barren. They actually thought He knew Sarah was barren when He made the promise and they thought He could do something about it. But now it was obvious that He knew nothing about the barrenness when He made the promise. In order for God not to be put to shame, they decided to help Him with the hand of Uzzah. Abraham saw sense in what Sarah said. They went ahead and applied the hand of Uzzah to the product of God. *Boom!* He didn't have to do it a second time to get the expected result. It was a male child. Finally, the promise of being the father of many nations was now a reality. God be praised!

No matter who or where the person is from, God will not share His glory with any man. He cannot afford to have His signature placed side by side with that of the hand of Uzzah on any product. So, God turned away. For thirteen solid years, there was no communication between God and Abraham. When heaven was sure the product the hand of

The School of Waiting

Uzzah produced had gone far away from the factory, then heaven gave Abraham another chance:

> *And when Abram was ninety years old and nine, the* LORD *appeared to Abram, and said unto him, I am the Almighty God; walk before me, and be thou perfect. And I will make my covenant between me and thee, and will multiply thee exceedingly.*
>
> —Genesis 17:1–2

Notice how the above Scripture was introduced. It tells us why heaven stayed away for that long. The first instruction heaven gave Abraham in order for him to be back on track was to walk perfectly before God. The word "walk" is taken from the Hebrew word *halak*, which means "someone who walks for another." The Hebrew symbol used is that of a man walking with a rod for strength and protection. What God was demanding from Abraham was for him to put aside his own walk and take on the walk heaven had prescribed. One's walk is to conduct one's life according to a certain pattern. God was telling Abraham to abandon his personal agenda and take on the agenda of heaven. The walk cannot be done by his own ideas or calculations. It had to be the way heaven wanted it. After God was sure He had gotten the first message, then God renewed the covenant of making him a man of many nations. Notice how verse 2 frames it. God had already made a covenant with Abraham at least ten years before (Genesis 15:9–15). The covenant had to be renewed in Genesis 17:2 because the hand of Uzzah had surfaced in Genesis 16. Again, it is clear to us that no matter who the person is, God will not permit His signature to be placed side by side with the hand of Uzzah on any of His products.

Abraham obeyed God and walked only the walk of God. With time, the product of God surfaced. God made sure that only His signature was on the product. But the product of the hand of Uzzah that Abraham employed still exists to this date. We can see the devastation caused by that product in our world today. God cannot permit the hand of Uzzah to be on His product. Heaven will wait until it is sure that there is no ounce of the hand of Uzzah in, near, or around a fellow before heaven will bestow its grace upon that person. God will not share His glory with any man, regardless of who that man is.

The Master in the School of Isolation

When heaven was satisfied with how Jesus handled the school of patience, heaven granted permission for Him to move forward. After many hours or days or months of praying and fasting to seek the face of God on what to do with the announcement made by the prophet John, one day, the Holy Spirit spoke. He gave a clear direction: "You have passed the school of patience. Move on to the school of isolation." He was cleared to go. He had satisfied the Examiners. It was time to move on to the next level:

> *Then was Jesus led up of the Spirit into the wilderness to be tempted of the devil. And when he had fasted forty days and forty nights, he was afterward an hungered.*
>
> —Matthew 4:1–2

> *And Jesus being full of the Holy Ghost returned from Jordan, and was led by the Spirit into the wilderness.*
>
> —Luke 4:1

His own isolation was to take place apart from the people. He had to leave the people who saw Him as a champion. His community had

The School of Waiting

grown since the announcement by the prophet John. It was now beyond His immediate family and followers. It now involved as many as heard John when he made the announcement. Heaven didn't need to orchestrate an event to force Him out. He made the choice to leave. As easy as this may look now, it was one of the most difficult exams to pass. We saw how Joseph cringed with fear when he was being separated from his people. We saw how Moses lost a great part of himself when he was forced to separate himself. Jesus made it look easy.

He was led by the Holy Spirit. It is one thing to be led; it is another thing to decide to follow. It should be noted that the Holy Spirit is not forceful in His leading. He just gives little promptings. One has to be sensitive to pick up on those promptings. The more one yields to these promptings, the easier it becomes to pick up on future promptings. Jesus immediately responded to the call to isolation despite the temptation to hold on to His community. He easily overcame the fear of losing His followers, unlike many who have gone before Him.

Going into isolation was just the beginning. Doing what should be done in isolation was the most important thing. Jesus performed excellently in the place of isolation. His performance became a syllabus for all to follow when in the place of isolation. When He got to His place of isolation, He was not busy holding on to His past, thereby losing His future. The accuser will bring many regrets and the fear of "what-ifs" and "what-if-nots." For example: "Many people used to listen to me before, but now everyone has deserted me" is a normal cliché the accuser uses in the place of isolation. Jesus didn't bother Himself about the community He left. He concentrated on His classes and quickly got down to business. Notice that the only thing the Holy Spirit did in the above passages was to lead Him to the place of isolation. The Holy Spirit didn't give further instructions. Jesus did what every man should do in the place of isolation. The first thing He did was to declare a fast. That kind of fast should only have a start date. The situation and circumstances one will face in the place of isolation will determine the end date. It must continue until the school of isolation is over; if not, it will be a difficult class to pass. The reasons unlimited fasting has to be declared in the place of isolation cannot be exhausted. The place of isolation is the place of temptation. It is a place where heaven will step aside to expose the individual to the tempter. How much of God's Word have you stored? How much of God do you have? How much pressure can you bear? How long can you contend with the accuser? The Word you have been teaching—do you live by it? Did you just memorize the Word, or have you been able to get it down into your spirit? These and many more questions must be answered to the satisfaction of heaven before you may leave the place of isolation. The only way to survive this kind of place is to declare war against the part of you that is likely to easily yield to the demands of the accuser and his demons. Another reason the tool of fasting must be employed at the place of isolation is what Mark pointed out:

And he was there in the wilderness forty days, tempted of Satan; and was with the wild beasts; and the angels ministered unto him.

—Mark 1:13

Notice what Mark said in the second half of the above passage: "He was with the wild beast." Why did that part appear? There is no word in the Bible that is idle. Every single word in the Bible was divinely planted by the inspiration and breath of the Almighty for our learning and development. The word "beast" is from the Greek word *therion*, which means "wild animal, metaphorically a brutal, bestial man, ferocious."

The School of Waiting

Apart from Satan and his demons, the individual in isolation will also encounter a beast. What does that mean for us? Jesus literally went to the wilderness for His own isolation. That may not be the case for most of us. The "beast" here represents irrational humans. People—both male and female—who are easily accessible by the devil to frustrate an individual in the place of isolation. This beast is used by the devil to bring out greed, lust, anger, murder, etc. The truth of the matter is that unless you have one of these beasts in you, there will be nothing to pull out of you when the beast of the wilderness comes to try you. Also, it should be of note that some of the people the devil uses as a beast, who are the conveyors of his agenda, are Christians! Most of them have been practicing Christianity for many years, and some even hold leadership positions in their local assemblies. In the few years I have been in this race, I have come to realize that the frontline of the devil's army are mostly Christians. The devil uses these Christians as his frontline attackers against other Christians. These are men equipped by demons to bring out the beast in other Christians. Unfortunately, most of these men don't even know that they are doing the devil's will. They actually believe they are fighting for God, and they do it with great zeal and aggression. If we want to point out things done by Christians serving in the devil's frontline army, space and time will not permit. One thing that has become fashionable is to use the tool of social media to point out ministers' faults, as if the one pointing out these faults is faultless. We see many people taking to social media to point out the faults of the ministers of God, calling them out by name and by ministry. Check that act very well—you rarely find God in it. Am I saying that ministers of God are above correction? The answer is no. But there is a way prescribed in the Bible for such correction:

Preparing for the Coming Glory

Brethren, if a man be overtaken in a fault, ye which are spiritual, restore such an one in the spirit of meekness; considering thyself, lest thou also be tempted.

—Galatians 6:1

Nowhere in the above passage does it say that the faults of the minister of God, or any Christian, for that matter, should be spread in the open air, under the sun for all the public to see. Why take to social media? It speaks of pride—pride in the sense that you are saying that whatever you are pointing out in the life of your fellow Christian is beneath you. You can't do such. So, you must let the world know how weak this fellow is to be doing such.

Back to the Master. In the place of His isolation, long before the beast showed up, He declared a personal unlimited fast. He didn't wait for His denomination to call for a fast. He didn't wait for a prophet to advise Him to fast. He imposed a fast on Himself. Fasting in the place of isolation, especially a long fast, strangulates the beast nature within you. Once this nature is strangulated and eventually destroyed, no matter what the external beast does to provoke you, it will fail. It will just be like flogging a dead man and expecting him to fight back. The man is dead; he can't lift a finger. This is why this curriculum is very important. Every beast within us must be eliminated before heaven can permit anyone to land at the floor of the valley.

Let's pick an example from the life of Joseph, when he was in isolation for a better understanding. When Joseph came to the conclusion that there was no hope of ever returning home, he settled into his new world. In no time, the favor of God brought him out. He became the chief slave in charge. Though he was elevated above all the slaves, he was not elevated above the tests he must pass. He had the test of beast

The School of Waiting

to contend with. Not too long after he ascended to the role of the chief of slaves, the beast in the place of isolation surfaced to sniff him. *Does he have part of us in him? Can we provoke him to act against his God?* Joseph has to provide answers to these questions and many more, in a way that must satisfy his examiners and put the devil to shame. Now then, Joseph was the slave of Potiphar. Potiphar was no mean man in the land of Egypt. He was an officer of Pharaoh. Hence, one might expect him to be rich and well-placed in society. He had many slaves to manage his estate. Male and female servants would have been a common commodity in his house. Joseph happened to be the head of all the servants—both male and female. The devil must have brought many beasts his way, but all failed. He tried him with the beast of greed, but there was no greed in him, so he didn't fall for that. He tried to get him angry and act out of anger, but that also was a dead end, because there was no iota of anger in him. The devil finally decided to use the ancient beast that worked for all men. But he noticed that Joseph had no interest in the female slaves under him, so he started looking for a more suitable prey to use.

> *And it came to pass after these things, that his master's wife cast her eyes upon Joseph; and she said, Lie with me.*
>
> —Genesis 39:7

He found one in Potiphar's wife. Surely, Joseph wouldn't be able to resist this one, especially if he wanted to maintain his position as the chief slave in the house. More so, what would make him think that this was not the place of his destiny? He was the boss here, and all the slaves answered to him. Potiphar didn't even care to know what was going on. He left his entire estate in the hand of Joseph. So, this could be the meaning of the dreams he had been having. She found no shame in lying with a slave. She had to do her master's bidding.

> *And it came to pass, as she spake to Joseph day by day, that he hearkened not unto her, to lie by her, or to be with her.*
>
> —verse 10

Every day she laid siege with seductive dresses and glances. But there was nothing within Joseph to which she could appeal. If lust lurked in Joseph, he would have fallen for her seductive gestures. She diligently did this every single day. But Joseph had dealt with lust in the place of fasting. As beautiful and as adorned as she was, nothing in Joseph was pulled to the trap. Joseph even refused to sit with her to have a conversation. Joseph completely avoided her. All the sexy pictures she posted on her Facebook and Instagram pages for Joseph to see were futile. Joseph did not even look at the pictures. If Joseph had paid attention to the pictures, the enemy would have built an image in his heart using the pictures as raw materials. A movie would have been shot in the theater of his heart. The director (the demon of lust) would be sure to play the movie over and over again for Joseph to see until it became a reality. But he refused to pay attention to the pictures. The ones she sent to his "phone" as "text messages" and "WhatsApp dms" went unread. Once, Joseph opened the WhatsApp message thinking she had an important message for him, only to see her picture. He didn't create a world of fantasy around the picture. He deleted it immediately and blocked her on all platforms. He dealt with the residue implanted on his imagination immediately, using prayer and fasting until it was completely wiped out of the memory of his imagination. His heart, mind, and imagination were completely clean and free of lust. Hence, when he went into the master's room to do the cleaning, nothing about her appealed to him.

The School of Waiting

He had taken the time and effort to deal with the lust within, making it difficult for the lust without to appeal to him. Joseph has given us a masterclass presentation on how to overcome both inner and outer lust: First deal with the internal lust, for then it will be easier to deal with the external lust.

Back to the Master in the place of isolation. Jesus dealt with every beast known to man in the place of isolation. He was tempted in *all* ways and yet was without sin. Notice that Jesus was taken to the zoo where all the animals were kept. He declared a dangerous fast of both food and water until all the beast within was completely dead. He was able to teach us from experience how to deal with the internal beast in one of His free masterclasses:

> *And if thy right eye offend thee, pluck it out, and cast it from thee: for it is profitable for thee that one of thy members should perish, and not that thy whole body should be cast into hell. And if thy right hand offend thee, cut it off, and cast it from thee: for it is profitable for thee that one of thy members should perish, and not that thy whole body should be cast into hell.*
>
> —Matthew 5:29–30

Considering the above passage, one will notice that Jesus is not asking us to literarily pluck out the eye through which lust captures pictures to the theater of our heart. He is actually talking about the inner eye, which watches the movie shot by lust after the outer eye captures the picture from the outside. You can't stop the outer eye from accidentally stumbling into nudity or semi-nudity. It is everywhere you turn—on your phone, on TV (even when you are trying to watch a decent show, they find a way of inserting indecent advertisements), on the street, in the supermarket, and even in the Church, the devil

Preparing for the Coming Glory

has people under his control who will do his bidding and even defend their actions. Anywhere you turn, the opportunity to take nude pictures with the camera of your physical eyes abounds. When these pictures are taken, lust processes it into a movie and brings it to the inner eye to view. It is this inner eye the soul uses to view the pictures taken by the outer eye—and this is the eye that Jesus is asking us to pluck out. When the inner eye is plucked out, over time, the demon of lust will find out that this fellow has no eye for the movie he is presenting. He will start looking for another avenue to cause destruction. That is exactly what Jesus was saying when He says to pluck the eye that offends.

Notice also the next verse in the above passage. This time He refers to the hand. How does He expect us to do that? In order to explain what Jesus meant with the cutting off of the hand, I will give a short story to illustrate. Many years ago, a man of God went to an area where some monks were carrying out certain devotional acts. He observed one who lifted his right hand for many hours. Upon inquiry, he discovered the reason why this monk lifted his right hand was because through that hand, he had killed some people. So, he was trying to inflict punishment on the right hand so that it wouldn't hurt anyone again. The man of God laughed at his foolishness and even made a remark about how foolish he was. Instantly, the man gave him a blow on the chest with the left hand for making such a remark. The man of God stepped back and explained to the monk that the agent killing the people he killed was the anger that is locked inside. The external hand was just carrying out the bidding of the internal hand. The man of God also made him understand that if he had a knife or a gun, he also would have been one of his victims. This is exactly what Jesus was saying. If the spirit of anger was not locked in the monk, there would be no inner hand to motivate the outer hand to kill. There would be no reason for the right

The School of Waiting

hand to kill anyone. Hence, the hand to deal with is not the outer right hand, which carried out the murder; it is the anger that pushed the right hand to carry out the murder. The beast on the outside only draws its strength from the beast on the inside. If an individual is able to deal with the beast on the inside through the curriculum heaven presents, there is nothing the beast on the outside can do to provoke that from the inside because there is simply nothing to provoke—just like we saw in the experience of Joseph.

Our Lord and Master has once more passed another test in the place of Isolation. There were many more to come. The aim of the devil is to prevent the individual from achieving purpose in the place of isolation. Jesus, when in the place of isolation, did not build a hut where He could lay His head. He was at the mercy of the weather. The sun smote Him by day and the moon by night. Sometimes it seemed as if God had completely abandoned Him. The sun represents the problems encountered when the man is out looking for the means to care for self and family. The moon represents problems on the home front, when he comes back home to seek rest. The devil knows that after the isolation comes the certification. Hence, he will come at the man with all he's got and from all fronts. While the man is busy trying to figure out the continuous bombardment of suggestion of what to do with the friends who pushed him into isolation, the beast in human shape is attacking left, right, and center. And while that is going on, he is getting bad news from work, how business is not doing well, how many customers are moving to other businesses, and all that. When the devil notices that all those things are not really getting to him, he employs the services of the moon by night. The devil uses those closest to him, those who should love him no matter his condition, will suddenly become hostile to him.

Preparing for the Coming Glory

It takes deep discernment to be able to pull the curtain back to see who is working behind the scenes.

Let's give an example for better understanding. There was, in our time, a great man of God who started his work with God as a pastor. He was doing very well, and the church he was pastoring was growing rapidly. He pastored for about twelve years, but then heaven decided it was time to move into the next phase of his ministry. Again, heaven orchestrated events that threw him into isolation. He was kicked out of the office of pastor and moved into the office of an apostle. It was a difficult time for him and his family. As he went from city to city to carry out the assignment of heaven, he met with great financial difficulties and opposition. That is the role of the sun in the place of isolation, to scorch and to bring pain, to make one decide to abandon one's mission and go back to the place of shelter. But he kept at it until one day he got frustrated and turned to God. He was doing great when he was in the shelter. Why was it now, when he was doing the will of God, that calamity came upon him? God told him that it was the devil holding back his finances. The sun's scorching can present in different ways. For this man of God, the devil was able to use the sun to hold back his finances. The moon was also used against this man of God. In his bid to fulfill his calling, he was always out of the house. This built resentment and unhappiness in his wife. Though she didn't verbalize it, it was creating tension. It's not easy for two persons' work on the home front to become one person's duty. The tension continued to rise in her spirit, and eventually, the man of God decided to give up the ministry and go back to pastoring. This would keep him more at home and available to his wife. But heaven was not happy with the decision. Heaven decided to take him home to permanently solve the problem. At this point the wife agreed to release him to do the mission of heaven. Any way you look

The School of Waiting

at it, she has lost him. She either loses him to death or to the mission field. It's her choice to make. Heaven waited until she made the choice. She decided to lose him to the mission field. After all, with that there would be the possibility of seeing him. That was how heaven dealt with the issue of the moon. So, this can present in various ways. The life of the Master is a learning point for every one of us, no matter the form it presents in our lives. Fasting, praying, and deep study of and meditation on the Word are necessary tools to survive this bombardment.

Finally, after forty days of continuous bombardment, the devil decided to launch the final blow. He brought his joker cards, the very ones that had defeated the first Adam. Unfortunately for him, this is the last Adam, not just the second. There won't be another. Jesus passed with flying colors. This joker is usually presented at the verge of breakthrough. The lust of the flesh, lust of the eyes, and the pride of life are the jokers, the best the devil's got. Let's spend a little time looking at how Jesus overcame and see if heaven has one or two things to teach us here:

> *Then the devil taketh him up into the holy city, and setteth him on a pinnacle of the temple, and saith unto him, If thou be the Son of God, cast thyself down: for it is written, He shall give his angels charge concerning thee: and in their hands they shall bear thee up, lest at any time thou dash thy foot against a stone.*
>
> —Matthew 4:5–6

Consider the above passage. The first statement the devil made was to ask whether Jesus was the Son of God. This was not an attempt to see if Jesus doubted being the Son of God. Just before Jesus made the trip to the wilderness, God said in an audible voice that Jesus was His beloved Son. Even if there had been no audible voice, there was no need to convince Jesus for He knew that He was from above. The devil was not attempting to make Him doubt His Sonship, either, for that would be easy to dispute. What the devil wanted Him to do was to get Him to act outside of God. That's where many of the anointed of the Lord fall. See how he put it to Eve:

And the serpent said unto the woman, Ye shall not surely die: For God doth know that in the day ye eat thereof, then your eyes shall be opened, and ye shall be as gods, knowing good and evil.

—Genesis 3:4–5

Note the above passage. The devil sold the fact that Eve would have power to decide what was good and what was bad. What could that mean? God is the Supreme Being. He reserves the sole right of defining wrong and right, good and evil. He is the standard. No other entity has that right or power. If anyone wants to take that position, then the person is trying to usurp the authority of God and take the position of God. That was the exact sin that drove the devil out of the sacred place—he wanted to be like God. Eve was drawn away by the temptation to be God, not realizing that she had already been created in the image of God. She only knew that she could not act as a god apart from God. The moment she tried to act as a god apart from God, she fell from glory, and the covering of God on her was lifted. That was the downfall of the first Adam. The trick has always worked. Now fast-forward to the last Adam, when the devil tried the same trick. He even gave Scriptures to back it up: "Angels have been given charge to make sure you are not hurt." But thank God for the last Adam. Jesus had the right response:

Jesus said unto him, It is written again, Thou shalt not tempt the Lord thy God.

—Matthew 4:7

The School of Waiting

What could Jesus mean by the above statement? He is definitely not saying the devil could not tempt Him. What He was saying is that when we, as sons of God, act apart from God, we are trying to tempt God. It is God who works through us to will and to do. If we take initiative because we want to prove to the world around us that we are somewhat important, then the authority of the One who works in us will be usurped and He will step aside to see how far we can go. This is a very common temptation the devil uses to pull men down day by day. Let's give two notable examples that made the news. Sometime ago, a man of God claimed that he wanted to show the world how powerful he was. He made an announcement from his platform that on such and such a day, he would be going into a lions' den to spend some time with the lions. He let the whole world know that he would exercise power and authority over the lions, just like Daniel did in the lions' den, and he would come out in one piece. Trust the news media—it quickly hit the headlines. On the D-day, cameras from all the news stations were present at a popular zoo in the city. The keepers of the zoo warned the man of God to change his mind and go back home while there was still time, but he insisted that he must show the world that his God had given His angels charge over him. He saw the people persuading him not to go as devils. He yelled at them to "get thee behind" him. The keepers unlocked the gate to the lions' den and left, and he opened the door and stepped in. The lions were initially confused. They stepped back. As soon as they did, the man of God lifted up his hands in victory shouting, "Hallelujah." The crowd cheered. But when the lions finally realized that fortune had shined on them, they pounced on the man of God and devoured him.

Many-a time the devil tempts us to act outside of God, showing the world that we are superstars. But we are absolutely nothing without

Him. Our Lord and Master, Jesus Christ, made Himself nothing without God. Who are you not to do the same? Someone said there is no great man of God anywhere; there is only the great God of the man. I agree with that statement.

The second case was the case of a group of young men who believed they had very strong faith, and they planned to show the world that what Jesus did, they could also do. With their strong faith, they asked to be taken out to the middle of the sea with a flying boat. When they got deep into the sea, they decided to walk out on top of the waves as Jesus did. Of course, they drowned. Their dead bodies were brought back home. Faith without a word from God is fake. The *only* factor that gives authenticity to faith is a word from God, not the Word of God. Look at how the Bible defines *faith*:

> *Now faith is the substance of things hoped for, the evidence of things not seen.*
>
> —Hebrews 11:1

Consider how it is written in the above passage. What gives substance to your faith is the word from God. It can be either written or spoken. (The spoken must agree with the written Word.) Without the substance, you are not acting in faith. There have been many who believed God for healing and died in the process claiming they had faith. The only thing that gives assurance to the fact that you have (or will have) what you are believing for is the word from God. Let's look at it from another angle. Say there is a philanthropist who puts a statement out there that he has a policy to bless widows, children, and the needy. He has even deposited billions of dollars into a charity fund to that effect. However, he has a fund committee that scrutinizes everyone who applies for the grant—to

The School of Waiting

be sure they truly qualify. Say a young widow went to the real estate market to buy a large piece of property without money or any source of income. When the bankers ask for a deposit, she says not to worry, she will get the funds from the philanthropist because she is a widow. Can you see how stupid that sounds? She has not applied for the grant. She is not even sure she qualifies. She has no word or letter from the scrutinizing committee that she has been granted the money. She just started to plan and act solely based on the assumption that because she is a widow, she would get the grant. That's exactly what it is like when we act outside a word from God. We don't have a word from God to say we have what we want, but we go about telling people that God will give us what we want. Meanwhile, on the other hand, if the same woman goes through the process and eventually interviews with the philanthropist and finally gets the grant, the evidence that she will get the money to buy the house is the letter from the billionaire. She can now confidently take that letter to the bankers as evidence of her down payment even though she doesn't yet have the cash.

The entire Bible is the Word of God. There are over eight thousand promises in the Bible for believers. Someone cannot just wake up and pick any one of the blessings and begin to claim it, however. The Word of God is just a letter, even though each of the words has inert power in it. The power in each word is activated by God Himself. That is when the Word of God becomes the word from God. The moment the very same Word you read every day becomes activated, that Word becomes the word from God. You can stake your life on the activated Word of God. That's not to say that we should only read the Word when we are looking to activate a blessing. The Word has life-giving ability. Reading it every day gives life to your soul and spirit. Meditating on the Word is a nonnegotiable act that your growth in the spirit depends upon. One of the ways the Word can be activated is through meditation. It may surprise you to know that God will not do anything apart from His Word. Hence, it is important to handle the Word of God with fear and trembling the same way our Master did. Jesus was presented with the opportunity to demonstrate faith without a word from God. The devil gave Him a Scripture, from the Word of God, as an anchor. But Jesus knew that standing on any portion of the Scripture and expecting God to be held to ransom by a word He did not give is a way to tempt God. Hence, if you must claim any promise of God in the Bible, meditate on it daily until it becomes activated in your spirit. Then you can be rest assured that you will get what you want. It should be of note that the two events described above as an example of how the devil is deceiving men of God are from different continents of the world. That goes to tell you how common this joker is. The devil has used it to destroy many lives just on their way out of isolation.

When coming out of isolation, because the individual has been fasting, studying the Word, and spending time with God, there is usually notable spiritual growth. The devil capitalizes on this growth to push the individual to begin to act as a superstar. It gives the devil great joy to see believers act outside a word from God. That was why his first statement to Christ was, "If you are the Son of God . . ." That is usually the best time to try this joker. When the anointing is at its peak, he makes you feel as if you have arrived and you can do anything since you are now the great power of God.

Another joker the enemy throws at men who are almost at the floor of the valley is the goods of mammon:

Again, the devil taketh him up into an exceeding high mountain, and sheweth him all the kingdoms of the world, and the glory of them; and saith unto him, All these things will I give thee, if thou wilt fall down and worship me.

—Matthew 4:8–9

Many a giant has fallen with this joker. Men are still falling because it works for the devil like magic. Jesus was taken in the spirit realm to see the entire kingdoms of the earth. Notice that it was not just the current kingdom that Jesus was shown. He was shown past kingdoms, present kingdoms, and the kingdoms to come. The devil promised Jesus all these and their glory. This would be wealth more than a generation could spend. This would be the power to control the past, present, and the future. All Jesus needed to do, the devil said, was to bow the knee. He was not saying Jesus should not go back to His ministry. He was saying all Jesus needed to do was to bow. Jesus could continue to preach His messages. He could continue to prophesy; He could continue to be called an apostle of Christ and the Son of God. He could continue to sing His songs. All He needed to do was just to bow. The world would see Him as a follower of God, but no one would know that He had bowed the knee. No one would know that the fountain of God within had been corrupted. He can still be the lead singer in the church, his songs can still be in the top of the chart, but the fountain has been corrupted. At that point, the devil had come to terms with the fact that this fellow now had the power of God. With this power, the fellow could do great damage to his estate and interest on the earth. The best way to mitigate the damage, the devil realized, was to corrupt the fountain. When this is done, a prophet may continue to prophesy, but as far as heaven is concerned, he is a soothsayer. A teacher will continue to teach, but he is now a setter forth of false and destructive doctrines. A pastor may continue to pastor, but he is now a recruiter of souls for the occult. A gospel singer may continue to top the chart but he is now a corrupter of souls and altars. This is a serious problem. There are many leaders in the Body of Christ today whose fountain has been corrupted, unbeknownst to their followers.

The main aim of the devil with this joker is to conduct an exchange program. Jesus had been endued with power to deliver souls to God. This power came with glory and grace to pull people from all over the world unto Him. If one is conversant with the New Testament, one will discover that the major consistent factor in the ministry of Jesus was that anytime He taught or preached, thousands of people would gather. He always pulled the crowd. That is the work of the grace and the glory that comes with an endorsement from God. What the devil aims to achieve with this temptation is clear. He cannot stop the endorsement; he cannot stop the people from coming, and he cannot stop the power from flowing from a clean source. What he now hoped to achieve with this temptation was to give Jesus his goods in exchange for the souls who would gather to hear from Jesus. Gold for souls. No one need know about this bargain—just bow the knee; You will get the gold, and the devil will get the souls. Let's look at how this joker played out in the lives of two prophets in the Bible.

Abraham was a notable prophet in his time. God Himself had called him a prophet, not any man:

Now therefore restore the man his wife; for he is a prophet, and he shall pray for thee, and thou shalt live: and if thou restore her not, know thou that thou shalt surely die, thou, and all that are thine.

—Genesis 20:7

Kings came to him to inquire of the Lord. One day, an unfortunate incident happened. His nephew and some other people were taken

The School of Waiting

as prisoners of war. The enemy captured their souls and put them in bondage. The prophet Abraham swung into action to rescue the souls from the strongman. When he was embarking on the venture, the devil didn't discourage him because he didn't believe Abraham would be able to rescue the souls. Four kings had tried and failed. How could one man succeed where four kings had failed? What the devil did not know was that this man was with God; hence He was in the majority. Eventually, Abraham was able to rescue the souls. That was when the devil came with this joker:

And the king of Sodom said unto Abram, Give me the persons, and take the goods to thyself.

—Genesis 14:21

Notice the bargain. It is not very different from how he presented it to Jesus: Take all the goods. They are Yours. There's only one thing You need to do: Bow the knee so that the souls under Your care will also bow. Take the gold and give him the souls. Thank God Abraham got the gist:

And Abram said to the king of Sodom, I have lift up mine hand unto the Lord, the most high God, the possessor of heaven and earth, that I will not take from a thread even to a shoelatchet, and that I will not take any thing that is thine, lest thou shouldest say, I have made Abram rich.

—verses 22-23

He had sworn to God. He knew that any gold from the enemy was a corrupter of true riches. The enemy did not give a free lunch. It was usually in exchange for something. And that something was usually more valuable than the lunch. What could be more valuable than human souls? Thank God Abraham refused the offer.

The second prophet to consider is Balaam. When Israel was in transit to the Promised Land, they came to a place near Moab. The king of Moab was afraid of them taking over his land. So, he decided to hire the services of Balaam. Before we continue, let's establish the fact that Balaam was a true prophet of God:

> *He sent messengers therefore unto Balaam the son of Beor to Pethor, which is by the river of the land of the children of his people, to call him, saying, Behold, there is a people come out from Egypt: behold, they cover the face of the earth, and they abide over against me: Come now therefore, I pray thee, curse me this people; for they are too mighty for me: peradventure I shall prevail, that we may smite them, and that I may drive them out of the land: for I wot that he whom thou blesses is blessed, and he whom thou cursest is cursed.*
>
> —Numbers 22:5-6

This is the first time the man Balaam was introduced in the Bible. Consider the manner of introduction given to Balaam. The king of the land of Moab confidently gave the credentials of Balaam. The top man knew that whomever Balaam blessed would be blessed and whomever Balaam cursed would be cursed. There are many points to unravel about the description given concerning Balaam. First, the fact that whomever he blessed would be blessed and whomever he cursed would be cursed was an authority that could only be given by God to His prophets as an insurance policy. The devil had no capability to bless. Therefore, if Balaam had been a soothsayer from inception, he would not have the

The School of Waiting

accolades of "whomever he blesses would be blessed." Let's look at an example of a man who was given this same accolade:

And I will bless them that bless thee, and curse him that curseth thee: and in thee shall all families of the earth be blessed.

—Genesis 12:3

Notice how that verse was framed. It starts with "bless them that bless thee." That's the exact way Balaam was introduced. The prophet to which the above passage refers is Abraham. We can therefore deduce that Balaam was a prophet of the caliber of Abraham or at least close to that. Going back to Numbers 22, notice that Balak wanted Balaam to curse Israel. He could have said, "For I know that whomever you cursed is cursed," before saying, "Whomever you blessed is blessed." But he didn't say that because that wasn't the coverage God gave Balaam. And that wasn't what he was known for. The coverage starts with "whomever you bless." Hence, Balak started by saying, "For I know that whomever you bless . . ." Now, the next thing to consider from the introduction of Balaam is the caliber of the person who gave the description. Balak occupied the highest office of the land. He not only knew Balaam; he also knows what he was capable of and the manner of grace and anointing he carried. There are different calibers of a prophet. There are different levels of anointing. Let's look at a passage that will give an idea of the caliber of anointing on Balaam:

Arise, shine; for thy light is come, and the glory of the Lord *is risen upon thee. For, behold, the darkness shall cover the earth, and gross darkness the people: but the* Lord *shall arise upon thee, and his glory shall be seen upon thee. And the Gentiles shall come to thy light, and kings to the brightness of thy rising.*

—Isaiah 60:1–3

Preparing for the Coming Glory

Notice the steps one takes in the manifestation of the anointing when the Word of God came to announce a man into his ministry. First, the Gentiles would come to the light of the newly announced man of God. Then when the light became brighter, it would attract kings, not just mean men. The man Balaam was known by the king, and not just the king of his own country, but the king of another country. One can only wonder how many other kings knew him. That tells us what caliber of prophet he is. We can safely say that at this point in time in his ministry, his light is far brighter than when he had started, and hence we can call him a "major prophet."

Now then, let's go back to the matter at hand. Balaam was hired to curse. As his custom was, he needed to inquire of the Lord whether to curse or not to curse. He did, but God refused to grant him permission to go. He relayed the message of God to the people without any problem. But Balak would not give in just like that. He understood the power of bargaining. The first set of people he sent out were servants. They did not fully represent the wealth of the nation. This time around, he sent the "Musk" and the "Gates" of his kingdom. It so happened that on a sunny afternoon, Balaam's servant came in from an errand and told him about a group of wealthy merchants coming into their town. They had the best cars, and they had lots of goods to sell. He had never seen a caravan of golden Ferraris before this time. These "merchants" became the talk of the town. Everybody wondered where they were coming from. Surely, the mayor must know about them. They were probably heading to the mayor's office.

Shortly after, these merchants parked their luxurious cars in front of Balaam's house. He looked out the window and wondered who they were, only to soon realize that Balak had sent more noble men to negotiate with him.

The School of Waiting

And Balak sent yet again princes, more, and more honorable than they. And they came to Balaam, and said to him, Thus saith Balak the son of Zippor, Let nothing, I pray thee, hinder thee from coming unto me: For I will promote thee unto very great honor, and I will do whatsoever thou sayest unto me: come therefore, I pray thee, curse me this people.

—Numbers 22:15–17

Notice how the passage above puts it. The princes sent were not just more honorable than the ones sent earlier. They were more and more honorable. The who's who of his kingdom. The ones whose wealth controlled the economy of his kingdom. Balaam quickly realized that the goods they carried was not for sale; they were a reward of divination. He was also made to realize that there was more where that came from, even up to the half of the wealth in the kingdom of Moab. In a split second, the devil took him to a high mountain and showed him the kingdom of Moab: "All these will be yours if only you can bow." Just give us the souls and take the gold. The neighbors had already gathered. Oh, what a time to be a prophet. He quickly became the talk of the town. More respect was given to him. The mayor of the town held an emergency meeting, and they decided to name a street after him. He had brought honor to the small town. A town that was not on the map now had princes of first-class caliber coming to visit.

The man of God bowed the knee. God had already told him concerning the request that the answer was a resounding *no*. Even if the king himself came down, there was no need to go and inquire again from the Lord. What was he expecting? That God would change His mind? The only reason he went back to inquire was because he had already bowed the knee. At that point, he crossed over from a genuine prophet to a soothsayer. He corrupted the fountain of his anointing by bowing the knee. He kissed the ring of Marmon, but he wanted to remain relevant in the agenda of God. His source had been corrupted. He'd heard what his itching ears wanted to hear: Go with the men. It was not God's will for him to go. That was why heaven concluded to take him out. Only mercy saved him. In the end, the Spirit of God refused to allow him to curse the Israelites. But because he had already gotten to a place of no return with Marmon by bowing the knee to the bargain of Satan, he could not just let Israel off the hook. He has to figure out a way to bring a curse upon them. He eventually came up with a piece of advice: Set a stumbling block before them, and their God will turn against them Himself. Smart! This advice echoed throughout the kingdom of darkness. They did a case study on it for years. This is a tool that can be used to pull many out of the way. From such simple advice, the devil and his team turned it into a way:

> *... which have forsaken the right way, and are gone astray, following the way of Balaam the son of Bosor, who loved the wages of unrighteousness.*
>
> —2 Peter 2:15

Notice how the way was named after the discoverer. This took hundreds of years of work to transition the advice into a way. But the devil and his team were not satisfied with the results "the way" brought. So, they did more work on it, and 'the way' became an error:

> *Woe unto them! For they have gone in the way of Cain, and ran greedily after the error of Balaam for reward, and perished in the gainsaying of Core.*
>
> —Jude 1:11

The School of Waiting

Notice also that the new model was named after the discoverer. Many have fallen with this joker. The devil and his team were still not satisfied with what they could get from the Joker, they worked more on it and came up with a better version—a doctrine:

But I have a few things against thee, because thou hast there them that hold the doctrine of Balaam, who taught Balac to cast a stumbling block before the children of Israel, to eat things sacrificed unto idols, and to commit fornication.

—Revelation 2:14

This is how the prophet Balaam came to bow to the demands of the devil. He gave out the souls and he took the gold—a trade by batter bargain. The fountain was corrupted. A man with the anointing to prophecy was now a soothsayer. Everyone that came undercover was also made to bow to the same god to which he bowed. Thank God the Master recognized this joker:

Then saith Jesus unto him, Get thee hence, Satan: for it is written, Thou shalt worship the Lord thy God, and him only shalt thou serve.

—Matthew 4:10

Jesus immediately commanded Satan to get out of His space. You don't give room for negotiation in this matter. Don't permit him to lurk around like he did in the case of Balaam, until you are eventually brought down. Act fast and kick the devil and his offer out of your space.

The Course Is More Important Than the Ministry

We have attempted to discuss some of the courses that must be taken in the University of Heaven. However, the list is inexhaustible. And the curriculum is usually tailored to each individual. Though we can learn from the successes and failures of those who have gone before us in this Kingdom, we may not get the same curriculum they did. The intention of heaven for every man is to bring situations and circumstances to each person that will remove the old nature with its accomplice and make us exactly like Jesus. The intention of heaven with everyone who accepts the offer of salvation is to make them an exact duplicate of Christ—nothing short of that. As long as a fellow is alive, heaven will keep bringing situations and circumstances to transition the person from an ordinary person who walked into the Kingdom through the door of salvation into an extraordinary person. Some exams may be repeated when heaven realizes that the initial exam did not achieve the set goal. Note that these seasons can repeat themselves over and over again in the life of a single individual for many reasons. It may be that previous exams were not successful in completely "un-fleshing" the individual, and so God calls for a retake of the course at a more convenient time. Whatever the reasons heaven finds to repeat a particular curriculum are, heaven will not stop until Jesus is fully formed in us.

I remember an event that happened many years ago. I know a fellow who was subjected to a repeat isolation class. The first time he was sentenced into isolation, heaven was not satisfied with the result of the exams he took. So, the Watchers called for another exam. This time, heaven decided that he must remain within the community he was serving while he retook the isolation classes. He had to remain in the assembly where He was asked to isolate until another instruction came from heaven. At first, he didn't make the move to isolate. But

The School of Waiting

heaven orchestrated events that drove him into isolation. It took about two years for another instruction to come. But those two years were years of great temptation. The devil used any and every person who was made available to him. On many occasions, at the general assembly of the community, the message for the day was about the process of this fellow's isolation, how no one should emulate that. While such messages were going on, all eyes of the congregation seemed to be on him and his followers. Unfortunately for him, he had a special corner where he seats with his followers. It was easy to locate him and his followers when such was going on. On one of those occasions, the preacher actually walked over to his corner and actually pointed at him in the illustration. Some in his company said it was as if the earth should have opened to cover them up from the shame and humiliation. Yet heaven refused to permit him to leave that assembly. He received several calls and advice from friends and loved ones who did not understand why he chose to isolate and yet remain in the community. Heaven refused to grant him permission to leave. He was to remain until the process was done. It might seem to the natural onlooker that he was taking a stance against the establishment while in actual fact he was just obeying simple instructions from heaven as he knew it at that time. He lost friends and loved ones, but he later realized that one of the things heaven hoped to achieve was to sever him from some of those relationships.

Then one faithful morning, while driving to the assembly, the Holy Spirit dropped in his heart that that very day would be his last day in the assembly. The Holy Spirit permitted him to tell one or two people about this decision. As soon as he got into the assembly, as a way of courtesy, he mentioned to the administrator that that day would be his last in the assembly. He also went to the department where he'd used to work, to announce his final departure. Shortly after he made the

Preparing for the Coming Glory

announcement, he was called into the office of the vice president of the assembly in the presence of some of the directors. Curses were practically rained down on him in the name of "advice" because the general assumption among all was that he was planning to establish his own assembly. Unfortunately for him, the Holy Spirit had simply instructed that that day would be his last in the assembly. So, just as instructed, he left the assembly. Those who were a part of the meeting and others who learned later that the meeting had taken place, concluded that he had left because of the meeting. After he left the assembly, many people from the assembly followed up with him for many years just to see if he had really left to start his own assembly. Up until the time of the writing of this book, I am certain that he is yet to start any assembly of his own. He is just a simple Christian who is trying to follow the instruction of the Holy Ghost that is directing the affairs of his life. Christ can take a willing heart through any situation in other to separate him from the world. The most important thing for all Christians in this life is to be like Christ. My path to becoming like Christ is definitely different from the path of others. There are almost no two paths that are exactly the same in this race. What matters is that everyone must learn to work out his own salvation with fear and trembling.

9

The Valley of Dry Bones

When heaven was satisfied with the results of Jesus, heaven certified Him. The angels blew the trumpets. The final announcement was made. Jesus was finally permitted to start His ministry as heaven was now confident that He would push *only* the agenda of God. By this time, all flesh was gone. The fellow had been left with just bones. But the bones still had marrow, and the marrow could still give life to the bones. That's far from the intention of God. The only thing that should give life is the Spirit of God. So, heaven must take the fellow back to the theater, where all marrow must be removed. The bones must be completely dry. No drop of moisture must be present.

Let's go back to the encounter of the prophet Ezekiel and see the intention of God for anyone who wants to be His servant:

> *The hand of the* Lord *was upon me, and carried me out in the spirit of the* Lord, *and set me down in the midst of the valley which was full of bones, and caused me to pass by them round*

Preparing for the Coming Glory

about: and, behold, there were very many in the open valley; and, lo, they were very dry.

—Ezekiel 37:1–2

Notice the description given to the bones. They were very dry, not just dry. The final step was for the bones to drop at the floor of the valley. The bones usually do not drop in one piece. They break into pieces at the impact on the floor of the valley, and they mix with other bones in such a way that no one knows which bone belongs to who. There are two factors, among others, that make the bones break into pieces on impact: First, the bones that eventually got to the valley were very dry bones, completely stripped of all flesh and every resemblance of personality. Because the bones are very dry, they become light and easy to be carried by the wind (the Holy Spirit). Second, because of their light weight, the wind of the Spirit is easily able to roll them down the mountain at a speed that will ensure they are completely broken at impact so that all self-reliance is completely destroyed. This is what heaven hopes to achieve with the last days remnant: complete unity between many nameless and faceless people. The unbelievers, observing from the outside, will see the glory of God as never before seen in human history before, but they will not be able to associate such glory with any prominent human name. This is the finest moment of the Church of God on earth, but yet no man will be able to take any ounce of the glory to himself. And no single individual will champion the revival like we have today. There will be many strange miracles through many faceless and nameless people, who are simple Christians and are just trying to please God.

Back to the prophet Ezekiel. He looked as the Spirit bade him to. He saw many bones scattered all over the valley. No skeleton was lying whole or intact. He was given the opportunity to walk through

The Valley of Dry Bones

the valley and see the bones at a very close range. He noticed that no skeleton landed at the bottom of the valley in one piece. Because they were completely dry, their impact in the valley led to their complete disintegration. Everything had been milked out of each skeleton, and the vessels had been completely destroyed. At this stage, the individual was beyond recognition. No one could tell who was who except through a DNA test. None of the skeleton was ashamed of what they have become. There was nothing to be ashamed of since no one knew who was who. Those who knew this fellow before and knew what this fellow was capable of in the past could no longer predict this new entity. He had been completely de-identified. The prophet started to imagine that, at one point in time, these bones were walking on their feet. Now they are just dry bones scattered all over the ground. Good for nothing. No one pays attention to them. They are irrelevant to the things that matter most in the society. At this point, the Lord cut the process of thought of the prophet short:

> *And he said unto me, Son of man, can these bones live? And I answered, O Lord GOD, thou knowest.*
>
> —verse 3

The Lord asked if the bones could come back to life. His mind could not comprehend how this could happen. They had all been stripped of everything that anyone could use to identify them. Even a miracle could not bring them back. Notice the response of the prophet to the question that the Father asked. If we are to analyze the response of the prophet or to paraphrase, his response is more or less, as far as I know, that these bones could not live anymore. He has searched through the archives of miracles in his mind and found nothing similar done in the past. Not even close. But then, this man was familiar with the ways of God. He knew there is nothing impossible for God to do. Hence, his response was, "Lord, You know." These bones have been through situations that have stripped them of self-reliance. They are completely dead to it. There is absolutely no reason to trust in self, for what is left from self is lifeless bones, extremely dry, and completely broken. It cannot even maintain wholeness. It has to hide itself in the midst of other dry bones. Each can only be identified by DNA. At this point in the life of the individual, ego is removed. He has been beaten to the extent that he has given up fighting and struggling. All the things he holds to, the things that define him, have been stripped away. So, he humbled himself. What makes a natural man proud to be part of a society has been taken from him. He has no more voice in the society, and no more personal ambition. He actually goes into hiding. When God eventually calls him, he will refuse because of his obvious inadequacies. Let's look at how this played out in the lives of our case study characters:

The Man Moses at the Valley of the Dry Bones

Now Moses kept the flock of Jethro his father in law, the priest of Midian: and he led the flock to the backside of the desert, and came to the mountain of God, even to Horeb. And the angel of the LORD appeared unto him in a flame of fire out of the midst of a bush: and he looked, and, behold, the bush burned with fire, and the bush was not consumed. And Moses said, I will now turn aside, and see this great sight, why the bush is not burnt. And when the LORD saw that he turned aside to see, God called unto him out of the midst of the bush, and said, Moses, Moses. And he said, Here am I. Now therefore, behold, the cry of the children of Israel is come unto me: and I have also seen the oppression wherewith the Egyptians oppress them. Come now therefore,

The Valley of Dry Bones

and I will send thee unto Pharaoh, that thou mayest bring forth my people the children of Israel out of Egypt. And Moses said unto God, Who am I, that I should go unto Pharaoh, and that I should bring forth the children of Israel out of Egypt?

—Exodus 3:1–4, 9–11

Let's talk a little bit about the above passage. Verses 5 to 8 were skipped for the sake of space and time. Let's do a little digging into the above verses. Moses spent the next forty years of his life tending the sheep of his father-in-law. Many would have looked at the man he had become and say, "This is just dry broken bones. What a waste. Someone who was supposed to be the emperor of the most powerful empire on earth wasted forty years of his life tending sheep. It must be of note that the shepherd job is the least job in the society in the days of Moses, like a janitor. It would have even been better if he owned all or part of the sheep. Unfortunately, this Moses had nothing to his name. The house in which he was living was rented, the wife he had was given without receiving bride price, the food he ate daily, all came from another man's table. At eighty, he has nothing to show for the life he has lived. His mates are heads of industries and heads of nations. And some of his mates have retired from active service with medals and monuments to show for their years of contribution to society. What a waste!! In the midst of this supposed waste, there is one thing he got that no one can take from him—he learned about God from his host. During one of the numerous disciple's classes, he had with his father-in-law, he asked, "Do you know where the mountain of God is?" Once in a while, he drove his sheep to the place and admired the mountain. What was God like? Oh, that I may know Him, and the power of His resurrection. Such was the heart cry of Moses. He kept going to view the mountain every now and then until finally, one day, He caught God's attention. By this time, heaven was satisfied with his training. He was not just a dry bone. This very dry bone had landed on the ground of the valley and had broken into pieces. He had lost the ambition of being the hero who would save Israel. His pride died a natural death. He could no longer rub shoulders with his mates. Anywhere he saw his mates, he hid. His life was nothing to be proud of. He had yielded completely to God, who alone could save. God is now satisfied with the level of progress he has made.

Note that the matter of sin did not appear at this point. It was expected that that would be the very first thing that will happen as you start your descent from the mountain. That's a nonnegotiable fact. If you cannot do away with your sins, you cannot even embark on the journey to the valley of dry bones. That's chemistry 101 in the University of Heaven, the entrance-level exam. If you don't pass it, you can't go anywhere with God. At this stage, what heaven is talking about is weights, desires that are not necessarily sin but do not align with the will and plan of God. For example, Moses may have worked in the field all day. It is much like how it would be for him to get home, eat, and land on the bed. But at the time he landed on the bed, the Holy Spirit can come and say now. It's my time. Spend the next three hours with me. If he takes the option of sleep, which is a legitimate need at that time, he would be acting out of the will of God. That's sin to him. Those are the kind of issues we are talking about.

Now then, Moses had satisfied the examiners. He has learned to wait until God comes, he has learned to throw his personal goals and agendas away. Everything that heaven wanted had been met. Now heaven could endorse this fellow without fear. He could represent heaven and its interest in the place of his assignment. Note verse 10. The herald went forth, and God laid out his assignment to him. Look at verse 11. His response was evidence of what he had been through. Who am I? He was now a nobody. This was a man who felt he was somebody and was already strategizing on how to carry out this very assignment that God is presenting. After being completely defleshed" and broken into pieces, lying uselessly in the valley, he saw nothing in himself that could make him a savior or a deliverer. This is the exact point to which God wants to drive us. It is a point where we see no ability in ourselves to do the work that is placed before us. It is a point where we are forced to completely rely on Jesus to work through us.

The Man Joseph at the Valley of Dry Bones

Let's consider how Joseph got to the same point where Moses found himself when he was at the burning bush. Joseph was thrown into prison after rejecting the bait of the "wild animal" in the "wilderness" of isolation. That itself was a show of God's mercy to him. There is no way a slave in those days would be accused of such an allegation and not be put to death. But the worst he got was prison. That's God's mercy right there. Now then, we do not know how long he spent in prison. But we know that after some time spent in prison, heaven made an attempt to bring him out.

> *But think on me when it shall be well with thee, and shew kindness, I pray thee, unto me, and make mention of me unto Pharaoh, and bring me out of this house: For indeed I was stolen away out of the land of the Hebrews: and here also have I done nothing that they should put me into the dungeon.*
>
> —Genesis 40:14–15

Let's give a little background to the above passage for better understanding. After Joseph had spent some years in prison, the Watchers

Preparing for the Coming Glory

decided it was time for him to come out. But first, there must be a passing-out exam. If he passed the exam, then they would let him go. But if not, he went back to prison for one or two more seasons, until the flesh that heaven wanted to deal with was removed. Only bones are allowed in the valley. Nothing more. Also the bone must be very dry. All its marrow must be removed so it has absolutely no chance of revival. So, heaven orchestrated a set of events to arrange for Joseph's release. Heaven had a special ability to use one event to achieve many goals. With this one event, heaven was able to run Joseph through all the necessary tests he must pass in order to be a certified 'Isolation' personality.

It so happened that two of Pharaoh's officials offended their master, and they were jailed in the same prison where Joseph was. Joseph is a fun guy to be with. They eventually came to love him. These were not ordinary men. They had the ears of the highest man in the land. They must have told tales of their escapades in the palace, how they made requests to the pharaoh and how he granted their requests. How people lobbied the pharaoh through them. How much they had made from lobbyists who wanted something precious from the pharaoh. At first Joseph made nothing out of their stories. After all, they were now in prison and there was no hope of coming out for all of them. They all suffered the same fate. But one day, the officials had dreams that baffled them. They didn't know that God had gifted Joseph in the area of dream interpretation. Their countenances were sad because there was no opportunity to get an interpreter. Joseph showed up at their cells and was able to interpret their dreams. Now, the series of exams must roll out. The examination committee had orchestrated this event to see what percentage of flesh was left in Joseph and how much more work must be done to get rid of it. Then, suddenly, Joseph remembered all

The Valley of Dry Bones

the stories the officials had been telling about, how they got things done for people by approaching the pharaoh on their behalf. This was his ticket to getting out of prison! After all, he had been good to them. It was now time for them to pay him back. That was the first thing Joseph did wrong. The devil whispered to him, "You can turn these stones into bread—if indeed you are highly favored by God and you are a master over all that are in this prison":

> *But the LORD was with Joseph, and shewed him mercy, and gave him favour in the sight of the keeper of the prison. And the keeper of the prison committed to Joseph's hand all the prisoners that were in the prison; and whatsoever they did there, he was the doer of it.*
>
> —Genesis 39:21-22

You have served them, you have taught them the ways of God, you have given them hope where there was none, you have wiped the tears of their eyes, you have brought them out of depression; if it was not for you, many of them would have committed suicide. On and on the devil went, reminding him of all the services he had done to all the prisoners. At no time had he made a demand from anyone. Now was the time. It was within his right to make bread out of these stones. Joseph took the bait. Look at it again:

> *And Joseph said unto him, This is the interpretation of it: The three branches are three days: Yet within three days shall Pharaoh lift up thine head, and restore thee unto thy place: and thou shalt deliver Pharaoh's cup into his hand, after the former manner when thou wast his butler. But think on me when it shall be well with thee, and shew kindness, I pray thee, unto me, and make mention of me unto Pharaoh, and bring me out of*

Preparing for the Coming Glory

this house: For indeed I was stolen away out of the land of the Hebrews: and here also have I done nothing that they should put me into the dungeon.

—Genesis 40:12–15

The request Joseph made to the official was summarized in the last two verses of the above passage. Let's shed some more light on those words to see if he will satisfy the Examiners. First, notice that he didn't ask for this favor until he had successfully interpreted the dream. When he saw that the official was satisfied with the interpretation then, his eyes were opened to the opportunity. We cannot tell how the official showed his satisfaction and appreciation. It might be that he was just nodding in agreement and satisfaction, or after hearing the interpretation, he lifted up his hands to his God in appreciation and then bowed at Joseph's feet. We cannot tell exactly what he did. But we know what Joseph did. Joseph saw a stone that God brought his way. God brought the stone so Joseph could beat it into the right shape and size so it could fit perfectly into its position in the Temple that God is building, but Joseph saw bread in the stone, and he took a bite. The examination committee closed their eyes to the sight.

Second, the statement in verse 14 was made out of the abundance of his heart. All the days he had spent with these officials, he must have said many "if-onlys." If only these guys would be released from prison, they could lobby for me. If only God would bring them out of prison, they could prove my innocence . . . But each time the thought of an "if-only" came, he killed it because there was no hope of them getting out of prison alive. But this day, through a supernatural encounter, it was clear to Joseph that one of them would be coming out alive. He quickly revived his thoughts. It was no longer a matter of "if only." It was now a matter of "when you get out." The devil is good at what he

The Valley of Dry Bones

does. He extended the hand of Uzzah to Joseph: "Get Pharaoh to get you out." The big question is, Who takes the glory for his release? The official, Pharaoh, or God? In this setting, it is obvious that the official would take the glory for his release. Joseph would forever be grateful to the official and to the pharaoh. In his closet, he would lift his hands in praise to God, but in public it would be, "If not for Senator so and so, if not for President so and so . . ." The examiners marked that particular work and found out that he had some flesh that God could not work with. God cannot manage to share His glory with anyone or anything. He cannot put His approval on a product that is not solely from His factory. This product, though it may look good, but it was not directly from the factory of heaven. The raw material might have been gained from the factory of heaven, but the finished product was from another factory. For this reason, heaven could not approve it.

Joseph didn't stop his request at verse 14. Really, there was no reason to continue, because what should have mattered most to him was getting out of prison. He had finally seen someone who had the ear of Pharaoh, and he had mentioned his plight to him. No need to dress it up. But he went on further in verse 15 to tell them the history of how he had been put into prison. The question that should ring in our minds is, how often had Joseph told this story in the prison? We cannot tell. It has now been at least ten years (we cannot tell for sure; we know he left the land of the Hebrews when he was seventeen and came out of prison when he was thirty) since Joseph had been stolen away, yet the memory still seems fresh in his mind. Only God knows how many times he played the scenario in his heart: Seeing his brothers laughing as they stripped him of his garment. Watching how they sold him without any form of remorse. They must have really hated him. He had built hatred and unforgiveness for them over the years. He had played the devil's movie over and over again in his heart. Heaven had tried to intervene by deleting the clips and by helping him to forgive. But he refused.

Forgiveness is one of the most important things to learn when walking with God. There are two types of forgiveness: man's way of forgiving and God's way of forgiving. In man's forgiveness, you can forgive, but you are not allowed to forget. That is not true forgiveness. It is almost impossible to forgive that way because each time the event is remembered, the same ill feeling you experienced at the time of the event wells up in your heart. Some say it is not possible to forget, especially when the event is very serious and painful. That may be somewhat true. But the way the brain works is amazing. No matter the event, what is fresh in the brain is what the individual gives attention to on a daily basis. For example, if you see a movie and you love the movie, you can play that movie over and over again in your mind. If you are asked about the movie two weeks after, you can relay almost exactly all the scenes in the movie. That's because you keep bringing the movie scenes up in your thoughts even though new events come up each day. But if you, even though you love the movie, decide to study for your exams and refuse to play the scenes from the movie in your mind for two weeks, when you are asked to relay the movie, you may be able to give a rough presentation, but it won't be as exact as if you had kept playing it over and over again in your mind. That's exactly how this works. When someone is offended, if that person refuses to take the bait of playing the offense over and over again, when asked about the offense after many days, he can only remember that someone offended him, but he will not remember all the details. In that case, since he can't remember the details, it's easy to forgive. But if the same person takes the bait of playing the scenario over and over again, day in and day out, he will remember the details of the offense even after fifty years, and in

The Valley of Dry Bones

that situation, forgiveness will be almost impossible. Though the person may verbalize forgiveness, as far as heaven is concerned, the person is yet to forgive.

The next logical question is, how does heaven expect us to forgive? Let's take our compass from the greatest sermon ever preached—the Sermon on the Mount:

> *And forgive us our debts, as we forgive our debtors. For if ye forgive men their trespasses, your heavenly Father will also forgive you: But if ye forgive not men their trespasses, neither will your Father forgive your trespasses.*
>
> —Matthew 6:12, 14–15

Verse 13 has been cut out for the sake of emphasis. Note the first verdict about forgiveness. A little background would help better our understanding. The Master was teaching His disciples the Kingdom principles. In order for you to be a citizen of the Kingdom of heaven, you must abide by the rules. The Sermon on the Mount is more or less the rules by which you must abide to be a citizen of the Kingdom. It is more like the constitution of the Kingdom. One of the cardinal issues of this constitution is the issue of prayer. You have to petition the great God when you have a request. The Kingdom has precepts of how to do that in its constitution. In this lecture, Jesus was teaching the newly sworn-in citizens how to petition the Judge through the tool of prayer. As He continued His lecture on prayer, He came to an essential part that had to do with forgiveness. Verse 12 tells us how to petition heaven for forgiveness of our sins. When we pray for forgiveness, we must ask the Father to forgive us just as we forgive our debtors. Think about that for a moment. Now then, verse 13 concludes the lecture on prayer as it is written in the constitution. But the issue of forgiveness is so

Preparing for the Coming Glory

important in the Kingdom that it is tied to your receiving the answers to your prayers. Out of everything He talked about during the lecture on prayer, He only came back to emphasize and elaborate more on the issue of forgiveness. In the lecture on prayer, He talked about things like knowing the will of God, asking for your daily bread, deliverance from evil, and all the other big matters. But He didn't come back to elaborate on any of those matters. But He came back to spend an extra two verses to talk about the issue of forgiveness. That's how important that issue is in the constitution. We could even go to prison over it.

Now, back to how we should pray. Jesus said to pray that God forgives us just as we forgive others. Imagine if the way we were to forgive was to verbalize it, but then to keep playing the scenario in your mind every day and everywhere. When we see the other person, we remember exactly what the fellow did, but we say we have forgiven such. If God were to forgive you in the same way, each time you came to Him in prayer, He would remember exactly what you did the last time. In fact, every sin you have ever committed is right before Him when you approach the bench in prayer. How do you think that will go?

Now let's consider how God forgives us of our sins and see if we can learn a thing or two about how to forgive:

He will turn again, he will have compassion upon us; he will subdue our iniquities; and thou wilt cast all their sins into the depths of the sea.

—Micah 7:19

Consider the above passage. He has cast all our sins into the depths of the sea. What that means is that His mind can be likened to a body as vast as the sea. When we ask for forgiveness, He takes the scene created when we were indulging in the sin and casts it to the bottom of that

The Valley of Dry Bones

"sea." When new information comes about us that is good, that information becomes fresh in His memory. The new information pushes our sins deeper down to the bottom of the sea. Hence, for Him to remember what we did wrong the last time, He will need to go down and dig really hard to find any sins we have committed in the past, because the newer information of our blood-washed life is bubbling up into His memory about us. That is exactly what heaven expects *us* to do as well. Every day we have fresh information stored in our memories, such that the old ones, though not deleted, will be archived in the depths of the sea of vast information. If you keep bringing up the issue, it becomes fresh in your mind, and newer information will be suppressed instead. Let's see another perspective to this:

> *As far as the east is from the west, so far hath he removed our transgressions from us.*
>
> —Psalm 103:12

See how our sins are treated by God. The distance between the east and the west is the distance God puts between us and our sins. There is no end to the distance between the east and the west. Hence, our sins are so far from us that it is impossible to comprehend. That is exactly how God expects us to forgive our neighbors.

Back to brother Joseph. In verse 15 of Genesis 40, posted earlier, he recounted how he had been brought to Egypt, though he didn't mention any names. But we can tell it was out of the abundance of his heart that he spoke. The examination committee marked his script, and he was found lacking on many counts: first, for invoking the hand of Uzzah for his rescue; second, for refusing to forgive his brethren fully; third, for attempting to make bread out of the stones of God; and the fourth count was due to how he responded when the two officials presented their problems to him.

Let's elaborate more on the count for better understanding and for our learning. As far as heaven was concerned, Joseph still had a bit of "me" in him. He had not yet gotten to the expected point that the committee wanted him to get to. He had made good progress on his descent from the mountain. A substantial amount of flesh was now gone, but the bones still had their marrow. They could still come alive and produce the same old life that had been cut away. Let's look at his response to the officials again:

> *And they said unto him, We have dreamed a dream, and there is no interpreter of it. And Joseph said unto them, Do not interpretations belong to God? tell me them, I pray you.*
>
> —Genesis 40:8

Notice how Joseph responded to the needs of the officials. He started with God—just like many do in order to show regard or respect or what-have-you to God so that other people think we are highly spiritual when, in actual fact, we are trusting in our own ability. Does not interpretation belong to God? "Tell me the dream, and I will take care of it." "I," "I," "I." Without Him, we can do nothing. "I" should not be in the picture. It is not okay to have "I" and "Him" in the picture. It's not a sign of respect, honor, or regard for God. Only He must be in the picture. You don't start with Him and end with yourself. You start with Him and end with Him. No part of the glory of God is allowed to be shared by anyone. All glory must go to God, and those at the receiving end must know that it is not a negotiable issue. There was still a part of the old that was alive in Joseph. If God must bestow His glory upon any man, that man must be a completely dry bone, a finished product

The Valley of Dry Bones

wholly made in the factory of God. Notice that Joseph was able to give accurate interpretations of the dreams even though heaven was not pleased with his test result. This goes to show that performing miracles is not necessarily a sign that God is with you or that God is pleased with you.

Before moving on with the story of Joseph, let's look at two examples, one from the Scriptures and one from our time, to elaborate more on the last statement about performing miracles. This is especially very important in this generation. The first is from the life of Moses:

And Moses and Aaron gathered the congregation together before the rock, and he said unto them, Hear now, ye rebels; must we fetch you water out of this rock? And Moses lifted up his hand, and with his rod he smote the rock twice: and the water came out abundantly, and the congregation drank, and their beasts also. And the LORD spake unto Moses and Aaron, Because ye believed me not, to sanctify me in the eyes of the children of Israel, therefore ye shall not bring this congregation into the land which I have given them.

—Numbers 20:10–12

Let's start by giving a short background to the above passage so we can better analyze it. When the Israelites left Egypt, they traveled through the wilderness until they came to a place called Kadesh. Unfortunately, there was no water in Kadesh for the people to drink. So, they cried unto their leaders, Moses and Aaron. Moses knew he couldn't supply the needs of the people. So, he went to the One who could supply their needs, and God told him exactly what to do. Now, let's consider what Moses did in the above passage. Moses gathered the whole of the nation in front of the rock. "Come and see what 'I' will do for you."

Preparing for the Coming Glory

Then, "You are all rebels. Must 'myself' and 'my brother' fetch you water from this rock?" He then struck the rock twice, and water gushed out. Water didn't trickle out; water gushed out. The congregation didn't see the great power of God; they saw the mighty works from a great man of God. Notice that even before the miracle came, Moses had already dishonored God. Yet that did not stop the miracle from coming. Only after Moses had finished showing off his prowess to the people, and gone back to his secret place with God, that he knew he failed. In the same way, Joseph got the miracle he wanted before the officials. What a great man of God he seemed to be. But back in his closet, alone with God, heaven revealed his failures.

The second story is of a great man of God who had a powerful healing ministry. It was so powerful that there was no record of anyone who attended his meeting without getting a miracle, no matter how sick the person was. His healing services were held for days, with thousands of people attending multiple services. He held five to six services in a day with thousands in each service, and no one was allowed to attend a service twice. One day, he stood at the pulpit to preach, and when he looked at the congregation, they looked to him like a sea of people without number. And then he made a statement that took away glory from God and apportioned it to himself: Now the whole world was under his feet. At that point, heaven backed out of his ministry. He went ahead and continued the service. Miracles flowed like never before. But that was his last service. He fell ill and never recovered until he died. God will not give anyone the privilege of sharing His glory.

Back to Joseph. We can now see the state of his life at this point in time. He failed some exams that could not be carried over—he converted the stones of God to bread, he invoked the hand of Uzzah, he refused

The Valley of Dry Bones

to forgive his brethren, and he touched the glory of God. The Watchers sat to deliberate on his case. They concluded that he must go back to class again to be lectured on those cardinal points of the Kingdom. The initial isolation had not achieved the goal that heaven wanted. He had to be sentenced to another period of isolation. Hence, he remained in prison for another two years.

After two full years of lectures and midterm exams, it was again time for Joseph to go through his final assessment. Within the past two years, opportunity had been given to Joseph to invoke the "hand of Uzzah" to orchestrate his release from prison. But he had learned his lessons this time. He refused to take it. He had learned to trust God to do what only He could do. He came to the conclusion that if God did not do it, then it would be better for it not to be done. He had decided never to help God accomplish His purpose for his life. He had also been dealt with in the area of forgiveness. Heaven took the time to lecture him on the way he was expected to forgive—refuse to take the bait of replaying the evil done to you. The memories had started to fade in his mind.

Now heaven was satisfied with the progress he had made. He had passed two of the tests he had failed in the last exam. It was now time to test one of the most important concerns of heaven—touching the glory of God. Would Joseph once again take the glory for performing a miracle? Would he ascribe what belonged to God to himself in a subtle way? Would he again show that he could do the supernatural with little acknowledgment for God? Let us see how heaven arranged this particular test:

And it came to pass at the end of two full years, that Pharaoh dreamed: and, behold, he stood by the river.

—Genesis 41:1

Preparing for the Coming Glory

God, in His infinite mercy, revealed what must happen to Pharaoh through dreams. His soul was troubled. No one could interpret his dream in the whole of his kingdom. We don't know if he had had dreams in the past, and whether or not the wise men in his kingdom were able to interpret them. But we can tell from the life of Pharaoh's officials who were in prison with Joseph that the wise men in Pharaoh's kingdom are able to interpret dreams. That was why they were sad they didn't have access to the wise men who could interpret their dreams. This time, all the wise men could not figure out what Pharaoh's dreams were. This already placed Joseph on a different plane. Then the chief butler was reminded of Joseph, who had interpreted his dream when he'd been in prison. Notice that he had not been reminded of this until Pharaoh had exhausted all his options! Heaven was setting the stage for an exam for Joseph, to see how he would behave. Joseph was hurriedly brought to the palace for the exam. He had no chance to prepare or think of what to say. Two years of class attendance and a series of midterm exams should have prepared him for this moment:

> *And Pharaoh said unto Joseph, I have dreamed a dream, and there is none that can interpret it: and I have heard say of thee, that thou canst understand a dream to interpret it.*
>
> —verse 15

The most important man at the time of Joseph had just made a phenomenal statement to Joseph. He had searched throughout his whole kingdom, and no man could solve the riddle of his dream. As far as the modern world was concerned, Egypt had the best of everything at that time. What the most powerful man on earth was revealing to Joseph, who was still a prisoner at that time, was that this problem could not be solved by anyone in the world. He made Joseph understand that

The Valley of Dry Bones

he was the last man standing: "Can you or your God solve this riddle?" This was the question posed to Joseph. There was silence in heaven and in the palace of Pharaoh. All pair of eyes were set on one man—Joseph. What was he going to say now? How was he going to answer?

> *And Joseph answered Pharaoh, saying, It is not in me: God shall give Pharaoh an answer of peace.*
>
> —verse 16

Glory to God! And shame to the devil! Behold the response of Joseph: The first set of words that came out of his mouth was clear: "It is not in me." Pharaoh must not look to *him* for he was a mere man—as ordinary as nothing. He was a completely dry bone that was not even whole. He was a broken bone that was good for nothing in the absence of the breath of God. Joseph didn't need to say anything else. He had already passed one-third of the final exam. Now he had taken attention away from himself. The glory of God had been presented to him on a platter. He looked at it and remembered what he had suffered the last time he'd touched the glory. His last desire was to go back to prison. Do you know that if Joseph had behaved as a super-champion, trying to prove to Pharaoh that he was the last man standing, he would still have been able to accurately interpret the dream? May God grant us wisdom to navigate this path.

The Watchers were still waiting to see what the final verdict would be. Joseph was only halfway through. That was not good enough to take him out of isolation. With that score, even if he was released from prison, he would still have to go back to isolation sometime in the future. So, the examiners still had their pens resting against their books, waiting to see what the final score would be. Now Joseph had refused to touch the glory of God. That was good. He had also taken the attention away from

Preparing for the Coming Glory

himself. That was also good. The question now in the minds of Pharaoh and his officials was: To whom should they look for the answer? Thank God Joseph didn't leave it hanging. He pointed them in the right direction. God was the One to whom Pharaoh and his kingdom must look. Heaven applauded. Joseph received a standing ovation from the host of heaven. He had crossed the first hurdle. He still had more to go.

Then Pharaoh told his dreams, and Joseph gave an accurate interpretation according to the Spirit. Pharaoh and his officials, the ministers, the senators, and the congressmen and –women, were fully satisfied with the interpretation. All the wise men in the land could not provide the answer. The priests and the magicians, who were representatives of the gods in the land of the living, failed to provide the correct solution to the dream. But Joseph, a mere prisoner, was able to easily solve the riddle without even asking for time to meditate or think about it. This was definitely one of the gods that had come to dwell among men, they thought. The hearts of all the noblemen melted before Joseph. At that point, his demands would be treated as the demands of the gods. Whatever he desired, even to the half of the kingdom, would be given to him without hesitation. These men had become stones before Joseph. What would he do now with these stones? He had many legitimate needs. He didn't belong in the prison. He must not go back there. These men had the power to speak the word that would bring him out. He needed to go back to Canaan, where the dream of ruling over his brethren would come to pass. Pharaoh could easily provide the chariots that would take him into the city in grand style. He needed gold to throw around as someone who had made it big in a foreign land. No nation had more gold than the one he had just put under his feet. These were legitimate needs that required Joseph's attention. The devil presented the

The Valley of Dry Bones

stones and made him see bread in them. Would he see God's precious temple in them? Now it was the time to see if Joseph would invoke the hand of Uzzah and convert the stones of God to bread.

> *Now therefore let Pharaoh look out a man discreet and wise, and set him over the land of Egypt.*
>
> —verse 33

Glory to God! Joseph refused the bait of making bread out of the stones presented to him. He did not ask to be let out of prison; neither did he ask for silver or gold. He scored a hundred percent on that test. At this point, what should have been uppermost in the mind of Joseph was to get out of prison. But he put his own problems aside. The nation needed to be saved from the devastating famine that must come. He offered a solution by the Spirit to the great men of Egypt. If his lot must be that he went back to prison, so be it. Personal ambition was dead. He had no desire to build his own kingdom. He had been completely "de-fleshed." Whether he lived or died, it mattered not. Whether he was in prison or out of prison, the only thing that mattered now was that God would be glorified. It was clear to the examiners that the hand of Uzzah had been dealt with. It was completely dead. Now heaven could move forward with Joseph.

Joseph finished giving his advice and turned to go back to prison. He was ordered to stand still before the king until he was given the permission to go. The examiners cleared Joseph. His files appeared before the great throne of God. God looked through it and saw that the product was solely made in the factory of God. God put His stamp on it. This was heaven-certified. The Watchers made the decree for his release. So it was written, and so it was done. This bone was now very dry. Its marrow had been sucked out. There was no hope of the bone ever coming back to life. Joseph was at the expected point—the point that heaven wants every man who can be used to be.

10

The Expected Point

Heaven had worked hard on the raw material that was presented to the factory through the door of salvation. That raw material had gone through a series of processes that had removed all impurities. What was left now was good for nothing in the eyes of men. This is the only kind of product that God can use. Everything and anything that will make anyone point a finger to any success, be it great or small, as the ability of a person must be taken out. *All* glory must go to God. All fingers must be pointed to God alone as the Doer of it all:

> *But God hath chosen the foolish things of the world to confound the wise; and God hath chosen the weak things of the world to confound the things which are mighty; and base things of the world, and things which are despised, hath God chosen, yea, and things which are not, to bring to nought things that are: That no flesh should glory in his presence.*
>
> —1 Corinthians 1:27-29

Preparing for the Coming Glory

Consider the above passage. Look at the first phrase. God only chooses the foolish. What does the word "foolish" means? The word "foolish" in the above passage is from the Greek word *moros*, which means "dull, stupid, blockhead." That's some serious stuff. That means the individual is good for nothing. On the other hand, the word "wise" is from the Greek word *Sophos*, which means "skilled, expert." What that passage is saying is that when something or someone proclaims to be an expert in any matter of life, that person has automatically inhibited God from working through his vessel in that area. God cannot use anyone full of self, no matter how good the skill or ability is. Unless the wise person empties himself completely to become foolish, he can *never* be a tool in the hand of God. Notice the second phrase is along the same line of discussion. If any man claims to be at the top and desires to be used by heaven, he has to allow heaven subject him to intense pressure that will help remove all the things that have secured him in that position. Only the base things of the world can be used by heaven. As long as there is still flesh on that bone, as long as the bone still retains its marrow, it *cannot* be a tool in the hand of God. The same passage gave us the reason that God will not do it under any circumstance. Look at verse 29. It is so that no one can glory before Him. It is His desire that His product retains only His signature. No trace of the hand of man must be seen in any of His products. That is the point God expects everyone to get to when we decide we will follow Him. I hear some ministers of God encouraging talented people to come and use their talent for God by working in the house of God. I am sorry to say that no matter how powerful a talent is, even though God is the Giver of it, He cannot use it. Otherwise, the individual will glory in the idea that he was able to achieve great things for the Lord with his talent. Heaven cannot tolerate such a statement. Heaven would rather bring that individual to the position where even if they beg him to use

The Expected Point

his talent for God, he will refuse to do so, not because he feels he is overqualified to work in a church, but because he feels inadequate to work for the Most High God. He would have learned by experience that the arm of flesh will always fail.

When a person arrives at this expected point, where the very dry bones are now lying uselessly in the valley, then God can work with them:

The hand of the Lord was upon me, and carried me out in the spirit of the Lord, and set me down in the midst of the valley which was full of bones, and caused me to pass by them round about: and, behold, there were very many in the open valley; and, lo, they were very dry.

—Ezekiel 37:1-2

The situation described above is a very hopeless situation. There is nothing any human ability can do to revive these bones. This is the point where science fails. This is the end point for all human wisdom and human abilities. This is the point where experts lift up their hands in surrender. It is at this point that the Father will go to work. It is time for God to release His glory—so that no man will be able to say, "if not for science or technology or the doctors or what-have-you . . ." This is the place where even the worst of all sinners are forced to admit that this was the finger of God. This is the point where the doubt of atheists about God will be cleared. He will be forced to admit that this was the finger of God:

And he said unto me, Son of man, can these bones live? And I answered, O Lord God, thou knowest.

—verse 3

Preparing for the Coming Glory

Notice the above conversation between God and the prophet. As far as the prophet was concerned, this was a hopeless situation. It did not even occur to him that God could do anything about it. He had worked with God for many years before this day. He had seen many miracles and strange things God had done. He knew how powerful God is. But yet, he could not bring himself to make any positive statement about the situation on the ground. God didn't tell him that the bones were very dry. God just told him to look at the bones. In the process of looking at the bones, he noticed that they were very dry. He could not bring himself to answer God's question in the affirmative. This was exactly where God wanted him to get to:

Again he said unto me, Prophesy upon these bones, and say unto them, O ye dry bones, hear the word of the LORD.

—verse 4

Now that it was obvious to all that this individual could amount to nothing, then when the glory of God shined through this individual, the world would know that this was nothing but the finger of God. This was not a great man of God; this was a great God of man. That is not to say that God cannot make a man great. God can and has made many men great. But when it comes to the glory of God, greatness belongs only to God. No man can touch it. Now then, notice the above passage. The first thing that the Father would do at this point was to release His Word. There was no dry bone in the valley of dry bones that would amount to anything if God did not release the Word. Let's look at some Scriptures for some examples:

Now in the fifteenth year of the reign of Tiberius Cæsar, Pontius Pilate being governor of Judæa, and Herod being tetrarch of Galilee, and his brother Philip tetrarch of Ituræa and of the

The Expected Point

region of Trachonitis, and Lysanias the tetrarch of Abilene, Annas and Caiaphas being the high priests, the word of God came unto John the son of Zacharias in the wilderness.

—Luke 3:1–2

John was in the valley of dry bones for many years. The news of the birth of a great prophet rocked the land when John was born. All of a sudden, no one heard about him again. People might have concluded that the prophecy about John would amount to nothing. He must have given the world around his family something to gossip about. Imagine someone with a great destiny, living in the comfort of his father's house, being an only child, to go out and live in the wilderness. Despite the wealth his father commanded, his diet was limited to locusts and honey. People have concluded that there was no hope for this fellow. This was a mad fellow. He refused to go to college; he refused to learn any trade. Marriage was not on his radar. A mistake must have been made somewhere. Where was the powerful prophecy that had gone before this man? Everyone in the Temple and in the community around them had witnessed Zacharias's dumbness for nine months. Was all of this for nothing? What about the miracles, signs, and wonders displayed at the naming ceremony of this precious child, John? Had that also been a fluke? Why was his life, after thirty years, nothing to write home about?

But a day came when the committee of the University of Heaven certified John. The Father sent forth His word, and he (John) became a global phenomenon. The men who held the oracles of God and were in charge of the Temple of God were forced to acknowledge that this was the finger of God. He became the greatest prophet of the New Testament. And in fact, Jesus confirmed that no man born of a woman was greater than John the Baptist.

Preparing for the Coming Glory

The second example is from the life of Joseph:

He sent a man before them, even Joseph, who was sold for a servant: Whose feet they hurt with fetters: He was laid in iron: Until the time that his word came: the word of the Lord tried him. The king sent and loosed him; even the ruler of the people, and let him go free.

—Psalm 105:17-20

Notice the above verses. Joseph had been roasting in prison, despite being a greatly talented young man. But it was obvious that heaven had no need for his talent. When he got to the expected point, however, the Father started to put His stamp on him. Notice what actually brought Joseph out of prison. Pharaoh, even though he was the king, had no power to bring Joseph out of prison. If he had, Joseph wouldn't have spent about ten years in prison. Only the word of God can make dry bones live again. Until God sent forth His word, Joseph remained in the prison. Until the committee of the University of Heaven had sent their certification notes to the throne of the Father, the word was not released to set Joseph free. Look at the above passage again—particularly verse 19. Until the time that the word came, Joseph remained in prison.

Look at another example from the life of Moses:

And the Lord said unto Moses in Midian, Go, return into Egypt: for all the men are dead which sought thy life.

—Exodus 4:19

Moses labored in the wilderness for forty years. When the Watchers finally certified him, they made a decree of his release from isolation. And after this decree God sprang into action. The pattern is the same for all dry bones. The angels of God proclaim the certification of the

The Expected Point

fellow, and God sends forth His word. After the word of God came to Moses, he was able to begin the ministry that was committed to him.

One should wonder, out of all there was to do with the dry bones, the first thing the Father did was to send forth His word. Why is that so? As mentioned earlier, God has a standard for every man. He sent His Son to dwell among us. This Son became the standard that all men who come to God must attain. The Father knows we cannot attain that height, no matter how hard we try. So, He subjects us to a series of processes that bring us to the point that we will give Him free passage into our lives. Then He sends forth His word. Who is this Word?

> *In the beginning was the Word, and the Word was with God, and the Word was God. The same was in the beginning with God. All things were made by him; and without him was not anything made that was made.*
>
> —John 1:1–3

From the above passage, it is clear to us that the Word whom God sent is Jesus Christ, His Son, the standard for all men. Look at the last phrase in verse 3. Nothing can be made without the Word. No product will come out of the factory of God without the touch of the Word. The ultimate desire of God is that *all* would conform to the image of His dear Son, Jesus Christ. Now that the bones have been completely de-identified, it is time for God to give them a new identity. That new identity can only be found in Christ. That is why it is the Word released who must do the rest of the work on behalf of God. This entity is now a new creature. The old is completely gone. Now the Word must be sent to give a new identity to the dry bones lying in the valley without an identity. None of the bones will amount to anything without the Word. The life-giving and life-sustaining substance within each bone has been destroyed with intense heat from the factory of God. If this new entity must come back to life, it has to be from a source that comes from without and not from within. So, going back to the prophet in the valley of the very dry bones, God put His word in the mouth of the prophet and asked him to prophesy as he was led:

> *So I prophesied as I was commanded: and as I prophesied, there was a noise, and behold a shaking, and the bones came together, bone to his bone.*
>
> —Ezekiel 37:7

As soon as the man of God released the word, Jesus went into action and begin to piece together the broken life. The life that was hopelessly hopeless was now being glued together again to be whole. But this time, it would become a new whole entity. The bone had no life in it, so there was no room for any form of resistance at this point. Wherever the Word leads, the bones just follow. At this point, there is nothing left to fight for in life. As it is said, he who is on the ground is never afraid of falling. This entity becomes a zombie—clay in the hand of the Potter. No form of resistance is given to the hand of the Molder. Look at how Jesus, the Potter Himself, puts it in this passage:

> *Then he told them what they could expect for themselves: "Anyone who intends to come with me has to let me lead. You're not in the driver's seat—I am."*
>
> —Luke 9:23 MSG

This is amazing. Can you see the advice the Potter Himself issued to the people flocking around Him? You have to get to that valley. And you cannot get to that valley unless you are completely "de-fleshed" and the bones are completely "de-marrowed" and dehydrated, until not a single drop of water is left. Not only that, but the bones must land on the ground with such an impact that they are broken into pieces, so that the fellow will not know what to do with his life except the Potter comes in to work. Now then, these bones have vacated the driver's seats of their lives. They have moved the decision-making faculty of their lives to the control of the Master. He determines, without any form of inhibition, what to do with every one of them. The Master then begins to bring the bones together. Even though they have been completely de-identified and no man knows which belongs to whom, He knows the formation of their DNA and can piece them together again without any error. The Potter finally puts the bones together to form a complete human skeleton. But this new entity is still lifeless, for the bones are still very dry, even though they now have the shape of a man:

> *And when I beheld, lo, the sinews and the flesh came up upon them, and the skin covered them above: but there was no breath in them.*
>
> —Ezekiel 37:8

Then, the Potter continues His work in this new entity. Jesus performs a bone marrow transplant in these bones using His own marrow as the donor. Though the bones may be those of Moses or Joseph or any other person who has passed through thick and thin to get to the valley, they now have the marrow of Christ, and the marrow must give the life of Christ to the bones. Now then, sinews are also transplanted into the new entity using Jesus as the donor. Sinews are a tough, high-tensile-strength band of dense connective tissue that connect muscles to bones. They transmit the mechanical force of a muscle contraction to the skeletal system, which in turn helps to coordinate the movement. This makes the man totally reliant on God in his core. Notice that this is put there by Jesus. It is part of His own sinew, transplanted into the new entity. Hence before the man can ever move, it has to be a God-ordained move.

> *For in him we live, and move, and have our being; as certain also of your own poets have said, For we are also his offspring.*
>
> —Acts 17:28

This man, who used to organize crusades without consulting God, who had a great ambition to build an empire for himself with branches all over the world—all without instruction from the Father—was now subjected to an entity that could not as much as move a limb without a word from God. This man, who went to marry anyone he liked, claiming that God did not choose a spouse for a man—had found himself in a place where his ability to make choices for himself has been destroyed. This man, who bought a car without informing Christ because he had the money and the brains to think for himself, was now someone who could not lift a finger except Christ permitted it. The sinews that coordinate the movement do not belong to him. If he must avoid internal chaos, he must move only when the Master instructs him to move. His entire being is in the One who transplanted His body parts to give his dead bones life. The conclusion of Paul in the above verse is that we are His offspring. The word "offspring" in the above passage comes from the Greek word *ghenos*, which means "descent from a particular people or person." This new entity can only trace his descent to Christ. The old descent through his earthly parent is gone. It was completely stripped off when he was rolling down the mountain. This is a new entity who is an offspring of the One who so graciously donated His body cells to bring him (the dry bones) back to life.

The Expected Point

Back to Ezekiel 37:8: the next thing the Lord will do is to clothe the fellow with flesh. That is, God now brought up the resurrected Christ in this brand-new man. Consider the word used in Ezekiel 37:6 to describe the action of clothing these bones with flesh:

And I will lay sinews upon you, and will bring up flesh upon you, and cover you with skin, and put breath in you, and ye shall live; and ye shall know that I am the Lord.

—Ezekiel 37:6

Notice the words used: "bring up." Jesus redesigned new flesh for this fellow, just as it was done when man was first created. But this time around, the flesh was not designed from clay. The Lord used a cell from His own flesh to clone new flesh. Through a single cell from His flesh, He was able to bring up flesh upon the new entity. Hence, this fellow was more or less Christ. The only part of this new entity that belonged to the man were the dead, dry bones, which no man could see externally. Look at how Paul put it:

I am crucified with Christ: nevertheless I live; yet not I, but Christ liveth in me: and the life which I now live in the flesh I live by the faith of the Son of God, who loved me, and gave himself for me.

—Galatians 2:20

Can you see how the current state of the man is described in the above passage? Due to the series of events the fellow went through to get to the valley, the old man was crucified on the cross. Dead. He can no longer live. There is now a new life. The new life is of the Son of God, who transplanted Himself into the dry bones to give it life. This is the Lord's doing, and it is marvelous in our sight.

Preparing for the Coming Glory

Now then, these former dry bones had the shape and form of a man. A new identity had been given. He was now a full-blown man. But he was still lifeless. The next thing the Father would do was to cause Breath to enter this new entity. At this point, the Holy Spirit takes over the task from our Lord Jesus Christ.

> *Who also hath made us able ministers of the new testament; not of the letter, but of the spirit: for the letter killeth, but the spirit giveth life.*
>
> —2 Corinthians 3:6

This new entity now has life only because the Spirit gives him life. The Breath is the Holy Spirit, and this Breath brought life. So, the revived bones no longer get life or their source of nutrients from its marrow. The marrow is long gone. Completely dry and dead when this fellow was rolling down the mountain. It now gets its nutrients from the Breath of God. His driving force is no longer self; it's now the inspiration of the Almighty. That's what keeps him alive. When the Breath from God stops for any reason, he becomes a dead man again, even though he might still be walking the face of the earth.

> *So I prophesied as he commanded me, and the breath came into them, and they lived, and stood up upon their feet, an exceeding great army.*
>
> —Ezekiel 37:10

This is a new product solely from the factory of God. God can confidently put His signature on this product. It no longer bears the identity of the "old" man. It now has the DNA of Jesus and the Breath of the Holy Spirit. The soul of this fellow is now fully and completely conformed to the image of Christ. The body is on the altar of the throne

The Expected Point

room, where it is being offered as a living sacrifice (Romans 12:1-3). As far as heaven is concerned, this is a nameless and a faceless entity. Only Christ can give him a new name. Hence, he becomes one of the fellows who must bear the name of the Lord (2 Timothy 2:19-21). Statements that used to anger this fellow in the past are now those statements that will receive a "bless you" from this man. This man used to argue with his wife in the past. But now he gladly accepts "defeat." The wife wonders what has become of her husband. Has he lost his manhood? The man who could not take any form of embarrassment from anyone in the past, now becomes someone who, when slapped on the right cheek, turns the left cheek to be slapped again, without a word to defend himself. Those who knew him when he had just started his journey in Christ are now afraid of what he has become in Christ. This is when the prophesy of Paul becomes fulfilled in the life of this fellow;

> *'Therefore if any man be in Christ, he is a new creature: old things are passed away; behold, all things are become new.'*
>
> —2 Corinthians 5:17

The next thing the Father will do is to cover the new entity with His glory. This is the final step in the equation of predestination, as stated in Roman 8:30:

> *Moreover whom he did predestinate, them he also called: and whom he called, them he also justified: and whom he justified, them he also glorified.*

The Father can confidently put His glory on this new entity because when He looks at this new entity, all He sees is Jesus. And it is not only God who sees this new entity as Jesus. When the world sees him, they will say this fellow has been with Jesus, the same way they spoke of Peter and the other disciples (Acts 4:13), or they will say this is a true Christian (Acts 11:26). Paul put it in a unique way:

> *To whom God would make known what is the riches of the glory of this mystery among the Gentiles; which is Christ in you, the hope of glory.*
>
> —Colossians 1:27

This entity is now Christ walking on the face of the earth again. This is not just one Christ. This is Christ in many vessels—an army of Christ. There is no way the gates of hell can prevail over this army. This is the army that God will use to destroy the works of Satan in these last days and to fight the final battle against evil. It is often said that Jesus is the answer for the world today, that Christ is the hope of glory for whom the world has been waiting. But we all know that Christ will not come back to this earth again except to reign in the millennium. Who, then, is the answer for the world today? What is the hope of glory for this generation? It is Jesus, manifesting through these dry and broken bones that have become a new entity through the Word from the Almighty—that is the answer for the world today. This new entity that has the DNA of Jesus and the Breath of the Holy Spirit is the hope of glory for whom the world is waiting.

Now then, notice that when the Holy Spirit came upon them to give them life, they became the host of an army. The purpose for the valley experience is to join the army of God in destroying the works of Satan (1 John 3:8). Enrollment is open to all—both current Christians and the entire world. This will be the new Body of Christ. Anyone who refuses to enroll in this army by refusing to go down to the valley will scarcely have any part in the end-time plans of the Lord. And it will

The Expected Point

be impossible to survive what is coming without having the DNA of Jesus and the Breath of the Holy Spirit. God is building a generation of Christians who will be devoid of superstars. Currently, we have pockets of men who have taken the painful trip down into the valley. And these men demonstrate the great power of God. But unfortunately, they are very few and far between worldwide. The majority of Christians are men sitting on the mountain, refusing to go down into the valley and eating from the very few generals of God. The majority of Christians seek God, get their miracles, and hear God through these superstars. Hence, we have one or two superstars in an entire nation, and the majority of the Body of Christ in that nation are just followers who have little or no knowledge about the God they purport to serve. In most cases, these superstars are go-betweens for the vast majority of the members of the Body of Christ. What we currently experience is what the Israelites experienced in the wilderness.

It is the intention of God for the entire nation to be a nation of priests. Every single citizen of the nation of Israel should have a direct relationship and his own connection with God. Every citizen of the nation of Israel should hear God directly for himself. But they rejected that picture, and another one was created. One tribe from the nation was picked to be priests to God, but that also failed. Finally, God picked a family to be priests unto Him, and this family became the "superstars" in the land because access to God seemed exclusively for them. If anyone wanted to seek God, they had to go through this family. This picture will not fly in these last days. A go-between now is never in God's agenda when dealing with man. He wants to have a one-on-one relationship with every single one of us. That is why God wants us to go down into the valley or be ruled out of His end-time plan. Look at how this Scripture puts the intention of God for the end-time Church:

Preparing for the Coming Glory

In that day shall the L<small>ORD</small> defend the inhabitants of Jerusalem; and he that is feeble among them at that day shall be as David; and the house of David shall be as God, as the angel of the L<small>ORD</small> before them.

—Zechariah 12:8

Let's take a short walk through the above passage. First, it starts with the words "in that day." Which day is it talking about? It's talking about the last days, the end times. So it is clear to us that this Scripture pertains to us today because we are living in the final seconds of the last days. Now then, let's go a little further with this Scripture. It says that during that time, God will defend the inhabitants of Jerusalem. There are currently two "Jerusalems." The first is the physical Jerusalem located in the Middle East, where the natural Israelites occupy the physical city, and the second is the spiritual Jerusalem, where the spiritual Israelites occupy a spiritual realm. The spiritual Israelites are those who have been washed by the blood of the Lamb and engrafted into the nation of Israel as blood-borne citizens:

That at that time ye were without Christ, being aliens from the commonwealth of Israel, and strangers from the covenants of promise, having no hope, and without God in the world: But now in Christ Jesus ye who sometimes were far off are made nigh by the blood of Christ.

—Ephesians 2:12–13

Notice how this passage describes how we became citizens of Israel. Verse 12 talks about how we are strangers to the family of God, Israel, because we are without Christ. But notice what it says in verse 13: By the blood of Jesus, we are brought near, and we are now fellow citizens

The Expected Point

of Israel. Although we cannot go to the physical Israel and begin to demand benefits from the Israeli government as citizens, we can go to the government of the spiritual Israel and begin to demand benefits as citizens because we have filed asylum from the tyrannical government of the devil and the government of the spiritual Israel graciously granted us asylum. Hence, we have been translated from the tyrannical kingdom of darkness into the Kingdom of God's Son, which is the spiritual Israel (see Colossians 1:13).

Now back to the Zechariah 12 passage. In the last days, into which we have already stepped, God will defend Jerusalem, which is the capital of both spiritual and natural Israel. The next issue to resolve is why there is a need for God to defend Jerusalem. There shouldn't be talk about actively defending Jerusalem if no attack is coming. That tells us clearly that there will be an attack against both the spiritual and natural Israel in the last days. As the nations of the earth gather to annihilate the nation Israel from the face of the earth, through what we call the Third World War, so shall they gather to wipe Christians from the face of the earth through what we call the great Tribulation and persecution. (Please refer to my book *The Truth about the Rapture* to understand the scriptural standpoint of the timing of the Rapture.) Hence, while the enemies of God, both physical and spiritual, are trying to annihilate God's heritage, wiping them off the face of the earth, God will rise to defend them.

The next question to ask is how He will defend both the physical Israel and the spiritual Israel. If you look again at the Zechariah 12 passage, you will notice a semicolon after the word "Jerusalem." That means the author was trying to describe how God intends to defend the two "Jerusalems." His plan is to make the weakest of us as strong as David. Think about that for a moment. David had the strongest army

Preparing for the Coming Glory

Israel had ever had to date. He never lost any battle all the days of his life. And the battles he fought were overwhelming. For instance, he was able to confront and destroy Goliath, a giant who terrified the entire army of Israel for forty days. Those were the kinds of battles David faced all the days of his life. What God was saying is that He will equip the weakest of us with strength such that no power of the enemy will be able to stand against us—the physical with weapons of destruction and protection, and the spiritual with spiritual weapons and power. Now back to the starting point. The end times is not the era when only one superstar will be going from country to country to preach the Word. The end times is an era when the whole Body of Christ will be so anointed that we will all go out to plunder the spoils of the enemy. We will be so strong and anointed that even the weakest of us will be as strong as David. That is why it is not negotiable whether or not to go down to the valley of dry bones. If you cannot get down there—no matter your reason—you cannot be a part of the army. The kind of strength we are talking about is not available in the realm of man. God has to work within man to bring about such strength. Notice what Zechariah says about the strongest of us: they will be like the angel of the Lord. You see, that kind of strength is not common among men. God Himself has to bring it about. In order for God to bring it about in any vessel, that vessel must first earn the approval of God. Approval cannot be given to anyone who has not become dry bones in the valley. In this era, there is no room for personal ambition or self-aggrandizement. You have to earn the signature of God by passing all necessary trials—tests—that will take you down into the valley. Again, notice that we did not mention the issue of sin. We are not deliberately closing our eyes to that. He who wishes to walk with God must put away all sin. This is a nonnegotiable fact. God cannot tolerate sin no matter who it is who commits it. Many pastors or

Church leaders try to explain it away. That doesn't change the position of God concerning sin—God is light, and in Him there is no darkness at all. Sin and God cannot coexist. Either you will cling to God and leave your sins behind, or you will cling to your sins and leave God behind. You can't have it both ways.

The Living Bones

Moving back to the words of the prophet Ezekiel, God gave him the final commandment concerning the bones in the valley. The result of the execution of the commandment shocked the prophet:

So I prophesied as he commanded me, and the breath came into them, and they lived, and stood up upon their feet, an exceeding great army.

—Ezekiel 37:10

Notice what the prophet saw. He didn't see a crowd of people. He didn't see multitudes from different races and cultures. He could not identify them by color or by social status at all. He couldn't differentiate the societal strata of the group. Instead, he saw an exceedingly great army. Men dressed in military attire with weapons of warfare in their hands were ready to destroy the gates of God's enemies, and he did not see any difference between them. They were all being coordinated from the same energy source. They were all made from the same flesh. It was the same spirit that had been put into them. They thought alike, walked alike, and behaved alike. Though their origin can be traced to all different races and cultures, and although they came from different strata of society, they had ears for only One: the commander in chief, Jesus

Preparing for the Coming Glory

Christ. And they all moved in perfect synchrony to the voice of that Commander. There was no one-man army. No special general. Only One is the general of this end-times army.

The next thing heaven does with this army is to put its glory on them:

Moreover whom he did predestinate, them he also called: and whom he called, them he also justified: and whom he justified, them he also glorified.

—Romans 8:30

Notice the last step in the matter of predestination: glorification. There is no way a bone that is clothed with flesh designed by God and Breath directly from the Spirit of God will not be clothed with the glory of God. We saw it in Genesis, when God created the first man. They were so clothed in God's glory that they didn't even need physical attire. They were naked, but they didn't see themselves naked until they departed from the glory. It will interest you to know that everyone who saw Adam and Eve in the Garden saw them as being clothed: the animals, the devil, the angels, and even God. God had to ask them a strange question when they said they were hiding because they were naked. The glory covering over them had been so thick that it formed a physical, tangible, and touchable barrier between their nakedness and the world around them (both physical and spiritual). This is similar to how God commanded Moses concerning the priests to make attire for them:

And thou shalt make holy garments for Aaron thy brother for glory and for beauty.

—Exodus 28:2

The Expected Point

See the instructions God gave Moses concerning the garments of the priest. The first purpose of the garments is for glory. The word "glory" in the above passage comes from the Hebrew word *kabod*, which means "honor, splendor." This glory attracts respect, favor, and blessings. Doors just open everywhere you go. This is the factor that makes people submit to their spiritual leaders. Great reverence is accorded to the man of God even from the highest authority in the land because of the glory on Him. The beauty, reverence, and submission this glory brings to the man of God is the reason that the Watchers decided to meet. It was concluded and agreed upon that the job of the examination committee was not yet done. It was clear to the Watchers that these dry bones could still receive marrow from an external source. And if the enemy could find a way to isolate one of the hosts and conduct a bone marrow transplant, it could then produce a member that was out of sync with the rest. This could cause serious problems for the army. We have seen such transplants occur in men who have gone before us, even after they had been certified by the Watchers.

Now then, the committee needed to come up with a curriculum to address this issue. Because the man of God had been "de-fleshed" was not a reason to prevent him from going through a higher level of study. His bones were dry and empty, making him more vulnerable than the others. The dryness and emptiness of the bones ensured a constant refill from the Lord. However, if permitted, the devil could also fill the bones, turning a true prophet of God into a soothsayer. We see this all over our world. So, let's take a little time to look at the higher learning institution set up by the examination committee of heaven.

11

The PHD Program

The Master's PHD Program from the University of Heaven

It so happened that at the last feast Jesus celebrated in the Temple at Jerusalem before His departure, He came into Jerusalem in grand style. This was done so that the Scripture might be fulfilled. Jesus, as the King of Israel, had to come into Jerusalem, and so He instructed His disciples on what to do:

> *And saith unto them, Go your way into the village over against you: and as soon as ye be entered into it, ye shall find a colt tied, whereon never man sat; loose him, and bring him.*
>
> —Mark 11:2

Notice the instructions He gave to them. The colt was a specific colt—not jjust any colt they found in the street. Also, there is another

Preparing for the Coming Glory

thing about this colt: no man had ever sat on him before If you know a little bit about donkeys and horses, you will know that it can be very dangerous to ride a colt that has never been ridden before. And Jesus' plan was to ride this colt from Bethany to Jerusalem, about two miles. To ride a colt that no man had ever sat on before for two miles would have been asking for far too much. Though no man had ever sat on this colt before, it is very possible that the owners had already subjected the colt to vigorous training. Before a man can successfully ride on a colt without causing harm to both himself and the colt, the colt must undergo a series of training sessions to prepare him for the task ahead. This training can last for months before the colt is ready to be sat upon. It is possible that this particular colt had been trained in that way. So, after subjecting the colt to months of training, the owners might have been ready to start riding on him. It was then the Master declared that He had need of the colt.

Another thing to note about this colt is that it could be likened to the dry bones we discussed earlier. In many ways, we can see the similarities between the dry bones and the colt. The dry bones were humans who were subjected to intense pressure to milk out any part of the self, worldliness, and lust from their nature. The colt also was like every other colt, but unlike the others, it had likely been subjected to months of intense training to make him ready for the Master's use. The dry bones, after receiving flesh from above, became new entities that no man had ever used before. In the same way, this colt, after receiving intense training, had been tied down, waiting for his first assignment.

Now then, after much bargaining with the owners, the disciples were allowed to take the colt, and they then brought it to Jesus. In those days, colts were a major mode of transportation on land. They helped to carry both burdens and humans from one point to another. There was nothing dignifying about them. They put their legs in the dirtiest areas of the land just to transport their owners from one point to another. They carried the heaviest of burdens just to satisfy their owners. But when this colt was brought to Jesus, it received a treatment no colt had ever received before.

> *And they brought the colt to Jesus, and cast their garments on him; and he sat upon him.*
>
> —verse 7

Notice the first thing they did when they brought the colt to Jesus. They cast their garments onto the colt. This was a show of honor, respect, and submission to royalty. They also did this to make Jesus comfortable. In those days, a garment was one of the most precious commodities someone could own. Some people, especially the poor, never owned more than five garments in their entire lifetimes. Items of clothing were not as common as they are today. Hence, to decide to do away with one of your most precious possessions would have been a very big deal. The colt had never received this kind of treatment before. And no other colt had ever received similar treatment. So this job must be very good for the colt. This was a colt that had humbly followed the two disciples, not knowing the kind of labor that awaited him. He had seen his fellow colts carry heavy burdens, and many of them were subjected to intense labor and hardship. Some of them even died under the weight of the burdens they carried. But here, no burden was put on the colt. Men treated it like a god. What a wonderful life it was now experiencing! Where this colt was coming from, it had not even been allowed into the house. It was left outside in the weather. Whether there was sunshine or rain, it was tied up outside and must not complain. When his owners permitted the

Preparing for the Coming Glory

disciples to take this colt away, fear likely engulfed the animal. At least it had known what to expect from its original owners, seeing how they treated their other colts. But these two guys—who didn't look rich—dragging it away in a hurry, to an unknown destination, spoke of his likely doom. But the treatment so far had been wonderful. (Note: this is the same way God will adorn His army with glory and honor before He rides on them.)

As if that were not enough, when Jesus finally sat on the colt after its adornment, surprisingly the colt didn't feel the weight of this Man. It was completely carried away by the happenings taking place around it. Suddenly at least twelve grown and able men shouted with great joy and reverence. They were all worshiping and dancing and singing before the colt. It must have been on top of the world at that moment. At first, it didn't know how to react, but later it began to enjoy the moments as they unfolded. It took its first step and was met with even more pleasant surprises. Each step it took out of the house was met with more praises and worship and celebration. It was beginning to enjoy this job! As it stepped completely out of the house, more surprises await it:

And many spread their garments in the way: and others cut down branches off the trees, and strawed them in the way.

—verse 8

It saw many people on both sides of the road, also spreading their garments. This time around, they were spreading their garments on the ground on which it was walking, its feet not touching the ground. Wow—the colt's father had walked on mud all the days of its life. Its mother and brothers walked on worse. Here it was, though, walking on the garments of humans, its feet not even touching the dirty and muddy ground. It concluded that this was no longer a job; it was his

The PHD Program

right. When only the Twelve had worshiped it in the house, it thought it was just an in-house thing. Now the colt was convinced that there was something special about itself. Everybody out on the street was treating it even better than the Twelve had treated it in the house. it was the superstar! The one the world had been waiting for! It had to change the way it walked. The colt applied a little bit of cat-walking and a little bit of bouncing, nodding its head in perfect synchrony to the praises being showered on it. Then it stopped. As soon as it stopped, the cheers grew louder. It looked to the left and to the right, and it saw countless numbers of people worshiping and celebrating it, much more than the Twelve had when it was in the house. Wow. Everywhere it turned, people were worshiping. Many were falling over each other just to have a glimpse of it. Some fainted when they touched it. The struggle to touch it was real. It had more than thirty strongmen surrounding it to prevent people from touching it. This journey must never end! It noticed another glorious thing the people did. They were cutting down branches of palm trees and waving the branches at it as it walks by. It was from this part of the world, and it understood exactly why they were doing that. The spreading of palm branches and garments were longtime customs. Dignitaries were welcomed this way, to show honor and respect. It is now clear that the colt was really someone special. The whole world was celebrating its very first entrance into Jerusalem. It must go to Rome after this!

> *And they that went before, and they that followed, cried, saying, Hosanna; Blessed is he that cometh in the name of the Lord.*
>
> —verse 9

Then something strange happened. The people started calling it a king. They were blessing the king who was coming into Jerusalem in the name of the Lord. This was now official. This colt's path was never going to be like those of its ancestors. It has broken even. It has finally hit the jackpot. It was now the king of all people. It kept hearing the security men shouting, "Give way to the king—give way ... give way!" It saw uniformed men stationed to make sure the procession was peaceful. "Those are my security agents," it whispered to itself. When they were almost to Jerusalem, it saw Roman soldiers with aggressive looks on their faces. At first, it was skeptical, thinking maybe its kingship was restricted to just the followers of this Man whom it carried. But later it relaxed. It noticed they gave a subtle bow to it and allowed it passage of way with its entourage. This was amazing! Its recognition was beyond the nation of Israel. The colt was known worldwide. It started to plan how to extend the frontiers of its kingdom to other parts of the world. It needed to open branches to reach the unreachable. It needed all people of all nations to acknowledge its lordship. It needed to change its name to a more dignified one, like Elijah or Samuel, to make it seem more respectable. The people couldn't just be calling him "donkey" anymore. They needed to put a title in front of its name as well: "Apostle Elijah"? No, that didn't sound right. "Prophet Samuel" That was more like it. He needed to hire a permanent bodyguard to watch over it every second of the day. People shouldn't just be able to reach it easily or at any time they wanted. It needed an administrative assistant, and of course, a PA. The people would need to make an appointment with its PA before they can see it for any reason. And the PA would have to give them appointments further out in the future—because it shouldn't be easy to see a great donkey of God like this colt. It also needed a special assistant to be in charge of all its travel schedule. It was going to be traveling a lot now. No one should be able to reach it directly on the phone. The administrative assistant would be very busy responding to calls from all over the world. It needed some beautiful ladies with well-tailored uniforms to serve it everywhere it went. Any nation it visited also must host a VIP reception for it. It could never stay in a hotel room that was less than the presidential suite. A payment and benefit package must be negotiated before it would minister anywhere. It would also be a sign of disrespect to use certain cars to convey this colt. If they must invite it, its flight ticket must not be less than a first-class one. The colt's list of privileges was soon endless.

These were the possibilities now available to a donkey who had been nobody and suddenly became somebody. Unfortunately for this colt, the next time it returned to the streets of Jerusalem, everyone was going about their business without even noticing it. It was wondering why no one noticed it anymore. The donkey should have noticed that the accolades given when it was walking to Jerusalem were not for it. The King of kings had chosen to ride on it—although it did not realize it. However, Jesus was not the one who walked on the garments the crowd had spread on the ground; the donkey did. But the garments were not spread on the ground because of the donkey. They were spread on the ground because of Jesus. When the people shouted, "Hosanna to the King," they were not referring to the donkey as being the king. It would be foolish to think the people were referring to it as a king. Even in situations in which the people could not see the King sitting on the donkey, they could see the influence and the hand of an invincible God through the ministry of the donkey. Every donkey in ministry must come to terms with the fact that whatever accolades it receives from men is because they saw the King of kings on top of it. It must come to realize that each time the people shouted "Hosanna to the King," it is not the donkey to whom they were referring. It was to the immortal and the invisible One sitting upon it to whom they were referring.

Preparing for the Coming Glory

The next logical question we need to ask is, What does the Master expect us to do when we are carriers of God's glory?

Then answered Jesus and said unto them, Verily, verily, I say unto you, The Son can do nothing of himself, but what he seeth the Father do: for what things soever he doeth, these also doeth the Son likewise.

—John 5:19

Notice what the Master says in the above passage. He Himself came to us as a human, born like every one of us. He was tempted in all ways we could think of, yet He was the greatest Bearer of the glory of God in the human world. If there is anyone to whom we should listen regarding this matter, it is the Lord Jesus. People flocking around His ministry did not see or hear God. They saw only Jesus (the donkey). They gave all worship and adoration to Him because of the works He did. It would have been okay for Jesus, being the Son of God, to say, like the donkey, that He is the greatest of all. But He didn't say that. Rather, He said that without the One riding on Him—the Father—He could do nothing. This is the position we must also take when at this junction. The most important time in the life of Jesus on earth was the time He spent with the Father in the place of prayer. He knew that if He must breathe, the breath must come from God on daily basis. So, while all men slept, Jesus would go to a secluded place and spend time communing with the Father. It was during this time of communion that the Father would tell Him His plan for the day. When you get to the point when you know that you are just a donkey, and that the glory you see is for the One riding on the donkey, then it will be easier to tell the devil to take his stuff and get out of your way. Jesus was bold to tell it to the public that He Himself was nothing. It is God who was riding on Him that brought about all the good works they were seeing. Hence, continual dependence on God, as the sole Source of our lives is the key to surviving the job of being the Master's donkey.

Again, if there is anyone to advise us on how to be a successful donkey at the Master's bidding, it is Jesus. He gave us another masterclass lecture on how to handle ministry success. The advice came in the form of a parable. Let's look at it critically to see if we can learn one or two things:

> *But which of you, having a servant plowing or feeding cattle, will say unto him by and by, when he is come from the field, Go and sit down to meat? And will not rather say unto him, Make ready wherewith I may sup, and gird thyself, and serve me, till I have eaten and drunken; and afterward thou shalt eat and drink? Doth he thank that servant because he did the things that were commanded him? I trow not. So likewise ye, when ye shall have done all those things which are commanded you, say, We are unprofitable servants: we have done that which was our duty to do.*
>
> —Luke 17:7–10

This matter the Lord is presenting to us in this parable is a very serious matter. In verse 7 of the above passage, Jesus gave us the picture of a master and his servant. This master seemed very rich. He sent his servant to plough his farm. The servant went to the farm and did a fantastic job. Many acres of land were covered by this faithful servant. The master saw the work that he did and was happy with both the work and the servant. Now then, if the master was happy with them, every servant expected to be allowed to take a break from work to relax and rest. But Jesus said in the above passage that that should not be what is expected from a good master. In verse 8, He explained what was expected of a good master. The master must not grant leave to the servant yet. The servant must still prepare the master's meal. After preparing the meal, the servant must bring the meal to the table and serve the master. When the master had eaten to his satisfaction, then the servant could go and take care of himself. In verse 9, Jesus concluded by saying that no servant should get a thank-you or any special treatment because he did what was originally in his job description.

With the above summary, we can now do justice to verse 10. Notice that Jesus, in verse 10, began to relate the story to the disciples. After going through a series of trials that had stripped a man of flesh, sin, and the world, the man became a very dry bone and found himself in the valley. The God of the valley poured His glory out on the mere man, and he became a wonder to his world. God recruited him into His army, and he became God's servant to command. God sent him to the labor field to heal and to deliver, to set people free from the shackles of the devil. He worked tirelessly to bring thousands of souls to Christ. Heaven was happy with this labor and with the servant. But this was not the time to go about feeling good about himself, saying that he was the mighty power of God. This was not the time to go on a mini-vacation. This was not the time to begin to accept higher titles and accolades. This was the time to go back to the Master of the field. This was the time to present himself to the Master for scrutiny. The army needed to return to base to serve the Master.

What does it mean to serve the Master?

To serve the Master means to minister to the Lord. The Lord also has needs, and His needs are expected to be met by us. These needs can be met in the place of ministering unto the Lord. Many times, Christians go into His presence to ask for this and that. Only a very few go to the Lord to have a conversation. What father is it who does not like to converse with his children? No father will be happy with a child who only wants something from him without wanting to spend time with him. The same is true of God. He created us to have fellowship with Him. He wants a relationship with us. When we come into His presence, He expects us to spend time just worshiping Him and enjoying His company. He wants us to just converse and discuss our days with Him. Men who spend such time with God tend to do more in the fields than those who just come to ask and take.

> *Now there were in the church that was at Antioch certain prophets and teachers; as Barnabas, and Simeon that was called Niger, and Lucius of Cyrene, and Manaen, which had been brought up with Herod the tetrarch, and Saul. As they ministered to the Lord, and fasted, the Holy Ghost said, Separate me Barnabas and Saul for the work whereunto I have called them.*
>
> —Acts 13:1–2

Consider the above passage. These men decided to go into the presence of God, not to ask for anything but to minister to the Lord. The word "minister" in this passage is from the Greek word *leitourgeo*, which means "to perform religious or charitable functions like worship, obedience, to discharge a public office at one's own expense." Note the last phrase: "at one's own expense." This is exactly what "ministering to the Lord" means. You go into the presence of God, not expecting to get something or to table a prayer to address one of your numerous needs. You go there because you just want to put a smile on His face. You just want to tell Him how wonderful He is and how good He has been to humanity. You just want to have a conversation. Notice that they were not just ministering to the Lord. They were doing it with fasting. That is a very serious matter. Fasting is alien to this generation. To get people to fast is a herculean task. When you eventually do get them to fast, they fast because they want something from God or because there is an emergency that they want God to address urgently in their lives or in the life of a loved one. Look at why these men were fasting. Was it because they had no needs? Or was it because they were not humans? No. They had needs like every one of us do. They had family and friends who needed one or two instances of help from above. But they put all those aside and concentrated on pleasing the Master. They even added fasting to their ministration to the Lord. The story of these men would not be complete if we don't look at what was written about them *before* they decided to minster to the Lord with fasting:

> *But the word of God grew and multiplied. And Barnabas and Saul returned from Jerusalem, when they had fulfilled their ministry, and took with them John, whose surname was Mark.*
>
> —Acts 12:24–25

Notice what was said about these men in verse 25, the last verse of chapter 12, just before chapter 13 begins: "They had fulfilled their ministry." What does that mean? Jesus, the Master, had handpicked them and sent them to one of His fields. They went there and worked their lives out. The harvest they experienced from the field was enormous. It was recorded that "they fulfilled their ministry." It means they achieved the exact standard that heaven expected them to achieve. God Himself looked at the quality of their work and marked it as 100 percent. There are very few people in the entirety of Scripture who are said to have "fulfilled their ministry." At a time when heaven was satisfied with their work, they should have been granted leave to rest. It should have been a time to relax from the hot sun they had subjected themselves to for so many months. But just as the Master advised in Luke 17:10, they first needed to come back home to serve the Master. These men followed the word to the letter. And they didn't only come to minister to the Lord, but they did it with fasting. There is no way God won't appear in situations like this. Notice verse 2 of Acts 13. The Holy Spirit appeared and spoke to them: "This is the next phase of your ministry."

The only way to please the Watchers after being certified as a dry bone is to adopt the principles Jesus gave in Luke 17. This must be a daily affair. No matter how glorious the work in the field was, the bone must realize that he is just a bone. It is the glory on the bone that is performing the work. Without that glory, no man would ever pay any attention to it. Who wants a skeleton in their space? No one. That is how the dry bone must continually see himself. The moment he sees himself otherwise, that is when he begins to fall. Our Lord Jesus Christ Himself said He was nothing without God. This is Someone who literally had the right to call Himself God. This is Someone who was the Co-Creator of all things, both in the visible and in the invisible world. Yet, when He was passing through the school of life, He descended "so low" so as to say continually, not only to Himself or to His disciples, but to the world around Him and whoever cared to hear, that He could do nothing without God. Every single miracle we see in His ministry, He publicly associated with God. And we all know He finished strong.

It is important for us to finish strong as well. The way out has been laid by the Master. We have to work never to get to the point the donkey reached. We must always realize that any reverence we receive is because of the One riding on us. If He steps down from the donkey, no one will pay attention to the donkey. Again, let's ask ourselves: Who wants a skeleton in their space?